'This book will be helpful to so many families and staff supporting daily on the ground. The book promotes humanity, the importance of the connections we make with each other, the ability to understand, read the non-verbal cues and help enable the person you are supporting to have really positive moments, increasing opportunity to build the supports for the best life possible for them.'

**Frances Steepe**, *Parent and advocate for using Intensive Interaction, Oxford, UK*

'Intensive Interaction is one of the most intriguing avenues of therapy for connecting with people seen as otherwise unreachable. The book offers a valuable – and I suspect, heartwarming – collection of papers showing the diversity of experience and practice using this method. Its importance lies also in attempts to frame it theoretically within Psychology, a connection which is valuable for practitioners and non-practitioners alike.'

**Vasudevi Reddy**, *Emeritus Professor, Developmental and Cultural Psychology Centre for Interaction, Development and Diversity, University of Portsmouth, UK*

# Integrating Intensive Interaction Principles into Psychological Practice

This book details how to use Intensive Interaction as a psychologically informed practice when working with 'seldom-heard' clients.

Although Intensive Interaction was originally developed for children with severe and profound learning disability, its use has expanded across age ranges and conditions, and is now utilised with children and adults including autistic individuals and people with dementia. Exploring the context in which Intensive Interaction has and can be used, specifically as a psychological approach, this edited volume covers therapeutic intervention on a one-to-one basis, as well as an intervention within other frameworks such as Trauma Informed Care and Positive Behaviour Support. Case examples are utilised throughout, alongside psychological theory, to demonstrate use in practice. Consideration is also paid to service contexts and how psychologists can introduce this approach in their local areas.

The first book on Intensive Interaction written by psychologists for psychological practitioners, this book will appeal to trainee and qualified clinical and counselling psychologists, and psychological practitioners including creative therapists and counsellors.

**Sophie Doswell** is a Consultant Clinical Psychologist who has worked in the NHS with individuals with intellectual disabilities and autistic individuals for over 25 years. She was introduced to Intensive Interaction early in her career and is passionate about its use within services as a way of connecting with individuals, alleviating distress and helping supporters.

**Maggie Ellis, MBE,** is a psychologist based at the University of St Andrews. She has worked with people living with dementia as a volunteer and researcher for 24 years, with a particular focus on facilitating communication between people with very advanced dementia and their carers.

# Integrating Intensive Interaction Principles into Psychological Practice

Edited by
Sophie Doswell and Maggie Ellis

Routledge
Taylor & Francis Group

LONDON AND NEW YORK

Designed cover image: © Maggie Ellis

First published 2026
by Routledge
4 Park Square, Milton Park, Abingdon, Oxon OX14 4RN

and by Routledge
605 Third Avenue, New York, NY 10158

*Routledge is an imprint of the Taylor & Francis Group, an informa business*

*British Library Cataloguing-in-Publication Data*
A catalogue record for this book is available from the British Library

ISBN: 978-1-032-98291-5 (hbk)
ISBN: 978-1-032-98289-2 (pbk)
ISBN: 978-1-003-59793-3 (ebk)

DOI: 10.4324/9781003597933

Typeset in Sabon
by Taylor & Francis Books

# Contents

# Illustrations

## Figure

## Tables

# Contributors

**Ditte Rose Andersen**: Psychologist and founder of Intensive Interaction Denmark, Denmark

**Arlene Astell**: Professor at Northumbria University, England.

**Ruth Berry**: Senior Clinical Psychologist at Lancashire & South Cumbria NHS Foundation Trust, England.

**Sophie Doswell**: Consultant Clinical Psychologist at South London and Maudsley NHS Foundation Trust, England.

**Sarah Dunstan**: Trainee Clinical Psychologist at the University of Essex, England.

**Maggie Ellis**: Senior Lecturer at the University of St Andrews, Scotland.

**Julie Elsworth**: Principle Clinical Psychologist (Retired) at Oxford Health NHS Foundation Trust, England.

**Graham Firth**: Intensive Interaction Project Leader (Retired) at the Leeds and York Partnership NHS Foundation Trust, England.

**Rachel Ann Jones**: National Programme Lead for Learning Disabilities at Improvement Cymru, and Visiting Professor at the University of South Wales.

**Christina Connell McGrath**: Assistant Psychologist at Essex Partnership University NHS Foundation Trust, England.

**Jules McKim**: Intensive Interaction Specialist Care Coordinator at Oxford Health NHS Foundation Trust, England.

**Judith Samuel**: Consultant Clinical Psychologist (Retired) at Oxford Health NHS Foundation Trust, England.

**Alison Spencer**: Consultant Clinical Psychologist at Hertfordshire Partnership University NHS Foundation Trust and Lecturer at the University of Essex.

# Foreword

I feel rather honoured to be asked to contribute to this significant collection. It is five years or so since I retired from active work in our field, or since I wrote anything about Intensive Interaction.

However, I do know this has been a good five years for Intensive Interaction. I am well aware that the dissemination of the approach continues to burgeon and flourish. This is due partly of course to the unstinting work of my friends and former colleagues in the Intensive Interaction Institute, some of whom are contributors to this volume. It is also due to the enthusiasm and commitment of other practitioners and family members who have similar passion for an approach which has a practical simplicity, but the most profound human effects.

It is rewarding to find that this volume has an emphasis on the setting of Intensive Interaction within psychological theory and understandings. Part of the logic of Intensive Interaction, it has seemed to me from the very beginning, is that the approach is partly derived from an extensive body of authoritative psychological research on how developing humans conduct the most complicated learning naturally.

This volume offers too, examination of a most significant challenge to Intensive Interaction, that of barriers to implementation. This is the potentially the most pressing issue confronting all of us devotees here. The barriers are many and these are the ones that have always seemed to me to be significant. Intensive Interaction is too simple and it is crucially reliant on the interpersonal facilities of the practitioner/partner. It was always a huge challenge to persuade services and perhaps practitioners, to look beyond the often technological interventions they favoured using. It could be a challenge to help them become relaxed, less driven in interventions and happily employ *themselves*, face, voice, body language as *the* crucial learning facility. I feel confident that all contributors and readers will find this scenario familiar.

Yes, Intensive Interaction has beautiful, simple principles of practitioner operation: tuning-in; minimalism, don't do too much; wait, let the other person lead; build the 'conversation' by responsiveness; use the other person's behaviours by reflecting back what they do or joining in, thus making yourself understandable. This style proved to be the key for creating enjoyable, fundamental interactions with people who have severe and complex learning difficulties, autism or other conditions causing them to still be at an early stage of communication development.

I so remember an incident when I was 24 and stupid, long before the commencement of any Intensive Interaction thoughts. My cousin Lena and I were attempting to help our aged Irish grandmother to recount some memories of her childhood in Ennis, County Clare – she could on occasion achieve some lucidity when her mind rested there. Lena had asked a question and my Gran was staring into space, frowning. After about 20 seconds, impatient, I prompted, asked another question. Lena the wise, elbowed me in the ribs, whispered: "Dave, don't interrupt her when she is thinking about the answer, you just restarted her." During the development of Intensive Interaction, this memory came to me often. There is thus much to be appreciated within this volume about the efficacy of Intensive Interaction for people with dementia and the challenge to the approach's adoption within services, leading to the development of 'Adaptive Interaction'.

Another key aspect of this book for me: it is so heartening to see included here chapters that describe the experiences of parents and families with their children or relatives of any age. Surely all of us Intensive Interaction aficionados greatly, nay, desperately, desire that the gifts Intensive Interaction can bring be as generally available to families as possible. We probably all have our favourite experiences or memories of the benefits the approach has brought to the everyday life of a family.

I also welcome a chapter focusing on what was a major facet of my professional working life. When the team I was within was working on the development of Intensive Interaction in the 1980s, many of our adult students were people who could exhibit well *extreme* behaviours of concern. This was within an institution and quite a few of our people were sectioned and detained under the mental health act due to the effects of their behaviour. The team members were very good, diligent record keepers. As we worked on and increasingly integrated Intensive Interaction into the fabric of our daily environment, there was a – now of course, unsurprising – side effect. Everybody became easier to be with. It was clear from the records that the number of difficult incidents was fading away Our students were exhibiting increased general well-being, self-esteem, positive general sociability, greater awareness, less social anxiety, having more fun, enjoying their daily experience. Each of them had ongoing access to their version of chit-chat and chit-chat is what human life is about.

To conclude, now reluctantly. As I study the book contents, I find many positive, detailed thoughts about Intensive Interaction gladly re-activating. It is a deep pleasure once again to feel like a fully-fledged member of this community of practice, however briefly, though my recall of the events of my working life continually conveys a great, quiet comfort. I believe this to be a gift for all of us in this work.

I congratulate the contributors to this book on their work and thank them for contributing further to my bank of memories. I also congratulate you readers for having the wisdom to be an Intensive or Adaptive Interaction practitioner, or perhaps, be considering becoming one.

Dr Dave Hewett OBE
Malvern, February 2025

# Preface

The idea for this book was developed at a meeting between a group of psychological practitioners, with a common interest in Intensive Interaction and/or Adaptive Interaction. On discussing the benefits of these approaches, we quickly realised the need for promoting their use to a wider audience. For example, although most of us work in the UK, we recognise a lack of more widespread psychological publishing on the benefits of using Intensive and Adaptive Interaction. As such, we aim to widen the appeal of this book and the approach to an international level.

Many of us have already published, and/or presented on this topic at local and national fora. However, we noted a reluctance for psychologists to fully embrace Intensive and Adaptive Interaction as part of their therapeutic repertoire. Indeed, we recognised that the majority of work in this area has been undertaken by colleagues in education and health including Dave Hewitt, Melanie Nind, Phoebe Caldwell, Graham Firth and Mark Barber. We recommend interested readers access the wealth of books, videos and other resources produced by these colleagues. Our intention is not to 'claim' Intensive and Adaptive Interaction for psychological practitioners. Rather, the aim is to combine, disseminate and promote the theoretical and practical knowledge gained by psychological practitioners over years. Ultimately, we aim to help psychological colleagues see the added value of utilising these approaches as an intervention.

We reference psychological theory, case studies and current study, including three new pieces of research conducted specifically for this book. As such, each chapter is written in a style that is specific to the authors and their respective backgrounds. We hope that this book encourages psychological practitioners new to Intensive and/or Adaptive Interaction to add the approach to their toolbox. We also hope and that the book will support those already using these approaches to further develop the use of Intensive and Adaptive Interaction as a psychological intervention through practice and research.

Sophie Doswell and Maggie Ellis

# Acknowledgements

Chapter Five : We would like to thank Dr. Catherine Crane, clinical psychologist, for her detailed and insightful suggestions.

Chapter Six : We would like to thank the participants for taking part in this study. We are grateful for their willing participation and desire to help others in the same situation. We would also like to thank Christina Connell McGrath for transcribing the interviews and helping with analyses.

Chapter Nine : We would like to thank Sophie Doswell, Jules McKim and Julie Elsworth for their input into this chapter.

Chapter Ten : We would like to thank Dr. Catherine Crane, clinical psychologist, for her feedback and suggestions.

# Chapter 1

# The history and development of Intensive Interaction

## What is it? ... and where did it come from?

*Graham Firth*

## What is Intensive Interaction?

### Definition

An early and concise definition of Intensive Interaction was put forward by the British Institute of Learning Disabilities (BILD), which stated that:

> Intensive Interaction is a practical approach to interacting with people with learning disabilities who do not find it easy communicating or being social ... In Intensive Interaction the carer, support worker, speech and language therapist or teacher works on being a better communication partner and so supports the person with learning disabilities develop confidence and competence as a communicator.
>
> (Accessed at: http://www.bild.org.uk/docs/05faqs/ii.doc on 13.10.07)

So, perhaps at its most basic level, Intensive Interaction should be seen as an interactional process that aims to develop and sustain positive and developmentally pertinent social communication for and with people who, for a number of reasons, find difficulties with interacting and being social.

Acknowledging the socially inclusive nature, whilst underlining the clear developmental aim of the approach, Melanie Nind and Dave Hewett (the originators of the approach) say that Intensive Interaction is 'an approach to teaching and spending time with people with learning disabilities, which is aimed specifically at the development of the most fundamental social and communication abilities' (Nind & Hewett, 2001).

### Who was Intensive Interaction designed for?

In the early stages of the development and dissemination of Intensive Interaction, the people who were then seen as potentially benefiting from the use of the approach were people with severe or profound intellectual disabilities, sometimes also combined with a diagnosis of autism. Indeed, the first groups of people with

DOI: 10.4324/9781003597933-1

whom Intensive Interaction was used during its development stage were those who were seen to be socially remote or passive. Therefore, the early recipients of Intensive Interaction were generally people who didn't tend to initiate social interactions with other people, and who might also engage in a variety of repetitive self-stimulatory behaviours. The approach was also used with people with multi-sensory impairments who were at that time perceived to be uninterested (or unable) to engage sociably with those around them.

### What are the aims of Intensive Interaction?

Generally, Intensive Interaction was then seen as an approach for providing people with positive and developmentally useful experiences of being socially included and emotionally connected, where previously such experiences had been absent. It provided people with opportunities to gradually acquire and develop the underlying and fundamental communication skills necessary to be social. Thus, Intensive Interaction enabled such people to socially interact and emotionally connect with those people closest to them, both physically and emotionally.

These Fundamentals of Communication (FoCs), as identified by Nind and Hewett (1994, 2001) are the foundational social communication skills and understandings that, in normal development, are generally learned before the development of symbolic speech. Therefore, a central feature of the approach is that Intensive Interaction is built around the social practices and understanding which most of us already possess, since they are those that we mainly intuitively use when sociably interacting with pre-verbal infants i.e., by being unconditionally responsive to what the infant does, and shaping our interactive behaviour to fit it within their current level of social understanding.

### What techniques are used?

Looking at the process in more detail, the generally accepted techniques of Intensive Interaction are therefore those associated with infant–caregiver interactions (Nind & Hewett, 1994). Melanie Nind (1996) identified '5 Central Features' of the approach:

1   The creation of mutual pleasure and interactive games – being together with the sole purpose of enjoying each other.
2   People adjust their interpersonal behaviours (e.g. their gaze, voice, body posture, facial expression) so that they become more engaging and meaningful to the person with a learning disability.
3   Interactions flow naturally in time – with pauses, repetitions and blended rhythms.

4    Accrediting intentionality: accrediting people, even with severe or profound disabilities, with thoughts and intentions, and responding to their behaviours as if they are intentionally communicative.
5    The use of contingent responding: following the person's lead and sharing control of the activity.

Actual sessions or periods of Intensive Interaction can vary extensively between participants and occasions, with the individual techniques being employed in very person-centred ways. Thus, the intensity, form and pacing of any interactive episode can vary widely within and across sessions, this being dependent on the current presentation of the participant.

Generally, these techniques used for Intensive Interaction, based on the 'infant–caregiver' model of interactivity, might include a combination of: the sensitive use of non-task associated physical proximity; contingent and responsive eye contact and facial signalling (sometimes with overtly dramatised or characterised facial expressions); some forms of socially significant physical contact (perhaps with a rhythmical basis); vocal echoing and responsiveness with clear and inclusive intonation; some form of behavioural mirroring and/or joint-focus activities or well-rehearsed game-like interactions.

So, when practically employing the approach, the practitioner uses the person's behavioural repertoire and personal interests, or motivating factors, as a starting point and guide. Thus, any interactional activity is either initiated by, or contingent on the positive engagement of the person. Also important are the general issues of tasklessness and mutual pleasure which set the demand-free agenda for any Intensive Interaction activity or session, rather than it being focused on the accomplishment of any predetermined outcome or structured task. Any social interactivity thus takes place within familiar and enjoyable interactions, where the content and the flow of the activity is defined by letting the person lead the interaction, with the carer, support worker, teacher or therapist responding to and joining in with the person's current behaviour.

### The philosophy of Intensive Interaction

It is perhaps an over-arching **Intensive Interaction philosophy** that sets the approach apart. Intensive Interaction has a clear value base in which people are seen as positive social agents, who should be valued on a human level for who they are, rather than be defined by what they can or cannot do. Kennedy (2001) suggests 'The difference between participation and compliance is at the very core of the Intensive Interaction approach'.

The socially responsive philosophy of Intensive Interaction could perhaps best be characterised as a combination of the following:

- A desire on the part of the practitioner (a carer or support worker, a teacher or a therapist) to sociably interact with someone with a communication or social impairment in a way that is meaningful to him or her, and through such interactions come to know the person better.
- A desire on the part of the practitioner to develop an equitable and mutually respectful relationship with the person.
- A determination on the part of the practitioner to socially and emotionally attune to the person and achieve the maximum level of social and emotional connection by allowing the person to dictate the form, intensity, and pace of the interaction.
- A determination on the part of the practitioner to create an emotionally secure and empathic social environment around the person, paying particular attention to the person's moment-by-moment feedback, in whatever form this might take.

Such a combination of the general philosophy and the practical techniques of Intensive Interaction might make the approach seem hypothetically complex, and thus difficult to practically apply, but because the approach is naturalistically based on the infant–caregiver model of interactivity, in practice most people find it unproblematic and often quite enjoyable. However, like many things in life, the skills of utilising Intensive Interaction tend to further develop with continued practice and subsequent supported reflection.

Perhaps of central importance to the Intensive Interaction philosophy, whereas some approaches started from a perspective of seeing a person with an intellectual disability and/or autism to be in some way an impaired or inferior version of some normalised ideal (i.e. someone who needs to be supported to change in some specified ways identified by practitioners with specified qualifications), Intensive Interaction starts with the premise that anyone can do it, and that anyone who receives it is already someone who is interesting and enjoyable to be with. As one parent once said of Intensive Interaction: 'through Intensive Interaction we can shift our vision of our sons and daughters from impaired versions of us, to fulfilled versions of themselves'.

## The history of Intensive Interaction development

In terms of setting out a richer and more contextualised picture of Intensive Interaction, a historical view of its development might be helpful.

### Before Intensive Interaction: what was going on?

In the UK, prior to 1970, children with severe and profound learning disabilities were statutorily deemed to be 'ineducable'. However, things changed with the Education (Handicapped Children) Act 1970, when responsibility for the education of this group of children shifted from the Department of Health to the

Department of Education. From this point onward, all children were entitled to some kind of education. Also at this time, for adults with severe or profound levels of learning disability, life-long hospital care was often accepted as the norm. There was little agreed understanding about how to support these individuals and thus the major focus was put on personal care. This phase of specialist care and provision has been described simply as *Tender Loving Care* (Ouvry, 1991) with little or no thought given to their possible educational or psychological development.

Then came a phase identified generally as one of *Stimulation*, aimed at usefully challenging the general perceived passivity of this 'Tender Loving Care' viewpoint. Thus, activities were developed to interest and in some ways perceptually or even physically stimulate the participants, for example via multi-sensory rooms and/or musical activities. However, such stimulatory activities didn't generally have any clearly defined educational or development aims. Thus, these individuals were often engaged in activities that they had not chosen and had little or no control over. Also, they were often given no choice, and probably had little or no understanding of the purpose of such activities.

The next identifiable phase has been labelled the *Behavioural phase* (Irvine, in Firth et al., 2010, p. 23), which attempted to address the inadequacies of stimulation by predeterminedly structuring activities and identifying externally formulated behavioural outcomes for the person. Thus, teaching became outcome or goal oriented, with specified learning targets being set for individuals and programmes written and carried out by staff. Again, the learner had little or no control over, or developmentally useful understanding about what was being done to them. It was during this phase, when special education use of 'behaviourism' was at its most educationally prevalent, that some educational, psychological and care practitioners began to question what they were doing, and why (McConkey, 1981).

### The Intensive Interaction development stage – Harperbury Hospital School

The early development work on the approach that has become known as Intensive Interaction came about due to the teaching staff at Harperbury Hospital School (in Hertfordshire, England) rejecting what they saw as the application of ineffective and ethically questionable behaviour modification techniques with their student group, young adults with severe or profound and multiple learning disabilities. They recognised that communication was their students' primary learning need as it was the key to all subsequent learning, but then also questioned why they were trying to teach representational signing to students who did not have any apparent understanding of symbolic language. They therefore saw little educational sense in what they were doing.

The staff team then employed an action-research methodology to initially identify their students' 'primary learning needs', these being the skills, understandings, and motivation to want to socially interact with those people around them. To achieve these learning outcomes, the staff team, led most notably by Dave Hewett and then Melanie Nind, started to collectively reflect on how they might best facilitate their students' learning, or further developing their 'fundamental communication' abilities (Nind & Hewett, 1994).

In 1981 the Harperbury team began to discuss and trial ways of building a curriculum that focused more on their students' social communication skills and understandings, rather than their deficiencies in the area of symbolic communication. They endeavoured to develop sociability within the classroom, and thus to begin to build positive and even playful relationships with the students. Early on, the idea of creating an 'Appropriate Communication Environment' (ACE) emerged; this ACE idea established the central and vital requirement for the staff to promote engagement by being more playful and responsive in their interactions with their student group. The Harperbury staff team also started to use what would now be termed 'video analysis', with staff looking back analytically at recently recorded video to reflect on the observable outcomes of their interactions, and also think about how they might improve their interactive practices.

In 1982, some of the staff began to look at the work of Clinical Psychologist Geraint Ephraim, who was working at another 'Hospital for the Mentally Handicapped' in the locality. Dr Ephraim was using an approach to developmentally informed care that he called 'Augmented Mothering' (1982). Dr Ephraim had developed this 'Augmented Mothering' approach by advocating for interactions based on a continued adoption of an 'caregiver–infant' model of interactivity, even into adulthood. During meetings with some of the Harperbury staff team, Dr Ephraim encouraged them to build on their work by accessing the then available literature on 'parent–infant' or 'caregiver–infant' interactions; this they did across the subsequent years.

Finally, by 1987, Nind and Hewett had become confident in clearly defining their approach, now called Intensive Interaction, and had seen compelling evidence of its educational efficacy i.e., highly significant positive outcomes for many of their students in the development of their fundamental communication abilities. That year they were invited to give a presentation on their work, to a conference called 'Interactive Approaches to the Education of Children with Severe Learning Difficulties', held at Westhill College, Birmingham. This conference is often cited as the beginnings of the *Interactive phase* of care and educational provision for people with learning disabilities.

This initial presentation on the Intensive Interaction approach was then followed by an article, 'Interaction as Curriculum', in the *British Journal of Special Education* (June 1988). It was at this time that the generally 'bottom-up', practitioner-led dissemination of Intensive Interaction began, with Nind and Hewett giving further presentations on the approach at a number of conferences and providing training sessions for staff teams from across the UK.

## The theoretical background to Intensive Interaction

The development of Intensive Interaction was underpinned by an increasing understanding of the developmental research and literature then available in the 1980s. Nind and Hewett looked particularly at the academic research and associated theory focusing on the development of communication and sociability within 'the interactive process in the natural model of infancy' (2005, p. 16). They identified three important themes that ran through their extensive search across this body of literature:

1   Early social and communication development takes place within a dynamic social process.
2   The developing infant is an active participant in their own social and communication development.
3   There are evidenced differences in the social learning environments created for infants with or without developmental disabilities.

Nind and Hewett went on to look in further depth at what they describe as the 'dynamic social context of early learning' (2005, p. 17). The overall picture then emerging was that of the infant being seen as an active agent within their own developmental process, rather than a passive recipient of caregiver stimulation. Also seen as intrinsic to the process of early interactivity (and therefore subsequently with Intensive Interaction) is the development of mutual pleasure; this also being the primary motivation for its continuation and frequent repetition.

   Overall, across their studies into the supporting academic literature, Nind and Hewett identified an interactive style that seemed 'optimal in terms of the developmental and learning outcomes' accruing for the child (2005, p. 25).

## The post-1988 dissemination stage

At this time, the responsive, naturalistic nature of Intensive Interaction was seen by many as extremely radical, drawing many responses as the approach became more widely recognised and practised, both positive and negative, from practitioners and academics in the field. Its introduction into care settings and classrooms where behavioural techniques were previously used caused some keen reflection, and sometimes resistance, among some staff. Carers and teachers were now being asked to join in with or reflect back to people's activities and/or behaviours that they had previously been taught to ignore, discourage or even prevent. Some staff were worried they might be reinforcing functionally ineffective or even inappropriate behaviours, rather than seeing a person's behavioural repertoire as a language they might acknowledge and use to make a social and emotional connection through.

   Another stumbling block to the early dissemination of Intensive Interaction in the 1990s was the principles of 'Normalisation', developed from work in

Scandinavia in the 1960s (Nirje, 1969) which were widely embraced by learning disability services at that time. Normalisation was a set of principles which looked to give people with learning disabilities access to living conditions and a culture of respect that fitted more closely to that enjoyed by most other people across society. Unfortunately, in many adult settings in particular, normalisation then evolved into a less nuanced set of 'age-appropriateness' principles which pointed services and staff to unreflectively promote activities based on a person's chronological age, rather than on what would be deemed developmentally appropriate i.e., activities at a level that someone with learning disabilities could understand and join in with. So, the introduction of Intensive Interaction with its basis in 'infant–caregiver' interaction models, into settings where 'age-appropriateness' principles had been, and perhaps still might be unreflectively applied was (and sometimes even now, continues to be) problematic. However, moving forward, the general dissemination process of Intensive Interaction was helped by the increasing acceptance of the 'person-centred' philosophy of care, which specified a person's care or educational needs on an individual basis. This made Intensive Interaction subsequently seem more relevant and/or appropriate to some services.

Across the 1990s, a range of publications promoted the use of Intensive Interaction, including research papers that began to demonstrate an evidence base and books describing Intensive Interaction from a range of perspectives including from parents, carers and professionals describing their day-to-day work using Intensive Interaction.

### A new millennium for Intensive Interaction

After 2000, Intensive Interaction started to become much more widespread in schools and services across the UK, with interest in the approach continuing to develop in a number of countries worldwide. In the early part of the new millennium, practitioners from various disciplines, including Clinical Psychologists (e.g. Samuel, 2001) increasingly added their voice and views into the body of literature supporting the approach, publishing research studies and important position papers that significantly moved Intensive Interaction forward. There is more information about the role of Clinical Psychologists, psychological practitioners and researchers in the development of Intensive Interaction in the following chapter.

At this time there was also a number of new books published, followed by the first video (Caldwell, 2002), and online Intensive Interaction learning resources becoming available.

Two important Intensive Interaction milestones occurred in 2009. First, Intensive Interaction was included in the then Qualifications and Curriculum Authority (2009) guidance document covering special educational provision in England and Wales. Also, in terms of adult social care provision, the UK Department of Health policy document 'Valuing People Now: A new three-year strategy for people with learning disabilities' (2009) explicitly stated that people with complex needs should have 'very individualised support packages, including systems for facilitating meaningful two-way communication' (p. 37), with Intensive Interaction being explicitly identified as the means of achieving such person-centred communication.

## Where is, and what is Intensive Interaction now?

Things have moved on since the first definitions of the practices and principles of Intensive Interaction were set out, with the conceptualisation and application of Intensive Interaction now becoming broader in terms of its use with a wider range of client groups. In addition to the initial groupings of recipients i.e. people with severe or profound learning disabilities and/or autism, Intensive Interaction is now used with wider groups of people who might more generally be described as having some form of communication or social difficulty. This includes those with multi-sensory impairments, those who have behaviours of concern (see Chapter 5), people with serious mental health problems, and some who evidence potentially trauma related psychological or psychiatric issues such as withdrawal, anxiety, depression and self-injurious behaviour.

Intensive Interaction is also being used with people who have already developed some or even high levels of symbolic speech and understanding but who for a number of reasons, e.g. autism or demand avoidance, might benefit from further developing their use and understanding of the more foundational aspects of human social interactivity.

Intensive Interaction is being used with people who have lost their previously attained abilities in the social domain due to late-stage dementia (Ellis & Astell, 2017; also see Chapter 6) or those in minimally conscious states or with profound disturbances of consciousness.

However, with the current use of Intensive Interaction now being seen to address the needs across so many groups, it should not be seen as some form of cure-all or magic wand; it still retains its original purpose, principles and practices.

No matter who Intensive Interaction is used with, or by whom, or within which care, educational or therapeutic context, there are still clear areas of agreement as to what the approach consists of and is its initial primary purpose. Initially the main stated focus of Intensive Interaction was the development of 'fundamental communication' skills and 'sociability'. However, more recently the approach is increasingly employed also as a means of rapport and relationship building, or as a way of just sociably 'being with' people who find difficulty in being social.

What a practitioner does, or thinks they do, when engaging in Intensive Interaction can be dependent on many things; it is very much influenced by the characteristics and history of the two people involved, their expectations of the process and their current context. But perhaps one way to look more generally at Intensive Interaction is to see it as an all-embracing humanistic

care philosophy which promotes issues of communication development, of unconditional social inclusion, of truly person-centred social responsiveness, and of equi-
tably sharing the power to define an appropriate form of sociable interactivity.

Such a general working philosophy of Intensive Interaction should be seen to
encompass the differing aims and professional roles of those who might wish to
employ the approach. Such a working philosophy is always there when the
Intensive Interaction approach is used to work with different partners or clients
and sometimes with quite radically different working contexts, agendas and
hoped for aims. Such a working philosophy might be used to frame a learning
environment to develop fundamental communication skills, or to develop
sociability and enhance relationship building, or it might be used to address
mental health issues in a therapeutic manner.

As Clinical Psychologist Dr Ruth Berry wrote:

> Intensive Interaction is different things to different people. For a teacher, it
> is a method of developing a pupil's communication skills. For a care
> worker, it is a way of spending pleasurable time with someone who can't
> hold an 'ordinary' conversation. For a Clinical Psychologist, it can be a
> way of establishing a therapeutic relationship with someone. By 'ther-
> apeutic', I mean a relationship that is intended to benefit the other person.
> (Unpublished draft)

How Intensive Interaction can be conceptualised as a therapeutic approach and
utilised by psychologists and psychological practitioners is the topic of the following chapter.

So, what sort of thing is Intensive Interaction now? Well, to recap, Intensive
Interaction is now considered to have a number of uses, namely, socially inclusive,
educational and therapeutic. The form that Intensive Interaction takes does not
necessarily differ between these three, but the aims of the practitioner probably do.
For direct care or support staff, including parents, Intensive Interaction may be a
primary tool for developing sociability and mutual responsiveness; for teachers,
educationalists and speech and language therapists it is primarily a tool for developing a learner or person's fundamental communication skills. A Clinical Psychologist is more likely to see Intensive Interaction as a therapeutic tool used to
alleviate a person's emotional distress and thus promote their emotional wellbeing. Of course, this is a simplification, as people who fulfil all of these roles
might also use Intensive Interaction to fulfil a number of aims simultaneously.

Interestingly, it should also be realised that the benefits of Intensive Interaction can go in both directions, with the more skilled communication partner, be
they family members, carers or support staff also benefiting from the improved
communication and social interactivity with the person they care for or work
with. However, as one of the originators of the approach, Dr Dave Hewett once
said, and as this book now also attests, the development and dissemination of
Intensive Interaction 'is still a work in progress'.

# References

Caldwell, P. (2002) *Learning the Language: Building relationships with people with severe learning disability, autistic spectrum disorder and other challenging behaviour* (DVD). Shoreham by Sea: Pavilion.

Department of Education and Science (1970) Education (Handicapped Children) Act. London: HMSO.

Department of Health (2009) Valuing People Now: A new three-year strategy for learning disabilities. London: HM Government.

Ellis, M. & Astell, A. (2017) *Adaptive Interaction and Dementia*. London: Jessica Kingsley Publishers.

Ephraim, G. (1982) Developmental processes in mental handicap: a generative structure approach. Unpublished Ph.D. thesis, Brunel University Foundation.

Firth, G., Berry, R. & Irvine, C. (2010) *Understanding Intensive Interaction: Context and concepts for professionals and families*. London: Jessica Kingsley Publishers.

Hewett, D. & Nind, M. (eds) (1998) *Interaction in Action: Reflections on the use of Intensive Interaction*. London: David Fulton.

Kennedy, A. (2001) Intensive Interaction. *LDP*, 4 (3), 14–17.

McConkey, R. (1981) Education without understanding? *Special Education: Forward Trends*, 8 (3), 8–10.

Nind, M. (1996) Efficacy of Intensive Interaction: developing sociability and communication in people with severe and complex learning difficulties using an approach based on caregiver–infant interaction. *The European Journal of Special Educational Needs*, 11 (1), 48–66.

Nind, M. & Hewett, D. (1988) Interaction as curriculum. *British Journal of Special Education*, 15 (2), 55–57.

Nind, M. & Hewett, D. (1994) *Access to Communication: Developing the basics of communication with people with severe learning difficulties through Intensive Interaction*. London: David Fulton.

Nind, M. & Hewett, D. (2001) *A Practical Guide to Intensive Interaction*. London: BILD.

Nind, M. & Hewett, D. (2005) *Access to Communication: Developing basic communication with people who have severe learning difficulties* (2nd edn). London: David Fulton.

Nirje, B. (1969) The normalization principle and its human management implications. In Kugel, R. & Wolfensberger, W. (eds) *Changing Patterns in Residential Services for the Mentally Retarded*. Washington DC: Presidential Committee on Mental Retardation.

Ouvry, C. (1991) *Strategies to Meet the Needs of People with Profound and Multiple Learning Difficulties*. London: BILD.

Qualifications and Curriculum Authority (2009) *Planning, Teaching and Assessing the Curriculum for Pupils with Learning Difficulties: General guidance*. London: QCA.

Samuel, J. (2001) Intensive interaction. *Clinical Psychology Forum*, 148, 22–25.

# Chapter 2

# An introduction to Intensive Interaction as a psychological intervention

*Sophie Doswell*

## Introduction

The previous chapter highlighted how Intensive Interaction grew as a communication and social engagement approach. During the early development, additional psychological benefits, for example the development of attachment (Bowlby, 1969) or improvements in psychological wellbeing (Seligman, 2010) do not appear to have explicitly explored. This is despite work on 'augmented mothering' by the psychologist Geraint Ephraim being fundamental to the development of this approach. Ephraim published a thesis (1982) and a publication on 'augmented mothering' (Ephraim, 1989) which promoted the importance of imitation and 'clicking together' when working with individuals who can be described as 'seldom heard'. Ephraim considered a wide range of theoretical concepts in his work and made specific reference to Bowlby's attachment theory (1969), and promoted the importance of developing a secure base. However, as Berry et al. (2014) note, Ephraim struggled to synthesise the theoretical underpinnings with his clinical work.

Ephraim supervised Phoebe Caldwell, who continued to utilise the approach developed by Ephraim, focusing on autistic individuals with intellectual disability. Caldwell describes Intensive Interaction as a 'technique that uses people's own body language to build up a non-verbal way of communicating with them' (Caldwell, 2008) and throughout her work has highlighted the value of Intensive Interaction in both social engagement and reduction of distress (Caldwell, 2013). Caldwell and colleagues have developed an approach using Intensive Interaction alongside an attention to sensory issues, called Responsive Communication (Caldwell et al., 2019). Responsive Communication aims to 'encourage effective emotional engagement and reduce behavioural distress'.

Melanie Nind, one of the early developers of Intensive Interaction, later acknowledged that emotion had not been at the forefront of thinking while Intensive Interaction was being developed, but stated that there are clear links between Intensive Interaction, emotional development and emotional wellbeing (Nind, 2012). With regard to theoretical underpinnings, Nind related Intensive Interaction to Bowlby's attachment theory, and recognised the benefits to staff

DOI: 10.4324/9781003597933-2

in developing positive relationships with individuals with intellectual disability through the use of Intensive Interaction. Nind also described Intensive Interaction as a 'therapeutic intervention'.

The authors of this book are psychological practitioners who have been using Intensive or Adaptive Interaction for many years, and have noted that despite one of the 'early influencers' in the development of Intensive Interaction being a psychologist and referencing attachment theory, and Nind's chapter clearly espousing the value of Intensive Interaction in relation to emotional wellbeing and attachment, the majority of psychologists do not appear to have embraced Intensive Interaction as a useful psychological approach. We are curious why Intensive and Adaptive Interaction, which the authors of this book believe are fundamental to meeting the psychological needs of individuals who are 'seldom heard', (including individuals with severe and profound learning disabilities and end-stage dementia), is not considered as a mainstream psychological intervention and taught to all applied psychology practitioners during the course of their training?

It appears there have been three main reasons that Intensive Interaction (and latterly Adaptive Interaction) has not been embraced as a psychological intervention: not being based on a clear psychological theory, lack of a robust psychological research base and therapeutic disdain for individuals who are 'seldom heard'. In this chapter we consider the theoretical and research challenges. With regard to therapeutic disdain, the reader is invited to explore Chapter 3.

## Intensive Interaction and psychological theory

Intensive Interaction can be seen through a range of theoretical lenses, and this appears to have led to a lack of theoretical clarity for psychologists. Harding and Berry (2009) described the psychological theories that may be useful in relation to Intensive Interaction:

> At the broadest level, Intensive Interaction is consistent with three major schools of psychological thought – humanistic psychology, attachment theory and positive psychology. All these approaches share a core tenet that positive human relationships are crucial to our sense of self-worth, ability to realise our potential, and our psychological well-being
>
> (p. 758)

Berry developed these arguments further across two book chapters in 'Understanding Intensive Interaction' (Firth, Berry & Irvine, 2010), describing how Intensive Interaction relates to the psychological theories of behaviourism, cognitive behavioural theory, humanistic psychology and psychoanalytic theory. In addition, Zeedyk and colleagues (e.g. Zeedyk et al., 2008) have highlighted the role of developmental psychology in helping us understand the psychological processes taking place while engaging in Intensive Interaction.

### Behavioural and cognitive behavioural theories

Behaviourism is included, according to Berry, as for decades this was the dominant school of thought in relation to people with intellectual disability, and Berry argues that Intensive Interaction has an important role in complementing behavioural approaches. This is demonstrated in Chapter 5, where McKim and Samuel described the use of Intensive Interaction within a Positive Behaviour Support framework.

Berry notes that cognitive therapy and Intensive Interaction share the principle of 'collaborative empiricism', which means working together to test things out. In addition, both cognitive therapy and Intensive Interaction have a focus on being guided by the client's emotional responses while recognising that the form is different, as Intensive Interaction uses physical proximity to determine and develop what the individual can tolerate, while cognitive therapy uses questioning and verbal reflections.

### Humanistic theories

Berry (2010) describes humanistic psychology, as having a 'root metaphor' as that of 'growth' and that the therapist creates the conditions that help the individual develop and change through the process of therapy. Berry argues that Intensive Interaction is consistent with these core concepts. Rogers' person-centred approach (1957; cited Merry, 2002) was explicitly identified as a humanistic approach that psychologists using Intensive Interaction identify as relevant to the approach (Berry et. al., 2014).

Berry (2010) pays particular attention to Maslow's hierarchy of needs (1943) as a psychological theory that has credibility with supporters working with people with intellectual disability. Maslow's theory postulates human needs have an order of importance, with physiological and safety needs taking priority, followed by love and belonging, esteem and self-actualisation. Maslow suggests that the priority needs must be met before the higher needs can be addressed. Berry posits that Intensive Interaction, as related to this hierarchy, can meet a range of needs identified by Maslow, including safety, love/belonging, esteem and self-actualising.

Maslow's ideas were the forerunner of the Positive Psychology movement, and Chapter 4 considers how Intensive Interaction can be conceptualised within this framework.

### Psychodynamic theories

While the importance of Intensive Interaction as promoting the 'fundamentals of communication' is highlighted in publications and research as described in Chapter 1, the consideration of the psychological impact of the failure to offer attuned communication has received less attention. However, psychological practitioners of Intensive Interaction see this as fundamental to understanding why Intensive Interaction is such a valuable intervention. Bowlby's attachment theory (1969) is considered a key theory by a number of psychologists using Intensive Interaction (Berry et al., 2014). In this context, psychological practitioners are highlighting the opportunity to develop a 'secure base' through the use of Intensive Interaction, and that individuals with severe and profound learning disability can then utilise this as a platform to engage more widely.

Siegel and Bryson (2020) have highlighted the elements to build secure attachment into '4 Ss', namely being Seen, Safe, Soothed and Secure. They also promote the importance of being 'present' in interactions as an important factor, which has clear resonance with the practice of Intensive Interaction and is why psychologists consider this approach to be a tool for building secure attachments. Of great importance is that a lack of a 'secure base', demonstrated where individuals are not 'seen' and engaged with in a way that is meaningful for them, is considered to lead to psychological distress. Reviews of the attachment literature have consistently shown that people with intellectual disabilities are at an increased risk of attachment difficulties (Hamadi & Fletcher, 2021; Van Ijzendoorn et al., 1999).

Samuel and Doswell (2021) wrote a chapter espousing the use of Intensive Interaction as an intervention as part of trauma-informed care for people with severe and profound intellectual disabilities, drawing on Skelly's attachment-informed Conditions for Security model (2017). This model highlights the importance of emotional availability, predictability, warmth, shared exploration and mutual enjoyment in developing positive attachments. In the chapter, Samuel and Doswell recognise that there are different ways Intensive Interaction may be utilised within a trauma-informed context, including through the development of relationships (promotion of positive attachment) and as a restorative intervention when individuals had experienced trauma such as through neglect or abuse that can cause attachment difficulties (a more 'therapeutic' approach).

These ideas are explored more fully in Chapter 3.

### Developmental theories

Suzanne Zeedyk is a research psychologist with a focus on the importance of communication and the role of connection in the development of babies and children. Zeedyk has written substantially on this topic, including editing a book in 2008 which includes describing the use of Intensive Interaction with a range of client groups with communication impairments, and utilising the work of developmental psychologists to provide explanations for the success of Intensive Interaction as an approach to promote communication and connectiveness.

Trevarthen (2008) in the chapter 'Intuition for Human Communication' describes the main findings relating to brain and physiological development that they believe are relevant to understanding the processes inherent in Intensive Interaction, with the aim of assisting psychologists wanting to 'help people with communicative impairments to have richer, happier lives' (p. 25). The starting position is that all human beings have an innate and intuitive capacity to use their bodies to communicate intentions and feelings. Child development research from the 1960s onwards demonstrated this intuitive sharing between infants and mothers, and also described the early engagement between child and caregiver that was considered the foundation of language, including rhythm and repetition. Murray and Trevarthen (1985) expanded this work to consider the psychological impact of this engagement, as they found that if the mother failed to show well timed and sympathetic responses to the infant's overtures, this led to withdrawal and distress in the infant.

Jeffries (2009) highlights the potential use of 'mirror neurons' to describe the processes taking place in Intensive Interaction. 'Mirror neurons' are cells that fire during both the execution and observation of motor behaviour and have been indicated as important in social condition and empathy (Enticott et al., 2019). Neuro-biological researchers note that while negative aspects of human social behaviour have been well researched, elements of pro-social behaviours such as 'affiliation' (that we see in Intensive and Adaptive Interaction) are less well researched (Alexander et al., 2021), but this is likely to be a valuable area for exploration over time.

### A trans-theoretical model of Intensive Interaction

It is clear that there is a wide range of psychological theories that can help psychological practitioners to conceptualise Intensive Interaction. While it may seem that having this range is a positive thing, allowing psychological practitioners from different schools of thought to embrace Intensive Interaction, in reality this breadth of theory appears to have also been problematic, as there has not been a unified psychological theory which has synthesised how to conceptualise Intensive Interaction. This may mirror Ephraim's apparent struggle to provide theoretical coherence with regard to his 'augmented mothering' on which Intensive Interaction was built. As Berry et al. (2014) note from their research with psychological practitioners using Intensive Interaction:

> without theory development and generation of an evidence base for a psychological or therapeutic model of Intensive Interaction, the approach is open to being dismissed as more commonplace than scientific.
>
> (p. 409)

In an attempt to overcome this barrier, a group of psychological practitioners who utilise Intensive Interaction have developed a model that we hope enables psychological practitioners to conceptualise Intensive Interaction within a psychological framework, while providing flexibility for the theoretical underpinnings to come from a preferred approach. This model can be found in Chapter 11.

## Research

A second area of challenge for the adoption of Intensive Interaction by psychologists appears to be the lack of robust psychological research demonstrating the value. This is directly relevant to the challenges of theoretical coherence describe above, as without this, an agreement regarding which outcomes should be expected and therefore measured cannot be reached.

Berry et al. (2014) noted that Intensive Interaction as an approach had not been present in psychological literature, and considered that this may have hampered adoption of Intensive Interaction within clinical psychology services.

Early on, Kellett and Nind (2001) recognised the challenges of undertaking quasi-experimental research in relation to Intensive Interaction, with particular issues highlighted in relation to informed consent, the ethics of withholding or removing an intervention considered to be helpful, issues with tools of measurement and ownership of data. Samuel (2001) notes that the analysis of Intensive Interaction outcomes contains the same challenges as psychotherapy process research and queries whether behavioural markers are an adequate measure to explore the participant's experience of Intensive Interaction. Samuel also notes the importance of measuring the impact on practitioners.

So, it is clear that there are challenges in undertaking robust research in relation to Intensive Interaction, and that consideration of adding a level of the psychological factors and outcomes increases complexity.

Despite these challenges, psychologists have undertaken psychological research in relation to Intensive Interaction in two key areas: participant experience and outcomes (typically through the case studies described below) and practitioner experience. More recently, efforts have been made to undertake more robust psychological research through systematic reviews and controlled studies, as well as considerations around outcome measurement.

### Case studies

Since the very early days of Intensive Interaction, even when the concepts were being developed, psychologists have undertaken case studies, however these have not typically explored or espoused Intensive Interaction as a psychological intervention, but focused on the more traditional social and communication development identified through using this approach. There are likely to be a number of reasons for this, including Intensive Interaction not having a shared conceptualisation regarding how to articulate this as a psychological approach and challenges of psychological measurement, especially with individuals with severe and profound learning disability who may struggle to describe their internal world.

Lovell, Jones and Ephraim (1998) published a case study describing Ephraim's clinical work, using Intensive Interaction with a man with severe intellectual disabilities. During Intensive Interaction sessions, the client initiated more physical contact, spent more time looking at people, demonstrated more joint attention and smiled and laughed more.

Around the same time, the clinical psychologist Judith Samuel published an early series of case studies with an Occupational Therapy colleague (Samuel & Maggs, 1998). Three cases showed the power of Intensive Interaction as utilised by professionals including clinical psychologists, but also highlighted potential barriers;

> In the case of Rodney, Levi and Stefan, a stranger was able to quickly interact with each of them in a way that day-to-day staff did not appear to do, either through ignorance of methods to use or through fear that such contact might be received with disfavour from management for not being in line with the assumed philosophy of the service.
>
> (p. 130)

A further case study, with an individual called 'Alice' described the introduction of Intensive Interaction into a service, and notes the inclusion of 'formal' weekly sessions from members of the multi-disciplinary team (more akin to therapy) and 'informal' sessions undertaken by support workers. Outcomes of this work were focused on communication and engagement (such as eye contact and physical proximity) rather than more explicit psychological elements such as attachment and wellbeing.

Elgie and Maguire (2001), at the time of publication an assistant and trainee clinical psychologist respectively, described work with a woman with severe intellectual disabilities and visual impairment, who engaged in serious self-injurious behaviour. Three areas for measurement were identified; the client 'reaching out', self-injurious behaviour and increase in vocalisations. The introduction of this new 'reaching out' behaviour was considered to be a 'sign of an emotional bond developing', which links clearly to attachment theory described earlier, although the authors do not explicitly conceptualise it as such. An increase in vocalisations is noted to be an indicator of communication development. No change was noted in level of self-injurious behaviour.

Brian Leaning, a clinical psychologist, and Tessa Watson, a music therapist and trainee clinical psychologist, reported the outcomes of a group intervention using Intensive Interaction (Leaning & Watson, 2006). A stated aim of the group was the development of emotional literacy, and to this end five outcomes were reported from their group. Three could be considered more traditional communication/social outcomes, namely eye contact with others, object orientated eye contact and active avoidant behaviour (e.g. moving or turning away). Two areas of measurement were more psychological in nature; smiling and self-stimulation (e.g. rocking, face slapping). They found participants demonstrated increased eye contact to others and to objects and a reduction in active avoidant behaviours. An increase in smiling was noted throughout the group and a reduction in self-stimulation was also reported. The authors conclude 'that this technique could be an essential tool in accessing meaningful contact and enhancing the emotional world of the participant'.

Chapter 6 describes the development, use and evaluation of a form of Intensive Interaction adapted for individuals with advanced dementia (Adapted Interaction). A significant difference with Adaptive Interaction is the recognition that with individuals with dementia, we are not expecting them to regain or develop skills, and therefore there is more of a focus on the 'here and now' and ensuring a positive connection between individuals with dementia and caregivers. Ellis and Astell published a single case study using Adapted Interaction, in 2008, and followed this with a multiple case study published in 2011.

Harding and Berry (2009) describe successful use of Intensive Interaction by a psychologist working with a woman who was more intellectually able than those described in previous case studies. The client had lived in hospitals since childhood and had a history of neglect and abandonment which had led to a range of difficulties including impulse control, difficulties forming relationships, self-injury and aggression towards others. Harding & Berry noted that the Intensive Interaction sessions seemed to provide the client with human connection that she enjoyed and within which she could exercise control in a safe way. Although not explicitly referenced, this clearly maps on to the development of secure attachment, and the attachment behaviours described by Siegel.

In a paper from 2013, Phoebe Caldwell and a psychiatrist Elspeth Bradley published a paper which described Intensive Interaction as an important element in supporting the mental health needs of autistic individuals (Bradley & Caldwell, 2013). Three case studies are highlighted, where Intensive Interaction is utilised alongside environmental adaptations. In Susan's case study, Intensive Interaction is utilised as both a direct therapeutic intervention on a one to one basis and is introduced to care staff, with a resulting reduction in a range of behaviours of concern including self-injury and screaming.

It is clear from case studies, which have been published over many years, that psychological practitioners have been undertaking Intensive Interaction and noting benefits from this approach. However, it may be that these have not focused sufficiently on the psychological benefits of the approach, and perhaps have not demonstrated robust enough outcomes to persuade psychologists of the validity of the approach.

### Systemic reviews and control group research

More recently, psychologists have made efforts to analyse the outcomes from Intensive Interaction utilising more robust methods. In 2015, psychologists Hutchinson and Bodicoat (2015) published a systematic literature review, analysing results from 15 quantitative and 3 qualitative papers. They concluded that 'studies were limited by the quality of reporting and difficulties conducting good quality, ethically sound research with participants … more research needs to be conducted before conclusions can be drawn regarding the efficacy of this approach'. This appears to underline the challenge that psychologists using Intensive Interaction have struggled with in the promotion of this approach.

Tee and Reed (2017) conducted research into Intensive Interaction with children with autism, utilising a control group, comparing a 20-participant 'treatment as usual' group of male children, with a matched group who also received Intensive Interaction over a six-month period. The Intensive Interaction group demonstrated a numerically greater reduction in child behaviour problems than the control sample; however, this difference was not statistically reliable. Other outcomes such as adaptive and social behaviours were not measured. It was noted that, the worse the child behaviour problems, and the worse the level of maternal depression, the fewer improvements were shown by the children following the Intensive Interaction programme. This research highlights that Intensive Interaction may not impact upon challenging behaviours, especially where the behaviours are significant, which is in line with the finding from Elgin and Maguire that Intensive Interaction did not alter the amount of self-injurious behaviour demonstrated.

Tee and Reed's finding regarding the level of maternal depression highlights a wider question regarding the parents, support workers and practitioners, including psychologists and psychotherapists offering Intensive Interaction. What is their experience of using the approach, and can this tell us anything about the helpfulness of the approach from a different perspective?

### Practitioner research

Psychologists have undertaken research with the regard to the experiences of practitioners and the impact that utilising this approach has on their attitude towards clients and how they feel about their work more widely. Where psychologists are promoting the development of attachment, focus on carers' experience is vital, as a significant association has been found between caregiver sensitivity (particularly in response to distress or fear) and child security of attachment (National Collaborating Centre for Mental Health, 2015). This takes on particular importance as the context of care provision in the UK is that many roles remain vacant, and reports demonstrate individuals are not receiving the quality of care they are entitled to (Care Quality Commission, 2022).

Therefore, one important area is how we ensure that those living and working with people who are 'seldom heard' can develop positive relationships with them, as we know that positive attachments are vital and that this is a group that is at risk of abuse if those supporting them do not understand their needs. The good news is that Intensive Interaction studies consistently report that staff develop improved knowledge of, and relationships with, the individuals they support through the use of Intensive Interaction. Berridge and Hutchinson (2021) undertook a systematic literature of nine papers exploring staff experiences of Intensive Interaction and found that Intensive Interaction is rewarding for staff, although implementation was sometimes perceived to be challenging.

Illustrating these challenges and benefits, Firth et al. (2008) describe the outcomes from training 29 care staff across four residential settings in the use of Intensive Interaction. Support was provided over a 6-month period post training. Responses indicated that staff felt rewarded by an Intensive Interaction episode that went well, but could struggle when individuals were less responsive. However, there were individual differences in relation to this, as one staff member described how successful efforts to engage a previously unresponsive individual had encouraged them to spend more time with that person. Pleasure experienced by clients as a result of Intensive Interaction led to staff enjoyment, which was recognised as being motivating for staff. The potential of Intensive Interaction as a relationship building tool was recognised by staff, although of interest is that not all staff perceived this as an appropriate goal.

Similar effects are found when a much less intensive training programme is offered. Zeedyk et al. (2009) trained twelve British teenagers who were volunteering with children living within Romanian Government institutions. The training took place during the first week into a two-week placement, split into two 30 minute sessions. The first included explaining the background and aims of Intensive Interaction, alongside a general description of the practice of Intensive Interaction; the second involved videos being shown to the volunteers to illustrate the approach in practice. Volunteers were asked to provide a narrative regarding their experiences of using Intensive Interaction, which were analysed by the research team. The comments of the volunteers showed that they could identify improvements in the children's communicative abilities once they began to use Intensive Interaction, with the most frequently cited behaviour being an increase in the children's attention to their partner. All volunteers reported observing increased engagement in the children, and that they had stronger motivation and sense of connection.

Clegg et al. (2020) surveyed over 50 day centre staff who had undertaken a day long training in Intensive Interaction and found that the majority of participants (92%) agreed that Intensive Interaction helps them get to know the person they support and that Intensive Interaction is a positive experience for them and for the person they support (91%). When 28 staff were interviewed and these interviews analysed, findings demonstrated that Intensive Interaction helps staff to build relationships with service users, and increase staff confidence and job satisfaction.

These benefits are also seen for staff working with adults with dementia. Ellis and Astell (2011) considered the effect of training caregivers in a nursing home in the use of Intensive Interaction techniques (Adaptive Interaction). The results state that after training staff members were able to recognise the individual ways in which the residents communicated and felt better equipped to respond appropriately. Further research (Astell, Shoaran & Ellis, 2022) indicated that caregivers trained in Adaptive Interaction learnt how to attend to individual residents, identify communicative behaviour and make a meaningful connection with them.

It appears that the benefits to practitioners are long lasting. Nagra et al. (2017) interviewed eight paid carers who had been trained in Intensive Interaction two to three years post training. Analysis of the interviews revealed similarities in responses, leading to a 'master theme' of emotional and practical endurance, with *empowerment, better understanding* and *perceived barriers to implementation* comprising subthemes. In relation to empowerment, staff commonly expressed increased confidence which led to an improvement in relationships, including a strengthening of the bond between client and carer. Carers also reported an understanding that 'clients should be able to 'let go and do what they would like in a safe environment', which has clear echoes of being a 'secure attachment base' for individuals. Realisation included that prior to Intensive Interaction they had little knowledge of their clients and how to communicate with them, but this changed following implementation of the approach.

### Opportunities for further research

It is clear that the research literature regarding Intensive Interaction, especially with regard to psychological outcomes such as wellbeing and the reduction of behaviours of concern, remains an area requiring further development, and a clear area which can explain the reluctance of psychologists to fully embrace the approach. A challenge therefore posed to psychological practitioners is how research into Intensive Interaction can be designed which is ethical and measures a wide range of meaningful outcomes that are relevant to psychological practitioners, including attachment behaviours in both the recipients of Intensive Interaction and the practitioners.

In Chapter 11, we consider a range of measures that could be useful in demonstrating the psychological benefits of Intensive Interaction for individuals.

It appears that insufficient importance has been placed on the robust and repeated finding that Intensive Interaction is important for staff, and that it improves knowledge of and relationships with individuals who are 'seldom heard', apparently leading to the conditions for positive attachments to be developed. This is an extremely important finding and should be espoused as a clear benefit of the approach, with associated measurement.

## Intensive Interaction in psychological practice

Despite the theoretical and research difficulties that have been highlighted in this chapter, psychologists using Intensive Interaction regularly have seen the psychological benefits that the approach brings, and have shared their enthusiasm for Intensive Interaction with the psychological community.

Judith Samuel wrote about Intensive Interaction within *Clinical Psychology Forum*, a publication for clinical psychologists (Samuel, 2001). As well as describing the development of the approach and the growing evidence base, Samuel described the introduction of the approach within a Community

Learning Disability Team (CLDT) and then to residential and day centre settings across the local area in the late 1990s.

In 2009, Cathy Harding, Ruth Berry and Luke Jeffries (2009) wrote about Intensive Interaction in *The Psychologist*, the British Psychological Society's monthly members' magazine. Jeffries noted 'Nind and colleagues ... claim that Intensive Interaction offers a positive way of gaining insights into a person's state of mental health and of promoting their emotional wellbeing' (2009, p. 757) and concluded that 'psychology can assist the debate on what Intensive Interaction is and how it works, and so further its potential use as an educational, *therapeutic* and social approach' (p. 759). Harding and Berry argued that Intensive Interaction 'has the potential to function as a powerful therapeutic intervention for people who struggle to use words to express their emotional state and for whom social interactions are difficult' (p. 758).

Ellis and Astell have published a number of papers aimed at highlighting the development and benefits of Adapted Interaction (e.g. Ellis & Astell, 2011, 2017) including in *The Psychologist* in 2015.

However, as described in Chapter 9, despite the attempts of psychological practitioners to 'spread the word' about Intensive or Adaptive Interaction, a recent survey of clinical psychology training courses (Dunstan, 2024) found that of 32 courses approached, only 12 of the 21 who responded said they taught about Intensive Interaction, and only one reported offering teaching on Adaptive Interaction.

To date, there has not been agreement as to how Intensive Interaction might be different when being utilised by psychological practitioners rather than, for example, educators or other professionals such as Speech and Language Therapists. To an outsider, watching a psychological practitioner utilising Intensive Interaction is likely to look identical to watching another practitioner using the approach.

In reality, what psychological practitioners report is three ways Intensive Interaction is used. One is the same as other practitioners, where psychologists are looking to communicate and connect with an individual. This is at the level of meaningful engagement. Psychologists may use Intensive Interaction to get to know clients they are due to work with using other models such as Positive Behaviour Support, or if spending time in a setting such as day centre, where they are engaging with a wide group of individuals but without the expectation to undertake psychological work.

A second area is linked to the first, and involves supporting others to undertake the use of Intensive interaction through elements of service development such as training, modelling, supervision and consultation. Chapter 10 describes this area of working in more detail. Often, when this service development is reported, the psychological aspects of Intensive Interaction have not been explicitly communicated to participants, but it is likely that this could be a useful addition, both with regard to the why (i.e. getting to know people, building positive attachments) but also explaining the benefits for staff. It may also help staff consider what they are hoping to get from using the approach, and understand that any positive emotions and experiences they have while using Intensive Interaction are valuable and are hoped-for outcomes, as well as any positives the individual experiences.

The final area where psychologists report utilising Intensive Interaction is where there is suggestion of psychological distress, perhaps seen in 'behaviours of concern' (see Chapter 5) and due to attachment difficulties and/or 'mental illness' where psychologists may draw on wider psychological experiences to undertake Intensive Interaction with a different purpose – to reduce distress and facilitate psychological growth (see Chapter 3 for further examples). This may look subtly different, for example offering a series of sessions at the same time and day which would look more like therapy as described by Samuel and Doswell (2021) in their chapter on trauma informed care.

## Summary and conclusions

As we move, in the following chapters, from theory and research into practice, there are a number of important considerations that have been highlighted through the work of psychologists described above.

- Psychologists appear to have rejected Intensive Interaction due to a lack of theoretical clarity describing the approach in psychological terms. We are hopeful that the model we have developed and describe in Chapter 11 will be a step towards overcoming this particular barrier.
- Psychological practitioners have not consistently identified and articulated the psychological benefits of Intensive Interaction, above and beyond elements of communication and social interaction. Alongside the model we have developed, we have suggested psychological measures that could be implemented with both the participant and practitioner.
- These challenges have meant research has not concentrated on measuring psychological outcomes, which may stop psychologists recognising the approach as having scientific rigour. Additional challenges have been noted with regard to robust and ethical study design, which must be overcome to build the evidence base. Further psychological research is required to counter these impediments.
- The outcomes from Intensive Interaction have focused on the recipients; however, there is a significant benefit for families and staff teams in using the approach which has not been given the importance it deserves. This area should be explored further as a benefit of the approach in its own right.
- In addition to the theoretical and research challenges highlighted in this chapter, psychologists are also subject to the barriers that have been more generally highlighted with regard to implementing this approach such as a resistance to engaging with individuals who are 'seldom heard' and a reluctance to make oneself 'emotionally available' to this group. This

detachment is described and discussed in more detail in Chapter 3. Barriers to adopting Intensive or Adaptive Interaction are the subject of Chapter 8.

The hope in writing this book is that we can bring together the psychological community to embrace Intensive and Adaptive Interaction as psychological interventions for individuals who are 'seldom heard', and those who support them.

## References

Alexander, R., Aragón, O. R, Bookwala, J, Cherbuin, N., Gatt, J. M., Kahrilas, I. J., Kästner, N., Lawrence, A., Lowe, L., Morrison, R. G., Mueller, S. C., Nusslock, R., Papadelis, C., Polnaszek, K. L., Richter, S. H., Silton, R. L & Styliadis, C. (2021) The neuroscience of positive emotions and affect: implications for cultivating happiness and wellbeing. *Neuroscience & Biobehavioral Reviews*, 121, 220–249.

Astell, A. J. & Ellis, M. P . (2011) The challenges of equipping care home staff with psychosocial skills: reflections from developing a novel approach to communication. *PSIGE Newsletter*, 117, 26–32.

Astell, A. J., Shoaran, S. & Ellis, M. P. (2022) Using adaptive interaction to simplify caregiver's communication with people with dementia who cannot speak. *Frontiers in Communication*, 6, doi:10.3389/fcomm.2021.689439.

Berridge, S. & Hutchinson, N. (2021) Staff experience of the implementation of intensive interaction within their places of work with people with learning disabilities and/or autism. *Journal of Applied Research in Intellectual Disabilities*, 34 (1), 1–15.

Berry, R. (2010) Some psychological theories of human behaviour. In G. Firth, R. Berry & C. Irvine, *Understanding Intensive Interaction: Context and concepts for professionals and families*. London: JKP.

Berry, R., Firth, G., Leeming, C. & Sharma, V. (2014) Clinical psychologists' views of Intensive Interaction as an intervention in learning disability services. *Clinical Psychology & Psychotherapy*, 21(5), 403–410.

Bowlby, J. (1969) Attachment. *Attachment and Loss, Vol. 1, Loss*. New York: Basic Books.

Bradley, A. & Caldwell, P. (2013) Mental health and autism: promoting autism favourable environments. *Journal on Developmental Disabilities*, 19 (1), 8–23.

Caldwell, P. (2008) Intensive Interaction: getting in touch with a child with severe autism. In M. Suzanne Zeedyk (ed.) *Promoting Social Interaction for Individuals with Communicative Impairments: Making contact*. London: Jessica Kingsley Publishers.

Caldwell, P. (2013) Intensive interaction: using body language to communicate. *Journal on Developmental Disabilities*, 19 (1) 33–39.

Caldwell, P., Bradley, E., Gurney, J., Heath, J., Lightowler, H., Richardson, K. & Swales, J. (2019) *Responsive Communication: Combining attention to sensory issues with using body language (Intensive Interaction) to interact with autistic adults and children*. UK: Pavilion.

Care Quality Commission (2022) *The State of Health Care and Adult Social Care in England 2021/22*. https://www.cqc.org.uk/publication/state-care-202122.

Clegg, J., Black, R., Smith, A. & Brumfitt, S. (2020) Examining the impact of a city-wide intensive interaction staff training program for adults with profound and multiple learning disability: a mixed methods evaluation. *Disability and Rehabilitation*, 42 (2), 201–210.

Dunstan, S. (2024) *Intensive Interaction and Adaptive Interaction Teaching: What can Doctorate in Clinical Psychology courses in the United Kingdom tell us?* Unpublished service related research report. Colchester: University of Essex.

Elgie, A. & Maguire, N. (2001) Intensive interaction with a woman with multiple and profound disabilities: a case study. *Tizard Learning Disability Review*, 6, 18–24.

Ellis, M. P. & Astell, A. J. (2008) Promoting communication with people with severe dementia. In M. Suzanne Zeedyk (ed.) *Techniques for Promoting Social Engagement in Individuals with Communicative Impairments*. London: Jessica Kingsley Publishers.

Ellis, M. & Astell, A. (2011) Adaptive interaction: a new approach to communication. *Journal of Dementia Care, 19 (3)*, 24–26.

Ellis, M. P. & Astell, A. J. (2017) Communicating with people with dementia who are nonverbal: the creation of adaptive interaction. *PLOS ONE*, 12 (8), e0180395.

Ephraim, G. (1982) Developmental process in mental handicap: a generative structure approach. Unpublished Ph.D. thesis, Brunel University.

Ephraim, G. (1989) *A Brief Introduction to Augmented Mothering*. Herts: Playtrac.

Enticott, P. E., Kirkovski, M. & Oberman, L. M. (2019) Transcranial magnetic stimulation in autism spectrum disorder. In Lindsay M. Oberman & Peter G. Enticott (eds) *Neurotechnology and Brain Stimulation in Pediatric Psychiatric and Neurodevelopmental Disorders*. London: Academic Press.

Firth, G., Berry, R. & Irvine, C. (2010) *Understanding Intensive Interaction: Context and concepts for professionals and families*. London: JKP.

Firth, G., Elford, H., Leeming, C. & Crabbe, M. (2008) Intensive interaction as a novel approach in social care: care staff's views on the practice change process. *Journal of Applied Research in Intellectual Disabilities*, 21, 58–69.

Hamadi, L., & Fletcher, H. K. (2021) Are people with an intellectual disability at increased risk of attachment difficulties? A critical review. *Journal of Intellectual Disabilities*, 25 (1), 114–130.

Harding, C. & Berry R. (2009) Intensive Interaction as a psychological therapy. *The Psychologist*, 22, 758–759.

Henwood, A., & Ellis, M. (2015) Giving a voice to people with advanced dementia. *The Psychologist*, 28 (12), 976–979.

Hutchinson, N. & Bodicoat, A. (2015) The effectiveness of intensive interaction: a systematic literature review. *Journal of Applied Research in Intellectual Disabilities*, 28, 437–454.

Jeffries, L. (2009) Introducing intensive interaction. *The Psychologist*, 22, 756–759.

Kellett, M. & Nind, M. (2001) Ethics in quasi-experimental research on people with severe learning disabilities: dilemmas and compromises. *British Journal of Learning Disabilities*, 29, 51–55.

Leaning, B. & Watson, W. (2006) From the inside looking out: an Intensive Interaction group for people with profound and multiple learning disabilities. *British Journal of Learning Disabilities*, 34 (2), 103–109.

Lovell, D. M., Jones, S. P. & Ephraim, G. (1998) The effects of intensive interaction on a man with severe intellectual disabilities. *International Journal of Practical Approaches to Disability*, 22, 3–9.

Maslow, A. H. (1943) *A Theory of Human Motivation. Psychological Review*, 50, 370–396.

Merry, T. (2002) *Learning and Being in Person-centred Counselling*, (2nd edn) Ross-on-Wye: PCCS Books.

Murray, L. & Trevarthen, C. (1985) Emotional regulation of interactions between two-month- olds and their mothers. In T. M. Field & N. A. Fox (eds) *Social Perception in Infants* (pp. 177–197) Norwood NJ: Ablex Publishers.

Nagra, M. K., White, R., Appiah, A. & Rayner, K. (2017) Intensive interaction training for paid carers: 'looking, looking and find out when they want to relate to you', *JARID*, 30 (4), 648–660.

National Collaborating Centre for Mental Health (2015) *Children's Attachment: Attachment in children and young people who are adopted from care, in care or at high risk of going into care.* London: National Institute for Health and Care Excellence (NICE)

Nind, M. (2008) Promoting the emotional well-being of people with profound and multiple learning difficulties: a holistic approach through Intensive Interaction. In J. Pawlyn & S. Carnaby (eds) *Profound Intellectual and Multiple Disabilities: Nursing complex needs* (pp. 62–77) Oxford: Wiley-Blackwell.

Nind, M. (2012) Intensive interaction, emotional development and emotional well-being. In D. Hewett (ed.) *Intensive Interaction: Theoretical perspectives*. London: Sage.

Ross, E. & Oliver, C. (2003) Preliminary analysis of the psychometric properties of the Mood, Interest & Pleasure Questionnaire (MIPQ) for adults with severe and profound learning disabilities. *The British Journal of Clinical Psychology*, 42 (Pt 1), 81–93.

Samuel, J. (2001) Intensive interaction. *Clinical Psychology Forum*, 148, 22–25.

Samuel, J. & Doswell, J. (2021) The use of Intensive Interaction in trauma informed care for people with severe and profound intellectual disabilities. In N. Beail, P. Frankish & S. Skelly (eds) *Trauma and Intellectual Disability: Acknowledgement, identification & intervention.* Shoreham: Pavilion.

Samuel, J. & Maggs, J. (1998) Introducing Intensive Interaction for people with profound learning disabilities living in small staffed houses. In D. Hewett & M. Nind (eds) *Interaction in Action: Reflections on the use of Intensive Interaction* (pp. 23–31). London: David Fulton.

Seligman, M. (2010). Flourish: positive psychology and positive interventions. *The Tanner Lectures on Human Values*, 31, 1–56.

Siegel, D. & Bryson, T. (2020) *The Power of Showing Up: How parental presence shapes who our kids become and how their brains get wired.* London: Scribe.

Skelly, A. (2017) Maintaining bonds: positive behaviour support and attachment theory. *Clinical Psychology Forum*, 290, 36–41.

Tee, A. & Reed, P. (2017) Controlled study of the impact on child behaviour problems of intensive interaction for children with ASD. *Journal of Research in Special Educational Needs*, 17 (3), 179–186.

Trevarthen, C. (2008) Intuition for human communication. In S. Zeedyk (ed.), *Promoting Social Interaction for Individuals with Communicative Impairments: Making contact.* London: Jessica Kingsley Publishers.

Van Ijzendoorn, M. H., Schuengel, C. & Bakermans-Kraneburg M. J. (1999) Disorganized attachment in early childhood: meta-analysis of precursors, concomitants, and sequelae. *Development and Psychopathology*, 11, 225–250.

Zeedyk, S., Davies C., Parry, S. & Caldwell, P. (2009) Fostering social engagement in Romanian children with communicative impairments: the experiences of newly trained practitioners of intensive interaction. *British Journal of Learning Disabilities*, 37, 186–196.

# Chapter 3

# Intensive Interaction, suffering and healing – from diagnosing and prescribing to connecting and engaging

*Ditte Rose Andersen and Ruth Berry*

## Background

### Intensive Interaction, connection and emotion

Intensive Interaction (Nind & Hewett, 1994) builds on the insight from developmental psychology that social and communication learning takes place through mutually joyful, sensitive dialogue in which the less experienced communication partner is allowed to explore and lead. They are encouraged to do so by sensitive responses that let them know that their interlocutor is listening in wonder.

Although Intensive Interaction can be described as a positive approach, it's not one that advocates a 'drive' towards positivity. Rather the tuned-in availability of the practitioner allows for genuinely mutual and joyful experiences to happen. Importantly, we argue, it also provides a space for the person to share those less positive emotions which we associate with suffering: pain, fear, overwhelm, anger, grief.

Communication-disabled people[1] (e.g. autistic, intellectually or multiply disabled people) often face life conditions which cause suffering. These conditions are not inevitable but arise from the way disabled people are positioned (Davies and Harré, 1990) and understood by wider society. Intensive Interaction has the potential to help people around the person (such as family, friends and care workers) connect with and act on the pain and suffering encountered. This can prompt supporters to better identify and potentially change the conditions affecting how disabled people live.

Here, we explore this potential of Intensive Interaction, drawing on psychological research and theories that stress intersubjectivity and knowing others through shared experience and engagement. We argue that Intensive Interaction can be understood as a relational space in which suffering can be shared and processed with others. Through theoretical discussion and case examples we show how Intensive Interaction has the potential to create such spaces within which human experiences can be *shared* and the person has an opportunity to *exert influence* over their life conditions, giving them more agency and options.

DOI: 10.4324/9781003597933-3

Interactions that involve openness and connection can both reveal and create the material for genuinely person-centred changes and improvements. We contrast this with alternative, more orthodox approaches which can involve diagnosis and a prescription made by the clinician/practitioner who retains a professional distance from the person.

We start by describing the kinds of adversity, pain and suffering experienced by many disabled children and adults and some of the factors which contribute to these experiences. We stress how detached ways of 'handling' this suffering exacerbate it. We then present Buber's thoughts (Buber, 1965, 2013) on how people exist in relations as a way to understand how Intensive Interaction offers an alternative to this detached stance. We argue that being met as a 'You' lessens suffering, in contrast to the negative impacts of being related to in detached interactions ('I-It' in Buber's terms).

## Adversity, pain and suffering in the lives of communication-disabled people

In this section we unpack the proposition that adversity such as trauma, abuse and pain are both more likely in the lives of those living with disability, and less likely to be recognised, or considered when trying to understand them. Furthermore, we argue that they are less likely to have access to the kinds of resources and relationships that can ease the distress arising from adversity.

### Lack of communication, connection and relations

Often, disabled children and adults will not have had successful experiences of communication with others. Many factors contribute to this. Atypical, infrequent or different signals may not be recognised as communication by the people around the person. Conversely, those around the person may not adapt their own communication to make it accessible. Review studies on early communication with disabled babies find that adults tend to adopt a communication style different from that used with typically developing children, characterised by less synchrony (LeClère et al., 2014), less child-led interaction, more object-focused and less purely social play (Rogers, 1998).

Bicknell (1983) writes about the potential impact on parents of their baby being born with a disability and how this can disrupt the attachment process, leaving these infants at greater risk of insecure attachments with primary caregivers. This may have implications for their ability to form attachments throughout their life (e.g. Sroufe, 2005) and increase the risk of an insecure attachment style, with a lower ability to regulate their own distress, or let others help or comfort them.

While powerful, parental attachment is not the only factor influencing the child's ability and interest in forming bonds with others. Reddy et al. (1997) point out that the baby seeks companionship with other adults, from its very first moments of life. The access to such broader companionship influences their later abilities to form bonds with others. Disabled babies may experience a lack of synchrony across contexts and people. This lack of access to communication puts people at risk of not forming and developing relationships at large early in life, and continually (LeClère et al., 2014).

Furthermore, it is not only early in life that we need to see, hear and feel others and to be seen, heard and felt by others. Intersubjectivity, in the words of Stern (2004) is a primary, motivational factor from infancy onwards. Regardless of early attachment, the absence of positive interaction and communication puts relationships at risk or prevents them from forming altogether.

Communication-disabled people also experience barriers to *accessing the kinds of relationships* which could help deal with adversity: there may be a lack of connection in everyday life as well as a lack of access to therapy. Some disabled people are deemed unfit for therapy, perhaps as a result of practitioners distancing themselves from the pain of disability (e.g. Bender, 1993). This can also be hard for family caregivers. In Firth's recent survey (see Chapter 7) one parent talks about the profound emotional challenge of relating openly to their child using Intensive Interaction: '*at the beginning [...] I found it very painful to do Intensive Interaction because it stripped away some protective levels of denial I'd had, regarding his abilities*'. The very pain of disconnection can make connecting harder. As psychologists we've also heard 'lack of abstraction skills' or 'lack of language' stated as reasons for not offering therapy to communication-disabled people.

### Losses, grief and sorrow

In their book on grief in intellectually disabled people, Danish priest Line Rudbeck and social worker, Susanne Hollund (2018) argue that this group experiences far more loss than most due to their life conditions. They may experience partial or permanent loss of people they love, e.g. when moving out of the family home before being emotionally ready, having to move to a new residential service and, not least, seeing members of staff come and go; temporarily because of shifts, or permanently due to staff leaving. Often, the person will have no control over these losses, and will be the one being left, not the one leaving at their own will. This may also create anxiety and wariness of future losses.

### Abuse

Studies find a manifold increased risk of abuse for both disabled children (Jones et al., 2012) and adults (Hughes et al., 2012). Many disabled children experience multiple cases of abuse (Sullivan & Knutson, 2000). In both our countries (UK and Denmark), recent years have seen horrible examples of abuse within the institutions meant to protect and care for disabled people (see e.g. Richards, 2020).

Neglectful or volatile treatment may also come in forms not properly recognised as abuse such as severe behavioural modification, extensive goal-blocking, unwarranted/insensitive use of force and restraint and manipulative practices.

### Bodily distress, ill health and pain

For some disabled people, bodily distress is more or less constant (Hewett, 1998). This could be due to epilepsy, mobility problems, pains and aches, sensory differences, hormonal states, and/or the adverse effects from drugs. This distress is often exacerbated by surroundings which are not adapted to the person (such as too-intense lighting, uncomfortable furniture) and not within their control (Hewett, 1998). Sleep disorders are also extremely prevalent with many disabled children and adults (Esbensen & Schwichtenberg, 2016; Korb et al., 2021).

### Unhappiness and negative interactions

An historical and current lack of access to communication and interaction impacts how you view and feel about yourself and may be detrimental to your outlook on life and your sense of identity. In the words of Daniel Stern (2004) *'Without some continual input from an intersubjective matrix, human identity dissolves or veers off in odd ways'* (p. 107). When unhappiness, anxiety and upset is expressed through what Geraint Ephraim termed 'exotic communication' (Ephraim, 1998) it is often labelled as 'challenging behaviour'. This view can dehumanise the person suffering. Statements, such as 'keep the person at baseline', 'return them to baseline' or, 'manage risks to self and/or other', discourage staff from seeing the person as someone expressing understandable distress. It also encourages a very fragmented view through which we address behaviours, risks and levels of arousal, rather than address a person. Such practices can make it difficult for both the person and members of staff to recognise each other as whole, human beings. We can end up handling challenges instead of listening to unhappiness.

The causes and kinds of suffering and adversity described above are an important context for the practice of Intensive Interaction. In using the approach, we are likely to encounter people who experience more, and more kinds, of suffering than most. Later, we'll return to the specific ways in which Intensive Interaction relates to, engages with and lessens suffering and adversity. But before that, we'll discuss how widespread ideas of disability and behaviour impact the ways in which disability services and practices deal with suffering and adversity.

## Diagnosis and prescription vs. connection and engagement

In our everyday lives, most of us seek connection, understanding and engagement with others to deal with, lessen or alleviate our suffering. The absence of company in itself can lead to poorer mental and physical health, with loneliness being associated with both higher morbidity and mortality rates from various diseases (Hawkley, 2022). Physical pain is known to reduce when we are touched, spoken to, or even just in the presence of significant, empathetic others (Duschek et al., 2020). With connection we are not alone in adversity. Support helps us understand our situation better, make changes or look after ourselves better. We propose, however, that some widely-applied approaches to disability can prevent, rather than promote connection.

### The impact of a medical model of disability

Disability, within a medical model, is seen as 'individual, personal tragedy' leading to attempts to 'modify', 'train away' or 'compensate for' innate impairments. This model also promotes labelling people and their behaviour, lifting actions and interactions out of their context, and putting abstract interpretations (diagnostic labels) into the foreground (Oliver, 1990; Michalko, 2002).

Similar arguments are made in the Power Threat Meaning Framework (Johnstone & Boyle, 2018) which seeks to challenge the focus on diagnosis (rather than distress), and shift practice towards engagement with the whole person (their history, meaning-making, experience of power & their survival responses). We see this whole-person engagement as a feature of Intensive Interaction and also want to draw attention to the issue of who holds the power in labelling. When people have no influence over how they're described, diagnosed and labelled this is disempowering and there is a high risk of descriptions not being in line with a person's preferences and self-understanding (see Botha et al., 2023). In contrast, using a description which 'feels right' to the person can restore power to them. We all detach and conceptualise to some degree. Concepts help us simplify experience and facilitate action. But when detachment dominates our understanding, we risk missing out on what it means to be human. Knowledge produced only by a detached stance can make engagement less likely. Versions and concepts of disabilities can span from medical language and diagnostic criteria to more everyday descriptions such as 'inflexibility', 'challenging behaviours' or 'repetitive use of language'. When we say, 'Theo has no real interest in communication. He only uses others as tools' we describe everyday interactions (or lack thereof) in a detached, diagnostic way. Such language makes us less likely to 'just offer company' for Theo. Furthermore, we locate the problem within Theo, making us less likely to consider what goes on between Theo and his surroundings. And if Theo disagrees, it will be hard for him to object, since his very way of making contact is seen as 'not communication'.

### The impact and power of labelling

Communication-disabled people are often met with practices aimed at identifying and describing *parts* of them: levels of functioning, abilities and weaknesses (e.g. through speech and language or psychological assessment), specific behaviours (e.g. through behaviour analysis) or traits and characteristics (e.g. through diagnostics).

It is often seen as crucial to organising services offered, that we carry out this identification and classification of 'deficient parts'. For example, we organise time-tables, pre-structured activities and work stations designed to compensate for 'executive dysfunction' or a 'lack of central coherence'. Or, we identify behaviours which 'need' to be restricted or promoted and organise activities to shape, extin-guish, or train such behaviours. Both accommodating to, or modifying specific, identified differences can create a highly controlled environment, capable of causing the kind of powerlessness described by Hewett (1998).

Reductionist applications of a behavioural approach are a widely-applied manifestation of this. Despite this approach being innovative at the outset (aiming to show that the ineducable were not, in fact, beyond instruction), the risk is that a person's humanity is lost when they are dis-assembled into a col-lection of behaviours that are analysed and then managed. Beth, a parent doing Intensive Interaction with her son Gary, reflects (in Hewett & Nind, 1988) how Gary was treated by professionals before Intensive Interaction, stating 'my son was performing obedience tasks but remained socially isolated, in a little tor-mented world of his own' (p. 215).

In a BBC documentary on behavioural approaches to autism (Robertson, 2013) we see an autistic three-year-old boy sitting on the floor with a therapist. The boy smiles stiffly and does not look at ease, while the therapist tries to get him to clap in a specific way. Having tried to meet the therapist's demands, he reaches for the chocolate milk and pastry in front of him, but is prevented from taking it. The boy leans over, loses posture and cries, but is 'neutrally' moved back to an upright position and asked, again, to clap. When he does it wrong, the therapist instructs him more sternly, claps louder. The boy winces at the sound, now crying loudly. The therapist tries to get him to look at the pastry and stop crying. When he cries louder, the therapist turns away with a closed face, shaking his head, saying 'nooo' in an unengaged, but dissatisfied way, until the boy stops crying. We suggest that aiming to have the boy 'behave in a socially acceptable way' is not neutral. There is a decision on what is acceptable. There is a decision to detach from the boy's own experience.

Behavioural approaches emphasise learning through conditioning and getting the person to comply with what is expected. Hewett (1998) points to some of the negative consequences of this: instead of being with the person and building on their immedi-ate interests and current abilities and sensibilities, we come to expect certain 'good' or 'appropriate' behaviours of them. Instead of working towards sharing power, we solidify our own position of power by deciding what the 'goal' is; rewarding what we want from the person, ignoring (or punishing) what we don't want.

### How labelling and detachment affects culture

Detached, diagnostic practices can be more or less formal, stemming both from specific psychological and educational approaches, and policies mandating target-driven, assessment- or test-based methods, focusing on measuring outcomes in both students/service users and staff. Local conditions and work culture also play a role. For members of staff, a sense of powerlessness, lack of resources and training combined with a 'raw' culture can push services and staff towards a more unreflective, behaviouristic way of being with communication-disabled people. When people express distress in ways that others experience as challenging, in the absence of a well-led and well-resourced culture which supports positive relationships based on a compassionate understanding of each person, instrumentalism, then cruelty and control over them often follows.

## A psychological understanding of others through engagement

The causes of suffering for communication-disabled people are various and multiple. We have argued that such suffering and adversity:

1    frequently has to do with or is exacerbated by the *lack* of connection;
2    is frequently met with approaches that involve detachment.

Addressing detachment and lack of connection in a disconnected and detached way, we are less likely to overcome detachment and disconnection. Fundamentally, human understanding comes about through engagement, a point made repeatedly within developmental psychology. This is why babies and their caregivers so easily engage in dialogue with each other. They do not figure each other out, before they engage with each other. Instead, babies and their caregivers recognise each other as persons through 'genuine dialogue' where caregivers act in ways that make sense to the baby, allowing the baby to be a subject in the interaction (Reddy, 2008).

### Second person psychology and its relevance to communication-disability

Reddy (2008) proposes that what she and others (e.g. Costall, 2006; Leudar & Costall, 2009) have termed an ecological or second person psychology and epistemology is needed to make sense of these early accomplishments. Psychology needs to take into account, in its understanding of people, that we are not objects or sets of data to each other, rather we are subjects meeting other subjects. Engaged understanding, not detached deduction, is the more common way in which people understand each other. This contrasts with both behavioural and cognitive psychology in which understanding is thought to come about either from a third-person perspective where people deduct the content of others' minds (intentions, motives, thoughts and feelings) or a first-person perspective in where we use ourselves as a template to 'simulate' what the other feels, thinks, wants, etc. (Reddy, 2008). Babies understand their social world not after making theories, simulating or deducting, but through actively engaging with others as subjects (Stern 2004; Reddy 2008).

Psychology has a long history of trying to detach itself from the phenomena it's trying to understand (Leudar & Costall, 2009; Costall, 2006). Thus, a detached view on how people understand each other is not exclusive to communication disability. But the nature of communication disability and the prevalence of the detached stance in disability services makes it urgent to address the ways in which we relate to and come to know communication-disabled people. Not least, because communication-disabled people do not have the means to overcome detachment in the ways most people do.

### 'I-You', 'I-it', disability and Intensive Interaction

Martin Buber (2013) was interested in how we exist in and through our relation to the world and each other. According to Buber, we do not exist separate from how and with what we relate. And in relating, we also shape and influence what or whom we relate to. We do this in two fundamental ways: we either speak the primary word 'I-You' or we speak the primary word 'I-it'. That is, we can either approach, perceive and act as whole beings, over against other whole beings, open to being affected by and moved by them. We do this when we speak 'I-You'. Otherwise, we can separate and distance ourselves from the other, pick out details and observations to label, categorise, change or manipulate. When we do this, we speak the primary word 'I-it'.

And these two ways of relating change *us*. When we speak the 'I-You', we're ready to be moved and changed by what and who we meet. When we speak the 'I-It', we're unwilling to be affected by the other person, and simultaneously determined not to affect ourselves. We relate less to the person as a 'who', and more as a 'what', which may feel safer: we don't risk being stirred or shaken. But it can create a harmful tunnel vision: we are certain of what we are looking for, but closed to what is really there.

We find that the distinction between these two ways of relating is pertinent to our discussion of how we get to know and understand disabled people. Consider, for example, the sequence with the boy being trained by a behavioural therapist. The boy isn't being responded to; not even when he loses posture and doesn't know where to turn. Nobody speaks 'I-You' to him. Instead, the therapist tries to 'elicit' behaviours from him, focusing on the 'relevant' parts of him, be it his 'unreasonable' crying or the 'correct' way of clapping. The boy in the sequence is, effectively an 'it' to the therapist, who in turn refuses to change or be moved by the boy.

Suffering is amplified when we are related to as an 'it'. Common practices such as applying behavioural descriptions, setting targets, testing, training isolated skills, and devising no-touch policies can all, to varying degrees, be seen as consistent with this way of relating. While no one can relate to others as 'I-You' all the time, there is a clear need to be wary of the extent to which 'I-it' is spoken in the lives of communication-disabled people.

### 'I-You', suffering and Intensive Interaction

We believe that the open-ended nature of Intensive Interaction helps us speak 'I-You' when we relate to communication-disabled people and their suffering. The principles of Intensive Interaction focus on holding oneself ready, being open and not driving forward whatever is (Nind & Hewett, 1994). The practitioner does not pick out separate parts to 'work on'. Instead, we take what the person does to be, or potentially be, meaningful. We are ready to be moved and changed by the person we're relating to (a characteristic of speaking 'I-You'). This immediacy of Intensive Interaction, where no 'alternative' or 'better' communication is required to start communicating, means that expressions of suffering are not redirected, interpreted or translated by the more experienced communication partner; not even when what the other expresses is difficult to hear. In the following examples we highlight how Intensive Interaction can be seen to help us relate to and be moved by the other as a 'You' and how this can, in itself, help us to move further away from an 'I-it' way of relating.

### Intensive Interaction enables compassionate, immediate responses to suffering

At a special school, I (DRA) was using Intensive Interaction with Ludvig, a then 15-year-old autistic boy. He was sensitive to all external stimuli and one day he accidentally knocked over a row of four metal seats while wanting to touch the velvet upholstery. The seats didn't fall on him, but the sound of them did. It was a sharp, ringing sound which made him roar and wail. Stressed and unhappy, he curled into a turtle-like shape. I moved down beside him, roaring with the same emotional tone and holding out my hand which he grasped almost immediately. Recognising his own 'language' in my roar, my sense is that he then felt safe enough to make physical contact with me and was no longer alone in his suffering. Exchanges of truly sad sounds ensued: this established more connection between us and was comforting to him, helping him to be more at ease while walking to his classroom where he found his blanket and settled down. I spoke 'I-You' during these minutes, using the principles of Intensive Interaction to tune in and keep tuning in to Ludvig as a whole person, even as he expressed things that were hard to hear and bear.

### Intensive Interaction can help us move from 'I-it' to 'I-You'

Visiting a residential service, I [DRA] met Ellen, a middle-aged woman who was severely intellectually and physically disabled, had cerebral palsy, strong near-sightedness and did not use verbal language or symbols. She occasionally made a 'ma-ma-ma' sound in little bursts. She blew raspberries and spent quite some time gripping and squeezing her tongue. Observing interactions with Ellen, I noticed that her key worker was often soft and gentle, and that some openness was present when her key worker spoke tenderly to her, smiled and softened her face. However, few of Ellen's actions were responded to as communication. She was spoken to, not with. Other members of staff dealt with her actions as 'parts', for example responding to Ellen gripping and squeezing her tongue, or blowing raspberries, by either ignoring what she was doing or, frequently, using her bib to 'help' her keep her tongue in. This is given as an example of 'I-it' relating. Ellen was not being met as an intentional, living 'You'. According to Reddy (2023), barriers to relating to another as 'I-You' may come from both directions: from 'I' not being present or the other's unavailability as a 'You'. In line with both Sabat's work on Alzheimer's disease (2001) and Michalko's work on disability (2002), communication-disabled people are often positioned in ways more likely to make them unavailable as a 'You'. When people like Ellen are seen primarily in terms of disability and deviance, their actions are more likely to be interpreted as signs to look on instead of human action to be engaged with.

When I sat down with Ellen, I felt that she quickly understood that I wanted to communicate with her. I leaned in and responded to her blowing raspberries by either doing the same or just showing that I enjoyed being with her and heard her. I had a strong feeling that Ellen felt confirmed by my responses. She became increasingly engaged in both her own actions and in my responses to them. She started turning towards me while blowing raspberries and she paused in response to my responses. She started exploring my face with some scrutiny and amusement! The dialogue became intense and rhythmical and Ellen engaged me in her 'ma-ma-ma' sound by looking at and listening to me as I chimed in. The emotional tone shifted as the interaction went on, Ellen started to look thoughtful and somewhat sad. She took my hand, looked up and said very clearly, 'Ma-ma-ma-ma'. She then curled her lips, looking as if she might be about to cry. Her sad expression came and went, our eye contact deepened and I positioned my hand and arm in such a way as to offer her comfort. I had a strong sense that there was a 'present moment' between us (Stern, 2004). Stern encourages us to pay attention to these shared, human experiences in therapy, as they have the power to both connect and change us. My words for trying to capture this moment are 'I sense you're feeling something you haven't for a long time, something you've missed. I feel your sadness, grief possibly, over not being heard, seen or touched. Maybe you miss the people who used to hear, see and touch you. Do you miss your parents?'. Ellen cannot articulate how she experienced this moment that we shared. But Ellen's key worker was in the room with us and told me her thoughts had been almost exactly the same. Specifically, she felt that Ellen's 'ma-ma-ma' vocalisation had sounded less like the Danish for food (mad) and more like mum (mor) to her. She had heard something new.

Afterwards, I noticed changes in the quality of the interaction between the key worker and Ellen. The softness in the support worker's face changed with Ellen's vocalisations and facial expressions. She laughed. She had fun with

Ellen. Ellen looked stronger and more competent. A dynamic had entered their being together. Ellen was now someone doing something and by being responded to, her actions took on the power to position her more as a 'You' where previously they had cemented her position as an 'It'.

### Intensive Interaction can be therapeutic – and point to the need for therapy

Sometimes, relating with the sort of openness described above may be enough to begin healing and ameliorating suffering. In other cases, it may put a practitioner in contact with profound or intense feelings that they do not feel equipped to contain or understand. Consideration should then be given to whether the person needs formal therapeutic input. In a sense this is commonplace. For most people, a friend can provide a comforting interaction in times of distress, but they may suggest more specialist support if they sense that this is needed. Frequently, however, communication-disabled people have little access to both friendship and therapy. Whenever practitioners become aware of emotional wounds and suffering, it is important to be reflective and conscientious in trying to figure out whether they can safely engage with it or whether access to a therapist (knowledgeable in Intensive Interaction) would be helpful.

### Intensive Interaction can promote justice and advocacy

Looking through the lens of social and critical models of disability, we have pointed out how relating in a diagnostic and detached way can take away people's power to change the circumstances causing pain or suffering. A person's expression of intentions, emotions and experiences may be read as 'meaningless' or labelled 'challenging behaviour' and 'managed'. Seeing expressions of discontent as an 'It' to be dealt with takes away a person's means to influence their conditions. Promoting the 'safe management of challenging behaviour' in the absence of a strong message about attending to what that behaviour is communicating, risks silencing the voices of those who cannot express themselves in typical ways. Conversely, connecting with 'exotic communication' (Ephraim 1998) can position the person as someone who can exert influence over their circumstances and can effect change. Through Intensive Interaction, knowledge is both accessed and co-created. The interactions can yield important information: what activities to offer, what changes to make, what resources to make available and what understandings to attach to a person's actions.

This is illustrated in the following case example. When Dave came into the hospital, what seemed most apparent to me [RB, working with a colleague, GF, who also writes in this book] was his acute sensitivity to stimuli which led to him feeling highly threatened. Even the presence of others was, to him, an intolerable demand. He went into 'fight' mode whenever anyone got close to him. There was a focus on keeping him alive and restraint was used in order to manage his 'challenging behaviours' so that he ate and drank. As an Intensive

Interaction Practitioner [GF] and a Clinical Psychologist [RB], we were employed to help figure out how we might offer interaction in a way that Dave could accept. Had these roles not been part of the hospital team, Dave may have had his needs for food, fluid and cleanliness met, but his need for a relationship could have remained invisible (hidden by the fear and fight response that was triggered by others getting close) and unmet.

We learned from Dave's parents that he had previously enjoyed books featuring sea creatures and outer space. We figured that reading to him about these would be a very low-demand relational activity. We sat as far away as practicable and other than saying 'Hello', 'Goodbye' and letting him know who was there, we didn't initiate any conversation. With very few exceptions he seemed to accept our presence. Through attuning to him and noticing any sign of attending, listening, tension and relaxation, we made choices on how close to be. Over months of carefully calibrated changes in proximity and activity he became more comfortable with our presence, less tense and more available to receive what we were offering. The first 'big sign' came when, one day, he answered our 'good-bye'. The day-to-day support workers seemed quite bemused and sometimes amused by what we were doing, particularly in the early days when Dave showed no visible response to our presence or our reading to him. They had a long history of working within a reductionist behavioural approach. Working with a relational approach in their presence, our work became part of advocating for Dave and his fellow-patients' rights to relationships. In this sense, responding to Dave's communication could also be seen as disability politics in practice. Previously, as described by Michalko (2002), the difference that Dave's disability made was that he was different. Now, Dave's different way of communicating made another kind of difference: through responses, his behaviours took on a social, communicative meaning. Our relating to him helped him be recognised as a 'You', not an 'it'.

To make Intensive Interaction accessible to the team, bespoke training, supervision and feedback was offered. The team frequently lost hold of the principles of Intensive Interaction when they were relating to Dave: for example making activities into a competition (how many times a ping pong ball could be kept aloft) rather than focussing on the mutual enjoyment of shared activity. As in wider society, the value of simply being together was hard to keep alive in the face of pulls to compete. We felt that the onus was on us to insist on Dave's right to simply be together. One way of doing this was to state in our formulation that his powerful behavioural response to proximity was not a sign that he did not want interaction, but a threat response and that his previous physical aggression was his way of expressing suffering. We never fully understood the reasons for these responses, but it did ease significantly over time (years) and with multiple inputs (including psychoactive medication alongside our relationship-building).

Psychologists play a vital role in developing and sharing psychologically-informed formulations which can serve as roadmaps for relational interventions that re-connect people to others and so reduce their suffering. These formulations also need to attend to the person's system. When staff have become 'raw' and 'brutalised', they too need compassionate understanding and support in order to have the emotional strength needed to be open to the distress of others.

### Intensive Interaction allows for a different I-it

Any 'You' will, according to Buber, eventually become an 'it' when the present moment has passed, but the reverse is only a possibility. Any 'it' may become a 'You', only if related to by the 'I-You'. There is a real risk that someone is never or rarely being met as a whole being. This is different to sometimes being met as a sum of qualities: relating as 'I-it' is an everyday occurrence, and one that allows us to sum up, reflect and move on. We do, and do need to, step back and look at things, instead of just being with them.

Doing Intensive Interaction with Dave allowed for 'I-You' relating, and it changed the balance between openness and 'looking on' in Dave's life (see Reddy, 2023). But it also changed the quality of the 'I-it' for Dave. Because we did do more detached work (e.g. analysis, assessment and formulations), there was an element of relating in an 'I-it' way. But it was a different kind of 'I-it' relating because the 'its' had been 'brought into contact with and melted down by the Thou' as they '[came] into being' (Buber, 2013, p. 43).

Intensive Interaction can be seen as a conscious step away from accepting that we should predominantly relate as 'I-it' vis-à-vis communication-disabled people. This shift, in itself, can help heal and lessen suffering. But the connection involved in 'I-You' relating also transforms and makes visible new (and potentially more mutual and meaningful) particulars and qualities which can have an impact on the system around the person: this might include recordings, individual plans, policies or organising of daily routines and activities or the physical environment. Intensive Interaction can inform, qualify and change other practices in the everyday lives of communication-disabled people; not based on guesswork, simulation or 'perspective taking', but based on knowing through engagement.

## Conclusions

In this chapter we have proposed that the adversity, injustice, and suffering in the lives of communication-disabled people can be both caused and exacerbated by diagnosing behaviours and prescribing interventions, instead of engaging with people. Drawing on both Buber and second-person psychology, we have argued that a detached understanding is prevalent in the practices and services that communication-disabled people encounter.

Through case examples we have shown how the 'I-it' way of relating to another's pain may instinctively feel safer, but that this detachment can prevent virtuous cycles of engagement and connection from forming. Turning to

Intensive Interaction, we argued that the approach involves an open, 'I-You' way of relating. We suggested that it is precisely this aspect which makes it healing and therapeutic.

Through Intensive Interaction we are put in contact with the conditions under which many communication-disabled people live. We must carry this knowledge into the contexts where decisions and changes are made and resources allocated. We encourage psychologists to consider how Intensive Interaction could impact and fit with formulations, to help the system around the person recognise them as a person and be open to the suffering of the identified 'client'. We also encourage psychologists, therapists and other practitioners to recognise the therapeutic potential of Intensive Interaction in daily practice as well as an aspect of formal therapy.

Intensive Interaction fulfils needs that, if left unmet, would make anyone feel lonesome, invalidated, bored, detached and disconnected; lives filled with shared stories, play, connection, self-expression, touch, movement and smiles are better lives. Thus, Intensive Interaction helps people get what they need.

But it also offers a unique and honest way to relate to what the person does not want, what they dislike, or find hurtful and unjust. Intensive Interaction allows us to connect over both joy and suffering. This is inextricably bound up with the 'engaged epistemology' and the open nature of the approach; the willingness to move and be moved. We've argued that this speaks to its affinity with a second-person psychology. We hope that our discussion inspires others to explore this aspect further, and that this helps deepen their understanding of both the theory and practice of Intensive Interaction.

Intensive Interaction sensitises us to the plight of the other; what it is like to be them. The very practice of Intensive Interaction can help us tune in to the detachment of current practices. We can begin to notice when we speak or hear others speak 'I-it' to a communication-disabled person. We can begin to recognise the process of detaching in everyday interactions and in the guidelines, policies, treatments and approaches offered. And we can say to the other: 'You'.

## Notes

1   In this chapter, we use the term 'communication-disabled people' as we want the ideas shared here to be seen as applying to this group of people which is wider than typical service boundaries allow for. In clinical practice, both authors work with people who are communication-disabled for diverse reasons and both aim to be needs-led rather than diagnosis-led (an important distinction which we expand on below).

## References

Bender, M. (1993) The unoffered chair: the history of therapeutic disdain towards people with a learning difficulty. *Clinical Psychology Forum*, 54, 7–12.

Bicknell J. (1983) The psychopathology of handicap. *The British Journal of Medical Psychology*, 56 (Pt 2), 167–178.

Botha, M., Hanlon, J. & Williams, G. L. (2023) Does language matter? Identity-first versus person-first language use in autism research: a response to Vivanti. *Journal of Autism and Developmental Disorders*, 53 (2), 870–878.

Buber, M. (1965) *The Knowledge of Man: Selected essays*. New York: Harper & Row.

Buber, M. (2013) *I and Thou*. London: Bloomsbury Academic.

Costall A. (2006) 'Introspectionism' and the mythical origins of scientific psychology. *Consciousness and Cognition*, 15 (4), 634–654.

Davies, B. & Harré, R. (1990) Positioning: the discursive production of selves. *Journal for the Theory of Social Behaviour*, 20 (1), 43–65.

Duschek, S., Nassauer, L., Montoro, C., Bair, A. & Montoya, P. (2020) Dispositional empathy is associated with experimental pain reduction during provision of social support by romantic partners. *Scandinavian Journal of Pain*, 20 (1), 205–209.

Ephraim, G. (1998) Exotic communication, conversations, and scripts – or tales of the pained, the unheard and the unloved. In D. Hewett (ed.) *Challenging Behaviour: Principles & practice*. London: David Fulton.

Esbensen, A. J. & Schwichtenberg, A. J. (2016) Sleep in neurodevelopmental disorders. *International Review of Research in Developmental Disabilities*, 51, 153–191.

Hawkley, L. C. (2022) Loneliness and health. *Nature Reviews Disease Primers*, 8 (22).

Hewett, D. (1998) Commentary: helping the person learn to behave. In D. Hewett (ed.) *Challenging Behaviour: Principles & practice*. London: David Fulton.

Hewett, D. & Nind, M. (1998) *Interaction in Action: Reflections on the use of Intensive Interaction* (1st edn). London: David Fulton.

Hollund, S. & Rudbeck, L. (2018) *Når udviklingshæmmede sørger : en bog om tab, sorg og trøst*. Forlag: Socialt Fagforlag.

Hughes, K., Bellis, M. A., Jones, L., Wood, S., Bates, G., Eckley, L., McCoy, E., Mikton, C., Shakespeare, T. and Officer, A., (2012) Prevalence and risk of violence against adults with disabilities: a systematic review and meta-analysis of observational studies. *The Lancet*, 379(9826), 1621–1629.

Johnstone, L. & Boyle, M. with Cromby, J., Dillon, J., Harper, D., Kinderman, P., Longden, E., Pilgrim, D. & Read, J. (2018) *The Power Threat Meaning Framework: Towards the identification of patterns in emotional distress, unusual experiences and troubled or troubling behaviour, as an alternative to functional psychiatric diagnosis*. Leicester: British Psychological Society.

Jones, L., Bellis, M. A., Wood, S., Hughes, K., McCoy, E., Eckley, L., Bates, G., Mikton, C., Shakespeare, T. & Officer, A. (2012) Prevalence and risk of violence against children with disabilities: a systematic review and meta-analysis of observational studies. *Lancet*, 380 (9845), 899–907.

Korb, L., O'Regan, D., Conley, J., Dillon, E., Briggs, R., Courtenay, K. & Perera, B. (2021) Sleep: the neglected life factor in adults with intellectual disabilities. *British Journal of Psychiatry Bulletin*, 1–7.

LeClère, C., Viaux, S., Avril, M., Achard, C., Chetouani, M., Missonnier, S. & Cohen, D. (2014) Why synchrony matters during mother-child interactions: a systematic review. *PLOS One*, 9 (12), e113571.

Leudar, I. & Costall, A. (2009) On the historical antecedents of the theory of mind paradigm. In Leudar, I. & Costall, A. (eds) *Against Theory of Mind*. London: Palgrave Macmillan.

Michalko, R. (2002) *The Difference That Disability Makes*. Philadelphia PA: Temple University Press.

Nind, M. & Hewett, D. (1994) *Access to Communication.* London: David Fulton.

Oliver, M. (1990) *The Politics of Disablement: A sociological approach.* New York: St. Martin's Press.

Reddy, V. (2008). *How Infants Know Minds.* Cambridge MA: Harvard University Press.

Reddy, V. (2023) Being open and looking on: fluctuations in everyday life and psychology. In Mezzenzana, F. & Peluso, D. (eds) *Conversations on Empathy: Interdisciplinary perspectives on imagination and radical othering.* Abingdon: Routledge.

Reddy, V., Hay, D., Murray, L., & Trevarthen, C. (1997). Communication in infancy: mutual regulation of affect and attention. In G. Bremner, A. Slater & G. Butterworth (eds), *Infant Development: Recent advances* (pp. 247–273). London: Psychology Press/Erlbaum.

Richards, M. (2020) Whorlton Hall, Winterbourne ... person-centred care is long dead for people with learning disabilities and autism. *Disability & Society,* 35 (3), 500–505.

Robertson, F., Herd, C., Macdonald, K. (Producers) & Robertson, F. (Director) (2013) *Autism: Challenging behaviour.* TV documentary. Accessed February 2017, from https://www.bbc.co.uk/programmes/b03gvnvm. Accessed August 2023.

Rogers, S. J. (1998) Empirically supported comprehensive treatments for young children with autism. *Journal of Clinical Child Psychology,* 27, 168–179.

Sabat, S. R. (2001) *The Experience of Alzheimer's Disease: Life through a tangled veil.* Oxford: Blackwell.

Sroufe, L. A. (2005) Attachment and development: a prospective, longitudinal study from birth to adulthood. *Attachment & Human Development,* 7, 349–367.

Stern, D. N. (2004) *The Present Moment: In psychotherapy and everyday life.* New York: W. W. Norton.

Sullivan, P. M. & Knutson, J. F. (2000) Maltreatment and disabilities: a population-based epidemiological study. *Child Abuse & Neglect,* 24, 1257–1273.

# Chapter 4

# Intensive Interaction and Positive Psychology

## Theoretical convergence

*Rachel Ann Jones*

## Introduction

This chapter explores the potential relationship between Intensive Interaction and the paradigm of Positive Psychology. My intention with this chapter is to equip the reader with a fuller understanding of the theory, research and application of Positive Psychology to strengthen our understanding of some of the processes that take place within Intensive Interaction. I will set the scene with a summary of Intensive Interaction, its positioning in psychological theory more broadly, before introducing Positive Psychology to the reader and the current evidence base within Intellectual Disabilities. I will then take a detailed look at some of the concepts of Positive Psychology that present opportunities for applicability within Intensive Interaction, such as positive emotions, meaningful relationships, flow, mindfulness, savouring and self-determination theory.

I approach this chapter through the lens of expertise in Positive Psychology and a clinical background of working with individuals with Intellectual Disabilities, including the use of Intensive Interaction. I note that Intensive Interaction is used and proven to be beneficial within wider populations than within my sphere of experience. I also approach this chapter with a bias as a Counselling Psychologist. Counselling psychology shares humanistic roots with Positive Psychology (Vossler, Steffan & Joseph, 2015) and an intrinsic tendency to look for strengths and positives within individuals.

For some time I have appreciated opportunities for convergence between Intensive Interaction and Positive Psychology. I hope by attending to this potential relationship, I offer up some alternative and complementary hypotheses for the outcomes and experiences of those engaged in Intensive Interaction, thus allowing for multidisciplinary ideas to flourish.

## Setting the scene

### Intensive Interaction

As previously described elsewhere in this book, Intensive Interaction is an approach that supports communication and facilitates the development of social

DOI: 10.4324/9781003597933-4

relationships for individuals with severe intellectual disabilities (Nind & Hewett, 2001). The approach promotes a practical way of being with people who are usually non-verbal or pre-verbal and seemingly 'out of reach'. At the core of this approach are concepts of enjoyment and pleasure combined with developing and maintaining meaningful social relationships (Nind & Hewett, 2001). The central aim of Intensive Interaction is to improve the quality of life of the individual by their developing skills in social interaction.

Intensive Interaction emphasises the importance of interacting with individuals at a developmentally pertinent level, as opposed to a chronological age level. With this acknowledged, it encourages practitioners to position themselves, and their way of being, in a significantly adapted way. The principles of Intensive Interaction are used in a variety of settings, across the lifespan and with a range of populations such as verbally capable individuals with milder forms of intellectual disabilities and or autism (Fraser, 2011), as well as more recently in dementia services (Harris & Wolverson, 2014; Astell et al., 2022).

There exist undeniable methodological challenges in developing an evidence base for Intensive Interaction and there is a need for further high-quality research (Hutchinson & Bodicoat, 2015, see also Chapter 2). These obstacles are not uncommon in the field of intellectual disabilities wherein standardised empirical methods of measurement and rigid adherence to models can effectively exclude this population (Jones, 2013). Single case studies and qualitative approaches ultimately provide the greatest richness in outcome data. That said, there is an increasing number of mixed methods studies of Intensive Interaction providing evidence for improved pre-verbal communication skills, increased initiation and maintenance of social engagement and enhanced skills in building positive relationships (Berry et al., 2013). Of note is the research highlighting how this approach has been found to be beneficial for building positive relationships between practitioners and recipients (Zeedyk, Davies, Parry & Caldwell, 2009). In some literature, a distinction is made between social and educational outcomes, while others have developed a model combining these perspectives such as the 'Dual Aspect Process Model' (Firth, 2009). Firth (2009) described how Intensive Interaction results in an increase in social inclusion and communication as a direct result of more inclusive responses to the person's communicative behaviour (Firth, 2009; Hutchinson & Bodicoat, 2015).

Harding and Berry (2009, p. 758) described how at its 'broadest level, Intensive Interaction is consistent with three major schools of psychological thought: humanistic psychology, attachment theory and positive psychology'. It is the latter of these psychological schools that I explore for the purposes of this chapter. I do so with recognition also, that Positive Psychology is ultimately considered to be underpinned by humanistic psychology (Heffron & Boniwell, 2011).

### Psychological theory and Intensive Interaction

Psychological theory has been slow to respond to developments in Intensive Interaction. Arguably, Intensive Interaction has been viewed in some services as primarily a communication approach for use by speech & language therapists or direct care providers. The approach is not yet widely represented in psychological publications and the extent to which it is adopted by psychologists is unclear (Berry et al., 2013). It is possible that the well-documented historical delays in the development of adequate psychological provision and specifically psychological therapy for people with intellectual disabilities (Bender, 1993; Bungener & McCormack, 1994; Kroese, 1997) has impacted the discipline's interest and understanding of Intensive Interaction.

As previously mentioned, Intensive Interaction has been adopted by an increasing range of professional groups, widening its reach from that typically seen as a central role for speech and language therapists or teachers. This is likely due to the expansion in application and increasing evidence base associated with the approach. In particular, psychologists working with individuals with intellectual disabilities have been taking an increasing, albeit gradual interest in Intensive Interaction (Harding & Berry 2009, see also Chapter 2). Although Harding and Berry (2009) have expanded the understanding of Intensive Interaction as a psychological therapy, there remains opportunity for further exploration of the psychological therapeutic elements of the approach. Despite recent advances in the delivery of psychological therapy for people with intellectual disabilities, those with profound and multiple intellectual disabilities often remain overlooked (Jones, 2013). Intensive Interaction could therefore provide a powerful psychological approach for this population.

### Positive Psychology

Positive Psychology is described as the 'scientific study of optimal human functioning [that] aims to discover and promote the factors that allow individuals and communities to thrive' (Seligman & Csikszentmihalyi, 2000, p. 5). Put more simply, Peterson and Park (2014, p. 2) argue 'Positive psychology is the scientific study of what makes life worth living'. The concept of Positive Psychology can be traced back millennia. The ancient Greek philosophers such as Aristotle, Socrates and Plato, explored the meaning of a good life and 'eudemonia', translated from Greek as happiness (Hefferon & Boniwell, 2011). Also contributing to the theory of Positive Psychology are Eastern traditions in their adding to the understanding of positive emotions, development of strengths, virtues, and values (Boniwell, 2012).

Abraham Maslow was credited as the first person to use the term 'Positive Psychology', in 1954 (Maslow, 1954). Victor Frankl (1959) and Carl Rogers (1961) are also often cited as central psychological figures exploring meaning in life. However, the term 'Positive Psychology' and concept itself lay largely dormant until revisited by Martin Seligman and colleagues some 40 years later. As President of the American Psychological Association in 1998, Seligman aimed to realign psychology's trajectory beyond that of pathology, resulting in a series of international summits and establishment of the Positive Psychology movement.

There was shared concern within the broader discipline of psychology that approaches had become preoccupied with disorder, dysfunction and illness with little regard for promoting wellness and understanding other constructs such as happiness, flourishing and optimism. As such, during the first part of the twenty-first century, Positive Psychology gained mass appeal and remarkable momentum, resulting in the beginning of a 'tectonic upheaval' in the world of psychology (Seligman, 2011, p. 1). Its success is thought to be due to a combination of an emphasis on high quality research and the turning of traditional pathologising approaches in psychology on their heads. Positive Psychology continues to thrive and is widely applied in a variety of different ways, often embedded in or underpinning approaches, as opposed to being adjacent to modern psychological theory. The intrinsic nature of Positive Psychology fulfils Seligman's original desire to facilitate the re-orientation of 'psychology as normal' as opposed to a distinct or stand-alone discipline (Seligman & Csikszentmihalyi, 2000).

Positive Psychology has received much criticism during its development. Hefferon & Boniwell (2011) explore the 'top ten' of such criticisms. Readers will note that both definitions of Positive Psychology, provided earlier, emphasise the scientific basis of Positive Psychology. Despite this, the paradigm has received criticism over the years for seemingly being pseudoscientific, based in pop-psychology and related to untested self-help books (Peterson and Park, 2014). Positive psychologists have worked hard to develop the emphasis on high quality research and evidence based interventions to address this criticism. With respect to its relative infancy, it is understandable that Positive Psychology has faced challenge, as the complexities of the paradigm have been explored in detail over time.

One of the more frequent criticisms questions Positive Psychology's relationship with the negative aspects of life. It has been argued that the focus on positives calls into question the relationship the theory has with the undeniable negatives which can also shape us in positive ways. Lomas and Ivtzan (2016) explored the 'second wave' of Positive Psychology. The authors unpack the complexities of the dialects of wellbeing describing the challenges of appraising things as either negative or positive. As such, Lomas and Ivtzan (2016) argue that the maturation of Positive Psychology requires a second wave, including an appreciation of the complexity of wellbeing. The authors emphasise that experiences, and ultimately wellbeing, is likely to be a complex combination or interaction of both positive and negative. In a subsequent publication, Lomas et al. (2021) describe progress being made towards a 'third wave' of Positive Psychology, with theory, research and application going beyond the individual to focus also on groups and systems. The authors also highlight the further need to broaden multicultural relevance to some of the theories, given their westernised bias. Despite changes in direction, the central principles of Positive Psychology have endured, and the exploration of optimal human functioning remains an important addition to psychology.

## Intellectual disabilities

One could argue that the specialism of intellectual disabilities has suffered the same preoccupation with deficits as mainstream psychology as illustrated by its focus on deficits and symptom treatment through psychopharmacology and applied behavioural models (Jones, 2013). In recent years, paradigmatic changes in respect to how individuals with intellectual disabilities are supported have shown a significant increase. This shift marks a move towards a strengths-based approach focused on enhancing positive experiences (Buntinx, 2014). The change in focus is evidenced in the ideological movements from Person Centred Approaches, Quality of Life Measures to Positive Behaviour Support. The relationship between this paradigmatic shift in intellectual disabilities and the advancement of mainstream Positive Psychology is interesting as both disciplines sit on parallel, yet converging trajectories.

People with intellectual disabilities have often been overlooked or even excluded by developments in mainstream psychological fields (Bender, 1993). However, Positive Psychology is an interesting exception to this, as evidenced by several publications. For example, 2014 saw the publication of *The Oxford Handbook of Positive Psychology and Disability* (Wehmeyer, 2014) which includes a review of intellectual disability approaches. Whilst the theoretical onus of this work is valuable in itself, direction for future research and practical clinical guidance are also needed. *Psychotherapy for Individuals with Intellectual Disability* (Fletcher, 2011) includes a chapter on Positive Psychology by Baker and Blumberg. The chapter uniquely suggests practical adaptations to some of the well-known Positive Psychology interventions to make them accessible for individuals with intellectual disabilities. There is, however, a bias in these suggested adaptations as they are implicitly aimed at individuals with milder impairments.

Inclusive research articles involving individuals with intellectual disabilities have also recently been published, marking a new focus in this area (Haigh et al., 2013). Haigh et al. (2013) interviewed adults with intellectual disabilities about what makes them happy. Participants' reports were clustered into themes including relationships, choice and independence, activities and valuable social roles. Participants also identified personal characteristics that kept them feeling happy, including optimism and managing difficult emotions (Haigh et al., 2013). There have been recent attempts to develop suitable outcome measures related to emotional wellbeing, such as the accessible self-reporting Clinical Outcomes in Routine Evaluation Learning Disabilities tool (Brooks et al., 2013). There is also at least one report of a Positive Psychology pilot group for adults with intellectual disabilities that has been published (Tomasulo, 2014).

As previously noted, the literature indicates a clear bias in this work towards those with milder impairments. Reasonable adjustments to language and complexity of tasks enable accessibility of the Positive Psychology theories to those with milder intellectual disabilities. There is no reason to doubt that these theories and interventions are just as relevant for this population as for those in general population. There is undeniably a wealth of research to be undertaken, replicating some existing studies from Positive Psychology, with adaptations to language and requirement for abstract thinking, being a place to start. A published systematic literature review would also be of value in identifying the work thus far.

There are several small-scale exploratory studies which have considered approaches to increasing happiness indices in people with profound and multiple disabilities (e.g. Lancioni et al., 2002; 2005). Happiness indicators were considered by to be smiling, laughing, positive vocalisations and excited bodily movements. The study concluded that structured stimulation sessions and mindful caregiving, among other things, increased happiness indices. This study embodies some of the methodological complexities of implementing Positive Psychology theory, research and practice with this population. There are clear, significant challenges to this work that are innate to the diagnosis of intellectual disability. They include the ability to self-report, reliance on informants, the need for abstract thinking, comprehension and expression, recency effects and memory problems amongst others. Furthermore, there are significant complications with simply identifying positive affect and wellbeing of people with more profound and multiple disabilities. There is undeniably a minimum level of cognitive development required for many aspects of Positive Psychology (Dykens, 2006).

With respect to some of these challenges in the applicability of theory, it is also worth considering a systemic perspective. Individuals with intellectual disabilities receive assistance from a variety of services and professionals throughout their lives, particularly family members and paid care staff. Positive Psychology could offer a useful framework for working with the systems around an individual with intellectual disabilities, in order to have a positive impact on everybody within the system. Indeed, evidence suggests that positive affect can be spread through systems (Fowler & Christakis, 2008).

Considering the fundamental principles of Positive Psychology, a population typically characterised by disability and impairment, undeniably has the most to gain from theoretical alignment. As such, there is a need for Positive Psychologists and those in intellectual disability services to work together (Dykens, 2006). The aim of this partnership is not only to learn about the application of Positive Psychology for individuals often defined by their 'deficits' but also for Positive Psychology to benefit from the existing knowledge base within the specialism of intellectual disabilities. No greater example of this exists than that of Intensive Interaction.

## Positive Psychology and Intensive Interaction

### Theoretical parallels

Both Positive Psychology and Intensive Interaction are theoretically constructed to explore building upon individual strengths and skills to enable each person to experience positive wellbeing. Yet only a couple of publications exist that make direct reference to the potential link between Positive Psychology and Intensive Interaction, and these references have been written from a broad theoretical perspective (Firth, Glyde & Denby 2020; Sandford 2011; Harding & Berry 2009). That aside, central to the theoretical frameworks of Positive Psychology and Intensive Interaction is the value of positive human relationships and their crucial role in subjective wellbeing. Whilst reference is made in publications to the positive emotional impact of Intensive Interaction, no overt relationship is then drawn to Positive Psychology. In depth exploration of the parallels between Positive Psychology and Intensive Interaction is absent from the literature, including viewing it specifically as a Positive Psychology intervention.

Positive Psychology Interventions are described as 'intentional activities that aim to cultivate positive feelings, behaviours or cognitions' (Sin & Lyubomirsky, 2009, p. 468). These activities serve as a cluster of tools and strategies with the primary focus on increasing positive feelings, thoughts and behaviour, and an emphasis on both short- and long-term effects. One of the motivations for the development of Positive Psychology Interventions was to address a perceived imbalance in 'psychology a usual' strategies, which have been criticised for aiming to solely ameliorate problems and focus on treatment, rather than prevention and enabling flourishing (Hefferon & Boniwell, 2011). There exists an extensive wealth of evidence in respects to Positive Psychology Interventions. A recent mega-analysis of the meta-analyses by Carr et al. (2022) supports the existence of an extensive evidence base supporting the effectiveness of such interventions. Positive Psychology Interventions have been evidenced to be effective in enhancing subjective wellbeing as well as reducing depressive symptoms (Boiler et al., 2013).

Intensive Interaction could be positioned directly as a Positive Psychology Intervention of its own. However, further evidence would be required to validate this proposition. Intensive Interaction may be capable of both enhancing subjective wellbeing, not only by cultivating positive experiences through social relationships and positive emotions, but also by reducing the negative symptomatology experienced by people with social and communication impairments. The key aim of Intensive Interaction is to support communication and develop positive social relationships. Positive Psychology research has consistently demonstrated that social relationships are one of the greatest predictors of subjective wellbeing (Hefferon & Boniwell, 2011). As such, one could conclude, that Intensive Interaction has the potential to improve the subjective wellbeing of recipients. However, the approach may also benefit the practitioner and generate positive emotions in both parties. Positioning Intensive Interaction as a Positive Psychology Intervention is novel. Yet, there are many anecdotal accounts that illustrate this position, as literature is littered with incidental accounts of its benefit to subjective wellbeing.

The following sections aim to stimulate discussion with respect to potential overlap, by highlighting specific existing elements of the Positive Psychology paradigm that have potential relevance to Intensive Interaction.

## Positive emotions

Goodwin (2012) described how just five minutes of 'in-the-momentness' with a pupil with profound and multiple intellectual disabilities could make an entire week of stressful work seem 'worthwhile'. Goodwin describes Intensive Interaction as offering 'joyful connections' through playful and affectionate activity within which each communication partner is rewarded. The literature is rich with anecdotal accounts referencing hedonic subjective experiences, intense engagements and shared pleasure in the experience. When connections occur, vocal sounds and movements align, and smiling or laughing may occur in both practitioner and recipient. Despite the obvious mutual nature of these interactions, the literature has not explicitly examined the benefits of Intensive Interaction in terms of the subjective wellbeing for both partners.

Whilst Hutchinson and Bodicoat (2020) reports experiences where Intensive Interaction results in difficult emotional responses and 'emotional overload' in staff, the overall experience produces positive emotional outcomes. Given the intersubjective nature of Intensive Interaction it would be natural to conclude that the experience of the individual with profound and multiple intellectual disabilities is similarly positive. An example of such, Kellet's (2003) case study of Jacob describes the impact of Intensive Interaction as creating for them a 'happier child' and how they discovered a 'delightfully humorous' character that they had not known before. Lovell et al. (1998) also described how an individual who following an Intensive Interaction programme became 'happier' and more willing to interact than he had before. As described by Harding and Berry (2009, p. 759) 'the sessions of Intensive Interaction seemed to provide Susan with human contact that she enjoyed'. In addition to increases in seemingly positive emotion, published case studies also describe reductions in negative experiences such as self-injurious behaviour, distressed behaviour, withdrawal and harmful stereotypy (Harding & Berry, 2009). In the general population, sharing positive emotions allows us to 'open up' to others, enhance relational bonds, as well as increase our sense of self (Waugh & Fredrickson, 2006). Research has also demonstrated that sharing positive emotions increases feelings of collectiveness in that we experience things less as two individuals but more as one (Hefferon & Boniwell, 2011). Not only is there a direct link between experiencing positive emotions and subjective wellbeing, research shows the sharing of positive emotion is known to facilitate feelings of connectedness to others, resulting in the formation of important social relationships.

There exist some interesting theories and research into the knock-on effects of positive emotions, most notably the broaden-and-build theory of positive emotions of Barbara Frederickson (2009). Research into this theory highlights how experiencing positive emotions opens our cognitive pathways, referred to as 'broadening'. The impact of broadening has been demonstrated in improvements to a variety of domains including intellectual, physical, social and psychological. Examples include development in problem solving, flexibility in thought, adopting alternative strategies for tasks, maintaining relationships, initiating relationships, goal orientation and improvements to sense of self and optimism (Falkenstern et al. 2009; Frederickson, 2009). As a result of these outcomes, further positive emotion is experienced, enabling further broadening effects, thus creating an upward spiral of personal resource development and positive emotion. Whilst it is recognised that not all Intensive Interaction evokes positive emotions, Positive Psychological theory could arguably explain some of the progress made and strengths developed as a result of Intensive Interaction.

### Social relationships

Whilst we are limited in our knowledge about what enhances subjective wellbeing for individuals with profound and multiple intellectual disabilities, it would be reasonable to conclude that social relationships have an important role to play. Research consistently evidences that regardless of personality style, social relationships enhance wellbeing in the general population (Froh et al., 2007). There is no reason to doubt that meaningful social interactions are not just as relevant for individuals with profound and multiple learning disabilities as for the general population. Indeed, it may be that social relationships have the potential for an even greater impact on this population's subjective wellbeing, given the limited access they often have to such meaningful encounters.

One parallel worth considering is whether Intensive Interaction could be an accessible version of Active Constructive Responding, as described by Seligman (2010). This is a means by which to interact with another individual for the mutual benefit of enhancing subjective wellbeing by paying attention to their experiences, personal views and feelings. Along with active constructive relationships, passive constructive, active destructive and passive destructive have been identified as relationship modes. Positive Psychology has evidenced that interventions such as Active Constructive Responding, socialising and active communication, impact positively on subjective wellbeing. Interestingly, in an examination of what distinguishes good relationships from poor relationships, Gable et al. (2004) found that Active Constructive Responding results in positive relationship formation and increased subjective wellbeing through an increase of positive affect and reduction in negative affect (Sin & Lyubomirsky 2009). Boniwell's tips for Active Constructive Responding chime loudly with Intensive Interaction, the key being 'paying close attention, listening, being interested and enthusiastic' (2012, p. 134).

## Flow

When considering and reviewing Intensive Interaction relationships, the Positive Psychology theory of Flow (Csikszentmihalyi, 2002) seems particularly relevant. Flow is described as the profound absorption in an experience, representing the optimum balance between skill and challenge (Csikszentmihalyi, 2002). Firth et al. (2020) describe some of the process that take place during Intensive Interaction, which relate closely to Flow. Firth et al. (2020, p.120) present accounts from Intensive Interaction practitioners that illustrate this 'skill and challenge' dialectic within Flow: 'decision-making is indicated as sometimes being intuitive in nature, and sometimes more conscious; sometimes moving between the two cognitive states as differing issues arise'. Intensive Interaction arguably invites flow, in those with developmental delay, due to its positioning between skill and challenge. But also within the practitioner themselves, who face an equal responsibility to respond accordingly within the moment.

## Mindfulness

A further thematic indication of Positive Psychology within Intensive Interaction is the time perspective, to live and enjoy the moment (Grace, 2017). It requires practitioners to share in the sensory 'here and now' world of individuals with profound and multiple disabilities. This perspective is far removed from the linguistic, cognitive, complicated lives that we lead. Time perspective as a concept in its own right has been considered a powerful influence on human behaviour, put simply the extent to which we operate positively or negatively in the past, present and future is considered to have a significant impact on wellbeing (Boniwell & Zimbardo 2015). Time perspective theory could have some interesting applicability to Intensive Interaction theory. Mindfulness has been positioned as an intervention to enable individuals to re-address their time perspective to the present. Intensive Interaction, by its very nature, could be described as possessing many elements of mindfulness.

Mindfulness is not one intervention, but rather a set of approaches (Keng, Smoski & Robins, 2011). Key parallels with Intensive Interaction include the emphasis on observing the world and the self in the present moment, non-judgement, patience and acceptance for what is. Mindfulness has an extensive evidence base, with research demonstrating improved behavioural regulation, emotional reactivity, increased subjective wellbeing, reduction in depression, anxiety and pain, to mention but a few (Keng, Smoski & Robins, 2011).

## Savouring

Another validated positive psychology intervention is that of savouring. Whilst similar to mindfulness and gratitude practices, savouring is considered distinct due to its emphasis on specifically generating positive emotion (Boniwell, 2012). Savouring is the skill of attending, appreciating and enhancing positive experiences that occur in life (Bryant & Veroff, 2007). At its core, savouring requires us to attend intently to our surroundings and '*stretch out the experience*' (Heffron & Boniwell, 2011, p. 164). Researchers have examined the core components of savouring, their underlying processes and the specific strategies that enable savouring. Several of the strategies described by Bryant and Veroff (2007) clearly resonate with Intensive Interaction, including: absorption (immersion in the moment); sensory-perceptual sharpening (focusing on certain stimuli and blocking out others); and sharing with others (sharing positive experiences with others directly influences levels of enjoyment experienced). Researchers have also examined the value of simply allowing savouring experiences to 'just happen' as opposed to evaluate and interpret them, but enjoy them as they arise, they describe that savouring should not be 'pushed' but allowed to naturally occur (Bryant & Veroff, 2007). This description resonates with the Intensive Interaction principle of not 'leading' or forcing within the relationship but pausing, observing and taking opportunity. Savouring has been shown to increase positive emotions and help regulate and ameliorate feelings of depression (Boiler et al., 2013)

### Meaning, accomplishment, gratitude

There is also anecdotal evidence that Intensive Interaction practitioners find meaning, purpose and significance in their lives by the very nature of the relationships they foster with people with profound and multiple disabilities (Harris & Wolverson, 2014). Intensive Interaction may also result in feelings of gratitude, not only directed to the other person in the shared experience, but also the practitioner for the life they have and abilities they take for granted in their own life. Intensive Interaction is arguably also linked with feelings of accomplishment, not least by accessing and engaging with individuals otherwise often disconnected from the social world, but also from a communication perspective; it enables skill development within individuals that is often overlooked for the acquisition of new abilities (Zeedyk et al., 2009).

### Self-determination theory

Self-determination theory is a positive psychology theory of motivation. Following many years of research, Ryan and Deci (2000) describe how self-determined development satisfies three core needs, that of autonomy, relatedness and competence; correlated with subjective wellbeing. Self-determination theory examines the distinction between extrinsic and intrinsic motivation, the stages or types of motivations, and the subsequent impact on subjective wellbeing. The premise being that the more self-determined an individual, or the more intrinsically regulated, the greater their subjective wellbeing.

Ryan and Deci (2000) developed a continuum of self-determination. The continuum describes six types of motivation that increase with their intrinsic and self-determined value as they progress up the continuum. At one end of the continuum there is *amotivation*, whereby an individual is completely non-autonomous, with no drive, and their needs are not being met. This is followed by four steps which are all extrinsic but progressing towards the final stage of intrinsic motivation. These next steps being that of *external regulation*, whereby motivation is exclusively external, thus controlled by rewards, punishments and conformity. Next on the continuum is *introjected regulation*, where motivation remains external but also has some self-control, the 'should do' rather than 'want to' motivation. This is followed by *identified regulation*, where self-determination begins to increase, whereby motivation is personally valuable in some way. Next is *integrated regulation*, engagement based on an increasing sense of who we are and what we can do. Then finally *intrinsic regulation*, where motivation is intrinsic and self-determined, driven by interest, enjoyment and satisfaction.

It is hypothesised that this continuum could be translated to offer potential insights into the processes that may occur within Intensive Interaction. It is proposed that Intensive Interaction, over time, enables and encourages the intrinsic motivation in recipients. Moving individuals in some circumstances from *amotivational* through to *intrinsically regulated*. Thus, by promoting self-determination and intrinsic regulation, the result is enhanced subjective well-being. Research, largely with children at key developmental phases, has shown many benefits of being self-determined beyond that of immediate increased wellbeing, including cognitive flexibility, creativity, self-esteem (Grolnick & Ryan 1987; Ryan & Grolnick 1986). Viewing the progress made during Intensive Interaction through the lens of self-determination theory offers another unique hypothesis as to the processes at play.

## Concluding thoughts

There are undeniable complexities with advancing the use of Intensive Interaction in an evidence-based world. We may have only a one-sided verbal account of the experiences of Intensive Interaction and of course this has yet to be empirically examined for the benefits on subjective wellbeing of the practitioner. This account, however, is not merely representative of the practitioner's experience. It is also arguably the intersubjective account of the two attuned parties. The reported experiences of the practitioner in the Intensive Interaction relationship gives us a glimpse into the experience of the recipient, a glimpse of something not often available given social or communication impairments.

When thinking about the needs of individuals with intellectual disabilities, it is possible to draw guidance from the Positive Psychology publications with respect to the universalism perspective of wellbeing and 'universal relativism' (Lomas, 2015). Understanding 'optimal human functioning' with people with profound and multiple intellectual disabilities requires considerable creativity and sensitivity in approach. Whilst we need to be careful about any presumption of universality in wellbeing, we can use the recognition that aspects of wellbeing have universal application, to the advantage of people who may benefit from Intensive Interaction, such as those with profound and multiple intellectual disabilities. Knowing what works broadly for the general population is of immense value. A universal perspective of the commonalities between people across cultures at a global level might offer useful perspectives in how we better appreciate methods of enhancing subjective wellbeing with harder to reach individuals. Whilst Lomas (2015) considers the relativism aspect as shaped by culture, perhaps in this context it could account for variation in social and cognitive impairment.

Whilst Intensive Interaction is increasingly used around the world, it is not widely available and embedded in service provision (Mouriere & McKim, 2017). If Intensive Interaction could be understood further from a Psychological Theory perspective, then this could be significant in terms of broadening its wider use and evidence base. The hope of this chapter was to not only to explore parallels but also seek momentum for attending to the relationship that exists between Psychology, by positioning Positive Psychology and Intensive Interaction together, and thus develop a forum with those with an interest to progress the psychological understanding of this phenomenon.

## References

Astell, A. J., Shoaran, S. & Ellis, M. P. (2022). Using adaptive interaction to simplify caregiver's communication with people with dementia who cannot speak. *Frontiers in Communication*, 6. doi:10.3389/fcomm.2021.689439

Baker, D. J. & Blumberg, E. R. (2011). Positive psychology for persons with intellectual or developmental disabilities. In R. J. Fletcher (ed.) *Psychotherapy for Individuals with Intellectual Disability* (pp. 67–90). Kingston NY: NADD Press.

Bender, M. (1993). The unoffered chair: the history of therapeutic disdain towards people with a learning difficulty. *Clinical Psychology Forum*, April, 7–12.

Berry, R., Firth, G., Leeming, C. & Sharma, V. (2013). Clinical psychologists' views of intensive interatcion as an intervention in learning disability services. *Clinical Psychology & Psychotherapy*, 21(5), 403–410.

Boiler, L., Haverman, M., Westerhof, G. J., Riper, H., Smit, F. & Bohlmeijer, E. (2013). Positive psychology interventions: a meta-analysis of randomized controlled studies. *BMC Public Health*, 13(1), 1–20.

Boniwell, I. (2012). *Positive Psychology in a Nutshell: The science of happiness*. Maidenhead: McGraw-Hill Education.

Boniwell, I. & Zimbardo, P. G. (2015). Balancing time perspective in pursuit of optimal functioning. *Positive Psychology In Practice: Promoting human flourishing in work, health, education, and everyday life* (pp. 223–236). Chichester: Wiley.

Brooks, M., Davies, S. & Twigg, E. (2013). A measure for feelings: using inclusive research to develop a tool for evaluating psychological therapy (Clinical Outcomes in Routine Evaluation – Learning Disability). *British Journal of Learning Disabilities*, 41(4), 320–329.

Bungener, J., & McCormack, B. (1994). Psychotherapy and learning disability. In W. Dryden (ed.) *The handbook of psychotherapy* (pp. 419–432). Routledge.

Buntinx, W. H. (2014). Understanding disability: a strengths-based approach. In M. L. Wehmeyer (ed.), *The Oxford Handbook of Positive Psychology and Disability* (pp. 7–18). New York: Oxford University Press.

Bryant, F. B., & Veroff, J. (2007). *Savoring: A new model of positive experience*. Psychology Press. doi:10.4324/9781315088426

Carr, A., Finneran, L., Boyd, C., Shirey, C., Canning, C., Stafford, O. & Burke, T. (2023). The evidence-base for positive psychology interventions: a mega-analysis of meta-analyses. *The Journal of Positive Psychology*, 19(2), 191–205. doi:10.1080/17439760.2023.2168564

Cooper, S-A. & Bailey, N. M. (2001). Psychiatric disorders amongst adults with learning disabilities: prevalence and relationship to ability level. *International Journal of Psychology Medicine*, 18, 45–53.

Cooper, S-A., Smiley, E., Morrison, J., Williamson, A. & Allan, L. (2007). Mental ill-health in adults with intellectual disabilities: prevalence and associated factors. *British Journal of Psychiatry*, 190, 27–35.

Csikszentmihalyi, M. (2002). *Flow: The classic work on how to achieve happiness*. New York: Random House.

Dykens, E. M. (2006). Toward a positive psychology of mental retardation. *American Journal of Orthopsychiatry*, 76(2), 185–193.

Emerson, E., Hatton, C., Baines, S. & Robertson, J. (2016). The physical health of British adults with intellectual disability: cross sectional study. *International Journal for Equity in Health*, 15(1), 11.

Ephraim, G. W. E. (1979). Developmental processes in mental handicap: a generative structure approach. Unpublished Ph.D. thesis, Department of Psychology, Brunel University.

Falkenstern, M., Schiffrin, H. H., Nelson, S. K., Ford, L., & Keyser, C. (2009). Mood over matter: Can happiness be your undoing? *The Journal of Positive Psychology*, 4 (5), 365–371. doi:10.1080/17439760902992415

Firth G. (2009). A dual aspect process model of Intensive Interaction. *British Journal of Learning Disabilities*, 37, 43–49.

Firth, G., Glyde, M. & Denby, G. (2020). A qualitative study of the practice-related decision-making of Intensive Interaction Practitioners. *British Journal of Learning Disabilities*, 49(2), 117–128.

Fletcher, R. J. (2011). *Psychotherapy for Individuals with Intellectual Disability*. Kingston NY: NADD Press.

Fowler, J. H. & Christakis, N. A. (2008). Dynamic spread of happiness in a large social network: longitudinal analysis over 20 years in the Framingham Heart Study. *British Medical Journal*, 337, 1–9.

Frankl, V. E. (1959). *Man's Search for Meaning: An introduction to logotherapy*. Boston MA: Beacon Press.

Fraser, C. (2011). Can adults on the autism spectrum be affected positively by the use of Intensive Interaction in supported living services? *Good Autism Practice*, 12 (2), 37–42.

Fredrickson, B. L. (2009). *Positivity: Groundbreaking research to release your inner optimist and thrive*. Crown Publishing Group.

Froh, J. J., Fives, C. J. & Filler, J. R. (2007). Interpersonal relationships and irrationality as predictors of life satisfaction. *Journal of Positive Psychology*, 2(1), 29–39.

Gable, S. L., Reis, H. T., Impett, E. A., & Asher, E. R. (2004). What do you do when things go right? The intrapersonal and interpersonal benefits of sharing positive events. *Journal of Personality and Social Psychology*, 87(2), 228–245. doi:10.1037/0022-3514.87.2.228

Goodwin, J. (2012). Living in the present. *PMLD Link*, 24(71), 31–33.

Grace, J. (2017). *Sensory-being for Sensory Beings: Creating entrancing sensory experiences*. London: Routledge.

Grolnick, W. S. & Ryan, R. M. (1987). Autonomy in children's learning: an experimental and individual difference investigation. *Journal of Personality and Social Psychology*, 52(5), 890.

Haigh, A., Lee, D., Shaw, C., Hawthorne, M., Chamberlain, S., Newman, D. W., Clarke, Z. & Beail, N. (2013). What things make people with a learning disability happy and satisfied with their lives: an inclusive research project. *Journal of Applied Research in Intellectual Disabilities*, 26(1), 26–33.

Harding, C. & Berry, R. (2009). Intensive Interaction as a psychological therapy. *The Psychologist*, 22, 758–759.

Harris, C. & Wolverson, E. (2014) Intensive Interaction: to build fulfilling relationships. *Journal of Dementia Care*, 22 (6), 27–30.

Hefferon, K. & Boniwell, I. (2011). *Positive Psychology: Theory, research and applications*. Maidenhead: McGraw-Hill Education.

Hutchinson, N. & Bodicoat, A. (2015). The effectiveness of Intensive Interaction: a systematic literature review. *Journal of Applied Research in Intellectual Disabilities*, 28, 437–454. doi:10.1111/jar.12138

Kellett M. (2003). Jacob's journey: developing sociability and communication in a young boy with severe and complex learning difficulties using the Intensive Interaction teaching approach. *Journal of Research in Special Educational Needs*, 3, 1–16.

Kroese, B. S. (1997). Teaching cognitive self-regulation of independence and emotion control skills. In B. S. Kroese, D. Dagnan, & K. Loumidis (eds), *Cognitive-behaviour therapy for people with learning disabilities* (pp. 67–85). Routledge.

Keng, S. L., Smoski, M. J. & Robins, C. J. (2011). Effects of mindfulness on psychological health: a review of empirical studies. *Clinical Psychology Review*, 31(6), 1041–1056.

Lancioni, G. E., O'reilly, M. F., Campodonico, F. & Mantini, M. (2002). Increasing indices of happiness and positive engagement in persons with profound multiple disabilities. *Journal of Developmental and Physical Disabilities*, 14(3), 231–237.

Lancioni, G. E., Singh, N. N., O'Reilly, M. F., Oliva, D. & Basili, G. (2005). An overview of research on increasing indices of happiness of people with severe/profound intellectual and multiple disabilities. *Disability and Rehabilitation*, 27(3), 83–93.

Lomas, T. (2015). Positive cross-cultural psychology: exploring similarity and difference in constructions and experiences of wellbeing. *International Journal of Wellbeing*, 5(4), 60–77.

Lomas, T. & Ivtzan, I. (2016). Second wave positive psychology: exploring the positive–negative dialectics of wellbeing. *Journal of Happiness Studies*, 17(4), 1753–1768. doi:10.1007/s10902-015-9668-y

Lomas, T., Waters, L., Williams, P., Oades, L. G. & Kern, M. L. (2021). Third wave positive psychology: broadening towards complexity. *The Journal of Positive Psychology*, 16(5), 660–674.

Lovell, D., Jones, S. & Ephraim, G. (1998). The effect of Intensive Interaction on the sociability of a man with severe intellectual disabilities. *International Journal of Practical Approaches to Disability*, 22, 3–8.

Maninder, K., Nagra, R. W., Appiah, A. & Rayner, K. (2017). Intensive interaction training for paid carers: 'looking, looking and find out when they want to relate to you'. *Journal of Applied Research in Intellectual Disabilities*, 30, 648–660.

Maslow, A. H. (1954). *Motivation and personality*. Harper & Row.

Mouriere, A. & McKim, J. (2017). *Integrating Intensive Interaction: Developing communication practice in services for children and adults with severe learning difficulties, profound and multiple learning difficulties and autism*. London: Routledge.

Nind, M. & Hewett, D. (1994). *Access to Communication: Developing the basics of communication with people with severe learning disabilities through Intensive Interaction*. London: David Fulton.

Nind, M. & Hewett, D. (2001). *A Practical Guide to Intensive Interaction*. Kidderminster: British Institute of Learning Disabilities Publications.

Peterson, C. & Park, N. (2014). Meaning and positive psychology. *International Journal of Existential Psychology & Psychotherapy*, 5(1), 2–8.

Rogers, C. R. (1961). *On Becoming a Person*. Boston MA: Houghton Mifflin.

Ryan, R. M. & Deci, E. L. (2000). Self-determination theory and the facilitation of intrinsic motivation, socialdevelopment, and well-being. *American Psychologist*, 55(1), 68.

Ryan, R. M. & Grolnick, W. S. (1986). Origins and pawns in the classroom: self-report and projective assessments of individual differences in children's perceptions. *Journal of Personality and Social Psychology*, 50(3), 550.

Sandford, R. (2011). Positive psychology and Intensive Interaction: exploring the links. *PMLD Link*, 23(3), 12–15.

Seligman, M. (2011). Flourish: positive psychology and positive interventions. *Flourish: A visionary new understanding of happiness and well-being*. Free Press.

Sin, N. L. & Lyubomirsky, S. (2009). Enhancing well-being and alleviating depressive symptoms with positive psychology interventions: a practice-friendly meta-analysis. *Journal of Clinical Psychology*, 65(5), 467–487.

Tomasulo, D. J. (2014). Positive group psychotherapy modified for adults with intellectual disabilities. *Journal of Intellectual Disabilities*, 18(4), 337–350.

Vossler, A., Steffen, E., & Joseph, S. (2015). Counselling psychology and positive psychology: towards a balanced integration. In P. A. Linley & S. Joseph (eds), *Positive Psychology in Practice*, 2, 429–442. Wiley.

Waugh, C. E. and Fredrickson, B. L. (2006) Nice to know you: positive emotions, self–other overlap, and complex understanding in the formation of a new relationship. *Journal of Positive Psychology*, 1(2), 93–106.

Wehmeyer, M. L. (2014). *The Oxford Handbook of Positive Psychology and Disability*. New York: Oxford University Press.

Williams, H. & Jones, R. S. P. (1997). Teaching cognitive self-regulation of independents and emotion control skills. In B. S. Kroese, D. Dagnan & K. Loumidis (eds) *Cognitive Behavioural Therapy for People with Learning Disabilities* (pp. 67–85). London: Routledge.

Willner, P. (2005). Psychotherapeutic interventions in learning disability. *Journal of Intellectual Disability Research*, 49(1), 73–85.

Zeedyk, S., Davies, C., Parry, S. & Caldwell, P. (2009). Fostering social engagement in Romanian children with communicative impairments: the experiences of newly trained practitioners of Intensive Interaction. *British Journal of Learning Disabilities*, 37, 186–196.

# Chapter 5

# Intensive Interaction in psychological practice for people who present with 'behaviours of concern'

*Jules McKim and Judith Samuel*

## Introduction

In this chapter we will show how Intensive Interaction has its place in supporting people with intellectual disabilities who present with 'behaviours of concern'. It is written in the context of the dual imperatives of reducing restrictive practices and the reliance on medication (NHS England, 2016). We present research, the service context and some case descriptions where Intensive Interaction has helped increase the person's quality of life and enabled continued community support rather than in-patient admission. We also offer some ideas for further research.

## Background

### Defining 'behaviours of concern' and relevance to Intensive Interaction

'Behaviours of concern' are also known as 'challenging behaviours', 'behaviours that challenge' and 'distressed behaviours':

> Behaviour can be described as challenging when it is of such an intensity, frequency, or duration as to threaten the quality of life and/or the physical safety of the individual or others and is likely to lead to responses that are restrictive, aversive or result in exclusion.
> (Royal College of Psychiatrists, The British Psychological Society & The Royal College of Speech and Language Therapists, 2007, p.10).

When the term 'challenging behaviour' was introduced, it was intended to emphasise that problems were often caused as much by the way in which a person was supported as by their own characteristics. Over time there has been a drift towards using it as a categorisation of people's attributes which cannot be changed, similar to the colour of eyes. However, as the Royal College of Psychiatrists et al. (2016) indicates, 'challenging behaviour' is a socially constructed concept and judgement is required to assess the behaviour's impact on the person and others.

DOI: 10.4324/9781003597933-5

It prompts a response by services to make appropriate changes to the environment and to the nature of the support provided. The intention is not to try to reduce the likelihood and/or severity of the behaviour without considering the inner person, their emotional state and the meaning and functions of the behaviour. Withdrawal and a lack of engagement with opportunities that may impact the person's quality of life should also be considered as 'behaviours of concern'. Services must focus on improvements in the person's well-being.

Intensive Interaction can enhance social inclusion as well as social and communication skills and both aspects improve quality of life (Firth, 2008). Intensive Interaction has the potential to be a useful intervention where an individual is displaying 'behaviour of concern', for example when an individual is experiencing social exclusion due to their behaviour or when difficulties with social and communication skills appear to be triggers for behaviour.

### Understanding 'behaviours of concern'

When an intervention is being considered, it is important to start with a detailed description of the 'behaviour of concern', its frequency, intensity and how long it has been occurring. Thereafter, its functions and meanings are sought (Herbert, 1981). Both physical and psychological factors need consideration. 'Behaviour of concern' may be more likely due to the person's relationship history, particularly where grief and/or trauma has been experienced. The ability to emotionally regulate also changes with developmental level (Frankish, 2021a).

'Behaviour of concern' may be associated with a genetic condition or an enduring mental health problem and/or may be a response to more transient conditions (Oliver et al., 2020). Transient conditions include:

- pain and discomfort
- sensory impairment and/or sensitivity to noises, tastes, smells, textures, lights and temperatures
- vestibular sensations (perception of balance and spatial orientation) and proprioceptive (perception of bodily movement, action and location) sensations
- emotional state: anger, anxiety, grief, low mood
- arousal level and sleep problems
- specific cognitive differences (compromised flexibility and inhibition and working memory)
- differences in social behaviour (including strong preferences or rejections).
- difficulties with communication make 'behaviours of concern' more likely
(Royal College of Psychiatry, The British Psychological Society & The Royal College of Speech and Language Therapists, 2007).

'Behaviour of concern' as a form of communication about a want or need is highly effective. It achieves results. Consequently, service responses may unwittingly reinforce it. The Positive Behavioural Support (PBS) framework (Gore et al., 2013) notes that the functions of 'behaviours of concern' include:

- to gain attention (social interaction either positive or negative from another person)
- to change sensory input (it feels good, it reduces pain, it meets a sensory need)
- to escape (from a demand, a person, a noise, a place)
- to gain something tangible (access to an item or an activity)

## Intervention

After initial assessment it is crucial to quickly address any transient factors such as pain and adjustable sensory triggers. It might also be possible to make rapid changes to the quantity and quality of the person's social experiences and in so doing meet social needs that might be underlying 'behaviours of concern'. Both the quantity and the quality of social interactions may require attention. Quantity is better described as availability: just the right amount of social contact at the right time to enable active support (Mansell & Beadle-Brown, 2012), in the form of both meaningful activity and relationships. Quality is provided by attuned support thus meeting the individual's particular needs, through an understanding of and response to their expressive communication, both verbal and non-verbal. Rather than leaving it to chance or hoping the right member of staff/carer is available, support workers can *become* the right member of staff by using Intensive Interaction.

Where a more comprehensive approach to intervention is required, the Challenging Behaviour Foundation (2023) recommends an eight-step process for creating a PBS plan. Such a plan provides caregivers with a guide to increasing an individual's quality of life and describes interventions both to prevent and to respond to 'behaviours of concern' and to reduce risk, at the at varying levels of arousal. The eight steps are as follows:

1  description of the challenging behaviour – describing the appearance, frequency, severity and duration
2  functions of the challenging behaviour – describing the reasons for the behaviour happening
3  proactive strategies – define and agree ongoing preventative support, ensuring the person is getting their needs met
4  early warning signs and strategies – define and agree best ways to avoid an incident
5  reactive strategies – how to respond to behaviours as safely and quickly as possible
6  post-incident support strategies – support to calm and avoid re-escalation
7  agreeing the plan
8  reviewing the plan

## The research and evidence base

### The importance of rapport in 'behaviours of concern'

PBS stresses the importance of developing rapport between a person and their network of support (Positive Behavioural Support Coalition UK, 2015). Carr et al. (1994) suggest that:

> two people have established rapport when their relationship is characterised by closeness, empathy and mutual liking.
>
> (p. 111)

A lack of rapport has been found to be linked to the likelihood of 'behaviours of concern' and can be improved through staff and care-giver training (Magito, McLaughlin & Carr, 2005). Kildahl et al. (2021), in their case study on an adolescent with autism, severe intellectual disability and self-injurious behaviour, noted:

> If it seemed like Philip preferred certain care-givers, these were encouraged to maintain the primary interaction with him.
>
> (p. 333)

Armstrong and Leahy (2022) introduced a skills-building package in special schools. They noted that before they could introduce this training, they had to build mutually enjoyable relationships based on the child's interests:

> The sharing of this enjoyment leads to the gradual building of a relationship and trust, and then to communication ...
>
> (p. 49)

Adams and Jahoda (2019) interviewed mothers of people with severe and profound intellectual disabilities about their experience of input from mental health professionals. The mothers talked about the importance of the therapeutic relationship being built by anyone working with their relatives. How the mothers describe this, the authors suggest, is 'a similar approach to Intensive Interaction' (p. 140).

When using Intensive Interaction, shared enjoyment is developed through playfully responding to the person and creating opportunities for turn taking. Together with learning the 'Fundamentals of Communication' (Nind & Hewett, 2001, p. 7), Intensive Interaction increases rapport. Thus, it is recommended at initial assessment, if the person lacks rapport with others and their social communication abilities are early/unknown, that Intensive Interaction is considered as an urgent proactive strategy (Samuel & Doswell, 2021; McKim & Samuel, 2021).

### Intensive Interaction, emotional availability and 'behaviours of concern'

Skelly (2017) draws attention to the use of attachment theory within PBS and describes a 'Conditions for Security' model, which, in addition to physical safety, includes the interactional features of 'emotional availability and pre-dictability, warmth, joyful mutual enjoyment and shared exploration' (p. 39). These are clearly the emotional benefits of Intensive Interaction (Hewett, 2018), which aims to develop skills in communication and the enjoyment of social interaction for people with severe or profound and multiple learning disabilities and/or autism.

Emotional development can be arrested because of trauma. Based on Mahler's model of emotional development, Frankish (2021b) presents a series of 24-hour social care interventions to provide the emotionally nurturing environment needed to enable individuals to grow emotionally and more in line with their cognitive development. Frankish suggests these interventions have similarities with Intensive Interaction:

> The principles are the same, to make real human contact with another person who has given up on expecting positive human contact.
>
> (p. 172)

### The role of Intensive Interaction in reducing 'behaviours of concern'

Bertulis et al. (1998) describe successful 'positive incident management' using aspects of behavioural approaches and Intensive Interaction for a residential school student, and Hewett (1998) presents Arnett's (1989) model of managing the stages of an incident paying close attention to the link between the style of staff behaviour and the student's arousal level. Sharma and Firth (2012) discuss the use of Intensive Interaction to reduce 'behaviours of concern' that have a communicative function in people with severe or profound learning disabilities. From their review of published case studies, they conclude that it can be effective.

In a systematic review of the literature, Hutchinson and Bodicoat (2015) indicated only limited support for the reduction in 'behaviours of concern'. They note that methodological limitations prevent firm conclusions from being drawn and recommend further research.

The use of Intensive Interaction with more intellectually able people with disabilities is exploratory, for example Moroza-James (2014, 2019) describes its use with her son with autism and behaviours of concern. Other parental views supporting the link between Intensive Interaction, emotional well-being and the reduction in 'behaviours of concern' are given in Chapter 7. In the context of providing meaningful activities, the use of Intensive Interaction is encouraged as a way to engage with people whose 'behaviours of concern' mean they are described as 'difficult to reach'. Harding (2021), in her chapter on providing emotionally aware care within the PBS framework, states:

Intensive Interaction [can be used] to build turn-taking skills … or increase sense of control and conversational games to aid development of sense of self and safe difference between people.

(p. 113)

McKim and Samuel (2021) describe the use of Intensive Interaction within a PBS framework for three service users. The role of Intensive Interaction in managing behaviours of concern for two individuals is described below.

## Service context

Within our local NHS Trust's Learning Disability Service, there has been an Intensive Interaction Service since 2010, based within the Psychology Department. This is described in Chapter 10. Over the years the input to people with 'behaviours of concern' has been to all parts of what constituted the Trust including direct social care, inpatients and community services. In 2017 the Intensive Support Team (IST) was created. This is a multi-disciplinary team with a proactive approach to improving the quality of life of people who present with 'behaviours of concern' and reducing hospitalisation (Department of Health, 2018). Alongside the IST the Intensive Interaction Service provides support to the individuals referred.

Although the descriptions outlined below are within this context, we hope the recommendations can be applied in any circumstance where support for someone with 'behaviours of concern' is being developed. For details of the referral process and standard operating procedure refer to Chapter 10.

## Case descriptions

Here we present two examples where Intensive Interaction was found to be a crucial component of the interventions provided to people who were at risk of placement breakdown due the presence of 'behaviours of concern'. Client details have been changed to protect anonymity. As the IST used the Challenging Behaviour Foundation (2023) eight-step model for PBS planning, these case descriptions are framed within this structure.

### Graham

Graham is a white British man with severe intellectual disability and autism who was 22 at the time of referral to the IST. He is a non-verbal communicator, but uses a few idiosyncratic gestures, objects of reference and understands some signs. He had moved to an annexe of a supported living house and visited his parents at weekends. Intensive Interaction was already part of his care plan, but this had not been maintained due to moves between provider organisations and changes to his staff team. IST involvement started after four months but the placement broke down a few months later. After two months in and out of a county residential home he was admitted to hospital, a long way from his family. A referral was made to the Intensive Interaction Service.

Input from the psychologists in the team, aside from the development of the use and confidence with Intensive Interaction, focused on supporting the staff and the family and ensuring good communication between the two. There was no other input from psychologists that had therapeutic benefits to Graham. The aim of reintroducing Intensive Interaction was to provide attuned social attention to reduce Graham's need to elicit this through harmful means.

During the 20 months in hospital, Intensive Interaction was reintroduced with guidance from the speech and language therapist. Discharge guidelines including a touch protocol were agreed (see Chapter 10 for further references to touch guidance). Staff training was completed and interactions videoed and analysed both individually and later as a group. The team's ability to reflect increased, confidence grew and fears about personal safety lessened.

### Step 1: Description of the behaviour

Graham's 'behaviours of concern' were an escalation of self-injurious behaviour (head-banging), physical attacks: hitting and throwing objects, and polydipsia (extreme thirstiness). There was concern that excessive drinking would lead to a seizure.

### Step 2: Functions of the behaviour

The functions of Graham's behaviour were determined as his strategies to seek tangible items, to escape from demands and uncomfortable environments and to seek social attention. A number of factors appear to have been difficult for Graham, including a key staff member who he was close to leaving suddenly, and having reduced activities at home and access to the community. Staff appeared to be scared of getting hurt by Graham so avoided interaction; there were also a number of agency staff working who did not know him as well and were therefore less able to read his mood.

### Step 3: Proactive strategies

Environmental changes were made to keep the staff safe and to keep tangible items out of sight. Psychiatric medication was reviewed. Graham's preferred interactions involved ripping paper, sharing colouring activities, bouncing on physio balls and repetitive physical contact games (pat-a-cake, head-shoulders-knees-toes). Staff availability was crucial, allowing him to lead, tuning in to assess micro-changes in his mood from vocal and body language cues, being relaxed and unhurried, giving him positive responses non-verbally, skilful positioning to allow him to approach while remaining safe and the use of vocal imitation and touch (high-fives, hugs).

*Step 4: Early warning signs and strategies*

Early warning signs were identified: tapping a finger on his hand; shielding his left eye with a hand; a deep frown; low grunts; hand flapping, toy banging, toy gathering. Staff learned to reduce verbal information and demands and give Graham more space. One staff member stayed available as complete withdrawal could increase his distress. Remaining in sight they would start one of his preferred activities ensuring it was visually obvious to him (ripping paper, stacking blocks, jigsaw puzzles), and importantly not asking or expecting him to join in. Graham might request interaction by either throwing a toy to staff, taking them by the hand or by joining in with what they were doing.

*Step 5: Reactive strategies*

When throwing items *at* staff began, staff withdrew further while remaining in the room, observing and waiting for Graham to approach them. If these behaviours continued, staff would leave the room and covertly monitor. Distraction and diversion were possible using Intensive Interaction: specifically ripping paper, with careful consideration to positioning, reduced eye-contact, relaxed body language and using no speech.

*Step 6: Post-incident support*

Staff remained available with reduced demand and verbal communication.

*Step 7: Agreeing the plan*

Following a best-interests process the plan was agreed by Graham's staff, family carers and clinicians involved. This plan was in both written and video form.

*Step 8: Reviewing the plan*

The plan was reviewed and the video version extended with additional footage. Intensive Interaction gave staff confidence to be with a person with an extremely negative reputation. Staff using Intensive Interaction did not experience so many serious incidents. It is important to stress, as outlined above, that the Intensive Interaction offered was dependent on Graham's mood and practical considerations of, for example, positioning, eye contact, the amount of mirroring used and the level of availability were adjusted accordingly. Rapport developed variably across the staff team. Preferred staff leaving and the presence of agency staff correlated with more incidents. Staff said:

He feels he has more control of what's happening, because he's leading it and he can see you responding.

(Support worker)

Intensive Interaction helped build and cement a relationship with Graham. He felt that people were with him. Previous task-orientated care changed to emotionally connected care.

(Support worker)

## Jane

Jane is a British Asian woman with moderate intellectual disabilities and autism and a long history of 'behaviours of concern'. She has verbal skills and her communication is developmentally more advanced than Graham's. She was 36 years old at the time of the referral to the IST. She lived with two other people with 24-hour domiciliary staff support and visited her family monthly. When Jane's father became ill and passed away the visits to her family stopped. Instead, remaining family members visited her. After four months Jane was referred to the Intensive Interaction Service.

Modelling, training and support for staff was given by the IST and the Intensive Interaction Coordinator. Written reflections and videos of interactions were created.

### Step 1: Description of the behaviour

Jane's 'behaviours of concern' were an increase in frequency and intensity of verbal threats, physical attacks (hitting, pushing, kicking, punching), property destruction, throwing objects and self-injury (banging her head on doors or walls).

### Step 2: Functions of the behaviour

She was thought to be missing her father's unique style of social interaction which included tactile games such as pat-a-cake. Staff were unsure how to respond to Jane's initiations of hand holding as the organisation had a no touch policy. They did not join in with her singing and rocking. Staff interpreted her verbal communication as functional rather than social. When Jane said 'Cup of tea?' it did not always mean that she just wanted a drink, it was often a social interaction she sought.

A reduction in accessing community activities, due to concerns around the risks involved, compounded her distress.

Other functions of Jane's 'behaviour of concern' were: her need for social contact; to get a specific item or a specific activity; to express her fear of transition/ changes to normal routine; to escape from demands; and situations that were overwhelming and over-stimulating due to sensory sensitivity, particularly the sound of the washing-machine on a fast spin.

### Step 3: Proactive strategies

Proactive support included an increase of 1:1 staffing hours and a review of psychiatric medication. Staff training on autism was updated. Staff alerted Jane if the washing machine was to be used and provided distracting activities.

The 1:1 staffing level allowed Intensive Interaction to be offered every 15 minutes. Techniques included verbal echoing and/or non-verbal turn taking (dancing and rocking). These interactions varied in duration from a few minutes to an hour.

### Step 4: Early warning signs and strategies

When increasing agitation was noticed, modifications included less verbal turn-taking. Verbal input was reduced to reflecting significant phrases that were indicative that she was seeking reassurance, for example: 'No rabbit no.' Physical contact initiated by Jane increased during escalation. It was found that firm reassuring hand holding by staff reduced the likelihood of an incident.

### Step 5: Reactive strategies

During an incident, firm hand holding on Jane's terms was able to be maintained. If required, a cushion was placed between her head and the wall. Positioning and vigilance enabled physical proximity to be continued safely. Verbal input and demand was reduced even further.

### Step 6: Post incident support

Jane's requests for interactions becoming more verbal and specific showed a return to her usual level of arousal.

### Step 7: Agreeing the plan

Following a best-interests process the plan was agreed by Jane's staff, family carers and clinicians involved. This plan was in both written and video form.

### Step 8: Reviewing the plan

Group supervision, initially described as uncomfortable, became constructive to reflect on their own and others' practice. Notably, Jane at first seemed to prefer interactions with the two senior male staff who may have reminded her of her father. They were also initially the more confident interactors.

The intensity and frequency of the 'behaviours of concern' reduced, and she returned to her previous community activities. Some 'behaviours of concern' remain but rapport with her network developed and her quality of life improved. The place of Intensive Interaction in securing these outcomes is captured in the following comments:

> If it wasn't for Intensive Interaction, I don't think Jane would still be living here in the community.
>
> (Service manager)

> Intensive Interaction has been our saviour. From the moment we attended our first session learning about this technique, it became a revelation to us. It made me view my whole relationship with Jane and the way in which I spent my time with her in a different light.
>
> (Jane's sister)

As with Graham, it is worth noting that for Jane it was not only the use of Intensive Interaction that made a difference. However, those implementing the approach thought that it had a significant role in the positive outcomes. What was crucial was *how* Intensive Interaction was offered and supporting the staff to understand that the starting point was to tune in to Jane and to assess her mood. In this way, the details of the technique were adjusted to offer engagement *on her terms*.

## Recommendations for practice

Rapport is the foundation of good support, upon which inclusion, well-being, quality of life and the development of communication and social skills are built. Recommendations for practice focus on the quantity and quality of social interactional support. At initial assessment, a person's relationship history must be explored: it is important to consider both historic and current influences on interactional preferences.

Aim for a rapid increase in the *availability* of one-to-one time when safe and possible to do so. This is for both proactive social contact and/or for reactive strategies as necessary.

Care-giver appearance, verbal and non-verbal behaviour, and the sensory input they provide can impact on the well-being of the individual. This may link to past experiences both constructive and aversive and influence current preferences. Where possible, through training and supervision, the person's network should adjust their interpersonal style, verbal and non-verbal communication in accordance with the person's preferences.

Matching person and staff interests can aid rapport building (Carr et al., 1994; Magito McLaughlin & Carr, 2005). The unconditional provision of enjoyable things and preferred items is important (Kildahl et al., 2021).

Training and follow-up support both from external clinicians, and, crucially, from local management introduces, maintains and sustains practice.

Building rapport can mediate where other causes/functions of behaviour are present: e.g. pain, anxiety, low mood (Oliver et al., 2020). Here Intensive Interaction may provide comfort, connection, grounding and distraction. Where there has been trauma, Intensive Interaction provides a frame for an external practitioner to provide therapy (Samuel & Doswell, 2021).

Where appropriate, and with suitable background information gathering (development level, risks, history, etc.), Intensive Interaction can be used as part of initial contact with clients. Rapport building is likely to improve the outcomes of all interactions regardless of the main focus or aim of the intervention.

Whatever planning process is used, the details must be agreed and reviewed. Consistency is key both in terms of the approach and the presence of preferred caregivers.

A local Intensive Interaction Coordinator is desirable to lead on training, supervision and mentoring. However, a senior clinician or manager with some ring-fenced time will be of immense benefit.

## Recommendations for further research

Further research would be useful to clarify both the physiological and emotional benefits of Intensive Interaction in relation to 'behaviours of concern'. Maes et al. (2020) describe the application of biofeedback, now within everyone's reach with personal digital fitness trackers. The understanding of the effects of Intensive Interaction on someone's arousal state as indicated by breathing and resting heart-rate would be illuminating.

The inclusion and prominence of unmet social needs in PBS plans could be usefully audited.

The mechanism behind increased rapport and quality of life warrants further investigation with increased methodological rigour. The use of case study methodology would be a useful next step after case descriptions such as McKim and Samuel (2021).

## Conclusions

Intensive Interaction has relevance for people with severe or profound intellectual disabilities and autistic people with high support needs who present with 'behaviours of concern', whether these behaviours are harmful to themselves and/or others or are presenting as social withdrawal. For such individuals it is essential that their support network addresses rapport at the earliest possible opportunity with careful planning and within a positive risk-management framework. In our experience there has been no-one with whom rapport and connection could not be built regardless of the nature of the behaviours of concern. Attempting to reduce behaviours of concern and *then* build relationships is the wrong way round. By examining the person's social and communication environment, rapid beneficial adjustments are possible where safe to do so. For a person who has experienced trauma, Intensive Interaction provides a framework for comfort and safety, as well as developing social communication skills.

It is especially important in the context of 'behaviours of concern' to provide good quality person-specific Intensive Interaction. The technical details must be adjusted to the person, their preferences, and their level of arousal, as outlined in the case descriptions above.

It is not enough to simply be doing Intensive Interaction. It needs to be of good quality and reflective practice is integral. The guidelines should be detailed, and video guidelines developed where possible.

Rapport should be a non-negotiable in all care settings. Lack of rapport has been identified as a context within which 'behaviours of concern' are more likely. Where rapport is lacking, and more positive relationships can be formed as a result of an intervention, there is an ethical imperative that such an approach is sustained.

## References

Adams, T. M. & Jahoda, A. (2019). Listening to mothers: experiences of mental health support and insights into adapting therapy for people with severe or profound intellectual disabilities. *International Journal of Developmental Disabilities*, 65 (3),135–142.

Armstrong, H. & Leahy, V. (2022). Skills building and clinical psychology: is there a role for clinical psychologists to support special schools in building 'key skills'? *Bulletin of the Faculty for People with Learning Disabilities*, 20 (2), 48–50.

Arnett A. (1989). *Dealing with Violence*. Hertfordshire Social Services Training Course Materials.

Bertulis, M., Norton, P., Jones, P., Cadwallader, C., Grounds, P. & McGreevy, S. (1998). Positive incident management: insights from staff involved and issues for the organisation. In D. Hewett (ed.), *Challenging Behaviour: Principles and practices* (pp. 17–33). London: David Fulton.

British Psychological Society (2016). *Psychological Therapies and People Who Have Intellectual Disabilities*. Leicester: The British Psychological Society.

Carr, E. G., Levin, L., McConnachie, G., Carlson, J. I., Kemp, D. C. & Smith, C. E. (1994). *Communication-based Intervention for Problem Behavior: A user's guide for producing positive change*. Baltimore MD: Paul H. Brookes Publishing.

Challenging Behaviour Foundation (2023). Information sheet: positive behaviour support planning: part 3 [pdf]. Retrieved from https://www.challengingbehaviour.org.uk/learning-disability-assets/03positivebehavioursupportplanningpart320192.pdf

Department of Health (2018). *Transforming Care: A national response to Winterbourne View Hospital: Department of Health Review Final Report*. London: Department of Health.

Donnelly, C. M., Elsworth, J. & McKim, J. (2015). An evaluation of an Intensive Interaction service. *Tizard Learning Disability Review*, 20 (3), 111–116.

Firth, G. (2008). A dual aspect process model of Intensive Interaction. *British Journal of Learning Disabilities*, 37, 43–49.

Firth, G., Elford, H., Leeming, C. & Crabbe, M. (2008). Intensive Interaction as a novel approach in social care: care staffs' views on the practice change process, *Journal of Applied Research in Intellectual Disabilities*, 21, 58–65.

Frankish, P. (2021a). Early development affected by early trauma. In Nigel Beail, Pat Frankish & Allan Skelly (eds) *Trauma and Intellectual Disability: Acknowledgement, identification & intervention* (pp. 55–64). Brighton: Pavilion.

Frankish, P. (2021b). Interventions based on the Mahler model of emotional development. In Nigel Beail, Pat Frankish & Allan Skelly (eds) *Trauma and Intellectual Disability: Acknowledgement, identification & intervention* (pp. 165–173). Brighton: Pavilion.

Gore, N. J., McGill, P., Toogood, S., Allen, D. *et al.* (2013). Definition and scope for positive behavioural support. *International Journal of Positive Behavioural Support*, 3(2), 14–23.

Harding C. (2021). Providing emotionally aware care in the positive behavioural support framework. In Nigel Beail, Pat Frankish & Allan Skelly (eds) *Trauma and Intellectual Disability: Acknowledgement, identification & intervention* (pp. 103–119). Brighton: Pavilion.

Herbert, M. (1981). *Behavioural Treatment of Children with Problems: A practice manual*. 1st edn. London: Academic Press.

Hewett, D. (1998). Commentary: managing incidents of challenging behaviour-principles. In Dave Hewett (ed.) *Challenging Behaviour Principles and Practices* (pp. 150–174). London: David Fulton.

Hewett, D. (ed.) (2018). *The Intensive Interaction Handbook*. 2nd edn. London: Sage.

Hutchinson, N. & Bodicoat, A. (2015). The effectiveness of Intensive Interaction: a systematic literature review. *Journal of Applied Research in Intellectual Disabilities*, 28, 437–454.

Kildahl, A. N., Bakken, T. L., Matre, A. E. W., Hellerud, J. M. A., Engebretsen, M. H. & Helverschou, S. B. (2021). Case study: identification of anxiety and subsequent intervention in an adolescent male with autism, severe intellectual disability and self-injurious behaviour. *International Journal of Developmental Disabilities*, 67 (5), 327–338.

Maes, B., Penne, A., Vastmans, K. & Arthur-Kelly, M. (2020). Inclusion and participation of students with profound intellectual and multiple disabilities. In Melanie Nind & Iva Strnadová (eds) *Belonging for People with Profound Intellectual and Multiple Disabilities* (pp. 41–58). London: Routledge.

Magito McLaughlin, D. & Carr, E. G. (2005). Quality of rapport as a setting event for problem behavior: assessment and intervention. *Journal of Positive Behavior Interventions*, 7 (2), 68–91. doi:10.1177/10983007050070020401

Mansell, J. & Beadle-Brown, J. (2012). *Active Support: Enabling and empowering people with intellectual disabilities*. London: Jessica Kingsley.

McKim, J. (2013). Developing the use of Intensive Interaction in the Oxfordshire Learning Disability NHS Trust (Ridgeway Partnership). *Clinical Psychology and People with Learning Disabilities*, 1–2, April, pp. 12–19.

McKim, J. & Samuel, J. (2021). The use of Intensive Interaction within a Positive Behavioural Support framework. *British Journal of Learning Disabilities*, 49 (2), 1–9.

Moroza-James, S. (2014). *Learning through Social Connection*. London: Thinking Autism.

Moroza-James, S. (2019). At home with Tom: maximising my son's potential with Intensive Interaction. In Mark Barber & Graham Firth (eds) *Delivering Intensive Interaction across Settings: Practice, community and leadership* (pp 129–139). Melbourne: private publication.

NHS England (2016). *Stopping Over Medication of People with a Learning Disability, Autism or Both (STOMP)*https://www.england.nhs.uk/learning-disabilities/improving-health/stomp-stamp/ [Accessed 23 February 2023].

Nind, M. & Hewett, D. (2001). *A Practical Guide to Intensive Interaction*. Kidderminster: BILD.

Oliver, C., Adams, D., Allen, D., Crawford, H., Heald, M. & Moss, J. (2020). The behaviour and wellbeing of children and adults with severe intellectual disability and complex needs: the Be-Well checklist for carers and professionals. *Paediatrics and Child Health*, 30 (12), 416–424.

Positive Behavioural Support Coalition UK (2015). *Positive Behavioural Support: A competence framework*. Retrieved from: pbsacademy.org.uk [Accessed 23 February 2023].

Royal College of Psychiatrists, British Psychological Society & Royal College of Speech and Language Therapists (2007). *Challenging Behaviour: A unified approach. Clinical and service guidelines for supporting people with learning disabilities who are at risk of receiving abusive or restrictive practice*. London: Royal College of Psychiatry.

Royal College of Psychiatry & The British Psychological Society on behalf of the Learning Disabilities Professional Senate (2016). *Challenging Behaviour: A unified approach – update*. London: Royal College of Psychiatry.

Samuel, J., Nind, M. E., Volans, A. & Scriven, I. (2008). An evaluation of Intensive Interaction in community living settings for adults with profound intellectual disabilities. *The Journal of Intellectual Disabilities*, 12(2), 111–126.

Samuel, J. & Doswell, S. (2021). The use of Intensive Interaction in trauma informed care for people with severe and profound intellectual disabilities. In Nigel Beail, Pat Frankish & Allan Skelly (eds) *Trauma and Intellectual Disability: Acknowledgement, identification & intervention* (pp. 121–134). Brighton: Pavilion.

Sharma, V. & Firth, G. (2012). Effective engagement through Intensive Interaction. *Learning Disability Practice*, 15(9), 20–23. doi:10.7748/ldp2012.11.15.9.20.c9380.

Skelly, A. (2017). Maintaining bonds: positive behaviour support and attachment theory. *Clinical Psychology Forum*, 290, 36–41.

Chapter 6

# Helping families to use the principles of Intensive Interaction with people living with advanced dementia

*Maggie Ellis, Christina Connell McGrath and Arlene Astell*

## Background

### How did this work come about?

The first and last authors of this chapter are psychologists with 50 years' combined experience of working with people with dementia, their families, and professional caregivers. In 2004 we were invited to a conference on the use of Intensive Interaction (II) with a range of clinical populations, e.g. deafblind individuals, individuals with profound and multiple learning disabilities and people living with severe autism. The talks were illustrated with video recorded examples of Intensive Interaction in practice and we were struck by the similarities we recognised between the individuals represented in the videos and those with advanced dementia, in terms of the communication challenges they face. The potential, connection and pure joy we witnessed in those videos altered the course of our careers.

Dementia is a progressive neurological syndrome characterised by a gradual loss of cognitive function. Individuals living with dementia experience changes that can impact memory, problem-solving, orientation, and language that worsen over time (Ellis & Astell, 2017; Alzheimer's Association, 2019). One of the biggest challenges faced by people with dementia and their families/caregivers stems from changes in communication skills (Azuma & Bayles, 1997). At the early stage of dementia, those with a diagnosis may experience word-finding problems and are likely to experience difficulties in keeping track of conversations (Hier et al., 1985). By the mid-stage of the condition, individuals find it harder to hold conversations, increasingly use "filler" words and phrases such as "uh-huh", "so that's that", etc. often to mask word-finding difficulties (Ramanathan, 1997). By the late stages, individuals living with dementia may become completely unable to use speech to communicate and struggle to understand the speech of others (Bayles, 1982). Combined with carers' reliance on verbal communication as a source of connection, this loss of speech and comprehension has a profound effect on relationships and caring dynamics).

DOI: 10.4324/9781003597933-6

Family members are known to experience ambiguous loss (a feeling that they have lost their loved one before they have died) and find it difficult to maintain their relationship with the person with advanced dementia (Sanders & Swails, 2009; Foley et al., 2019). Although by the later stages, remote memory (memory of past events), working memory (the ability to manipulate information in a short space of time) and language are significantly affected by dementia, there exists evidence to suggest that so-called "emotional memory" remains intact (Duffy, 1999). Duffy (1999) argued that this may be why a person with advanced dementia (PwAD) may be unable to identify a significant person in her life or the nature of their relationship but nonetheless retains an emotional impression of their past relationship. However, Duffy (1999) also noted that this knowledge may be of little consolation to a loved one who has been mis-identified. Family members who visit their loved ones in care facilities typically experience a loss of hope and feelings of despair when they feel as though they are unable to connect with their family member (Duggleby, Schroeder & Nekolaichuck, 2013). Conversely, professional caregivers who are required to develop caregiving relationships, are challenged in terms of forming new con-nections or maintaining existing ones with individuals who appear to be uncommunicative. As such, bids to communicate with people with advanced dementia decrease over time and become largely functional in nature, i.e. rela-ted only to activities of daily living (Bowie & Mountain, 1993).

Some PwAD exhibit persistent actions which often involve making "signature sounds" or the stimulation of their own bodies, such as rubbing their leg, chewing their fingers, pulling at items of their clothing or patting either them-selves or external objects with their hands (Kitwood, 1997). Perrin (2001) pos-tulated that these actions should be regarded as self–stimulatory in nature occurring in response to the failure of the environment to provide the PwAD with occupation and a feeling of security. As such, the PwAD retreats into her own world where these repetitive actions provide stimulation that possibly represent her "last desperate bid to remain psychologically alive" (Kitwood, 1997, p. 75). These repetitive actions are typically misinterpreted as "random", "meaningless" or even "challenging" by professional carers, and family mem-bers (Klimova & Kuca, 2016). Therefore, such actions are typically ignored or even discouraged by carers and family members, leading to complete social withdrawal in the PwAD.

The importance of the aforementioned self-stimulatory/social actions demonstrated by people with advanced dementia has been previously high-lighted by Validation Therapy (VT: Feil, 1993). VT was created in the late 1960s as a method for communicating with older adults and was later adapted in the 1980s to focus on individuals with Alzheimer's disease (Neal & Briggs, 2003). The core idea of VT is to acknowledge and affirm an individual's sub-jective reality. As such, VT may often involve using the actions of the person with dementia to communicate with them. Feil (1993) developed a set of vali-dation principles for caregivers to follow, reflecting the essence of the theory.

These include recognising that all actions have meaning and that individuals should not be forced to change their behaviour. Caregivers are also encouraged to accept each person non-judgmentally and to regard all individuals with dementia as valuable, regardless of the extent of their impairment (Feil, 1993).

Feil (1993) identified several potential benefits of VT for people with dementia, including improved speech, facial expressions, communication with others, and a reduced need for physical restraints or psychotropic medications. However, there is limited scientific evidence supporting its effectiveness, particularly regarding outcome measures (Day, 1997; Neal & Briggs, 2003). Despite this, the foundational principles of VT – such as maintaining and supporting the residual communicative abilities of people with dementia – suggest that the techniques used may help evoke positive emotions and improve self-esteem. These outcomes, in turn, may positively influence quality of life. It can be argued that consistently validating a person's emotions and personal reality makes almost any situation meaningful and aligns with Kitwood's (1990) concept of person-centred care. Specifically, VT views the person with dementia as a complete individual with a history and emotions, focusing on maximising each person's remaining abilities.

Self-stimulatory actions in people with advanced dementia in VT would be viewed very similarly by the II community. Indeed, comparable acts witnessed in individuals with profound and multiple learning disabilities would be regarded as part of the "language" of the individual, i.e. the "fundamentals of communication" (Nind, 1996). We argue that in this respect, PwAD are no different. Indeed, Kitwood (1997) made a similar point almost 30 years ago in arguing that:

> In the course of dementia, a person will try to use whatever resources he or she still has available. If some of the more sophisticated means of action have dwindled away, it may be necessary to fall back on ways that are more basic, and more deeply learned; some of these were learned in early childhood.
>
> (p. 75)

From this perspective, making repetitive sounds and movements, turn-taking, laughing and using a range of facial expressions may potentially be used as a basis of communication between PwAD and their caregivers/families. By using the individual's own repertoire of fundamental communication skills to communicate with them, we introduced the principles of II to the world of dementia.

## Adaptive interaction

### How does it link to Intensive Interaction theory?

We have been using the principles of II to work with individuals with very advanced dementia for almost 20 years. We realised early in the process that our approach, although based on II, is slightly different.

The main differences are:

1   We cannot assume that relationships can build over time (owing to the severe impact of dementia on memory). As such, interactions must be developed in the moment, meaning that the communication partner must *adapt* to whatever the person with dementia is doing at any given time.
2   Our aim is to simply connect with the person living with advanced dementia. There are no educational or long-term relationship-building goals.

Owing to these differences we thought it prudent to name our "variant" of II, Adaptive Interaction (AI).

## Research background

Over the last 20 years, we have conducted several studies noting increased communicative actions in individuals with advanced dementia when engaging in AI as compared to control and other comparison conditions (e.g. Astell, Shoaran & Ellis, 2022; Ellis & Astell, 2004; Ellis & Astell, 2011; Ellis & Astell, 2008). More specifically, in AI sessions, PwAD made more attempts to communicate compared to control and comparison conditions. AI sessions also elicited positive affect such as laughter that was absent in control and comparison conditions (Ellis & Astell, 2017). These findings further supported the use of AI, demonstrating its potential for promoting communication and facilitating relationships with PwAD.

Via our training company Astellis (www.astellis.co.uk), we have educated professional caregivers, speech and language therapists, psychologists and nurses in the practice of AI far and wide. Training has been conducted all over the UK, the Republic of Ireland, Canada, the U.S.A. and Bulgaria and interest continues to grow. Post-training, learners report feeling more confident in terms of interacting with PwAD and more willing to attempt interactions. Trainees often note that they feel differently about communication, recognising that it is much more than speech.

As previously noted, family carers face a unique set of issues when it comes to communicating with their loved ones with advanced dementia. As such, in recent years we have developed and evaluated our own training programmes for family members caring for their loved ones at home or for those who visit in nursing homes. Owing to the social restrictions imposed during the pandemic, we took the family programme online, providing four two-hour sessions across a four-week period. To pilot the training, we collaborated with Age UK, offering free sign-up to carers who had already taken part in the "Empowered Conversations" programme (https://empowered-conversations.co.uk/). This training was conducted as an evaluation of the programme and its impact on informal caregivers/family members of individuals with advanced dementia. All potential participants were offered the opportunity to take part in the programme without being part of the research.

## Method

Training took place online once a week for four weeks via Microsoft Teams. Each session lasted for two hours with a different focus each week. Week one focused on the impacts of advanced dementia. Week two addressed the perspective and world experienced by the PwAD. Week three focused on recognising the person's retained communicative skills and week four developed this further, identifying his/her communicative repertoire. The training was collaborative and conversational in nature with participants engaging with each other and the trainer throughout. The programme required trainees to practise specific elements of AI between the training sessions. Feedback on these practice sessions provided lively and engaging discussion every week.

The participants (eight women, two men) were all family caregivers (50–67 years old) of an individual living with dementia (60–86 years old). Of the individuals with dementia, eight had severe dementia, one had moderate dementia, and one had mild dementia as rated by the trainees using the Clinical Dementia Rating Scale (Morris, 1993). Participants completed the Zarit Burden Interview (Zarit, Reever & Bach-Peterson, 1980) and Dementia Attitudes Scale (O'Connor & McFadden, 2010); before and after the training and were invited to take part in a group interview pre- and post-training.

The qualitative elements of the research are of particular relevance to the current chapter. Through exploration of pre- and post-training interviews we can fully understand the nuances of each person's experiences, challenges and wins. Although each individual provides a unique perspective, the impact of AI training across the board is significant and sometimes surprising. Several of the participants cared for family members who retained some speech, and as such took part in the training to pre-empt the need to use AI. For this chapter, we have chosen to tell the stories of two participants who care for individuals who are almost completely non-verbal and for whom AI training was both timely and relevant. Couple 1 are Mark (husband/care partner) and Lucy (wife/care recipient). Couple 2 are Kate (daughter) and Bella (mother). What follows are the stories of the participants in relation to the challenges they face in maintaining their relationship with their loved ones living with advanced dementia and how training in AI helped them to view communication from a different perspective. Individual perspectives are provided in response to interview questions and are edited to remove filler words and hesitations.

## Materials

The following questions were asked by the first author pre-training:

1   What challenges do you face in terms of communicating with your loved one?
2   How do you deal with these challenges?

3   What would you like to be able to improve in terms of communicating with your loved one?
4   What are your hopes and expectations for the training?

The above questions were repeated during the post-training group interview to assess any change in response, except for question 4, which was reworded to evaluate the training itself:

4.1 How has the training met or failed your expectations?

## Results and discussion

### Mark and Lucy

Mark cares for his wife Lucy at home. They are a couple in their mid-60s with a strong relationship that Mark tries very hard to maintain. Lucy is living with advanced dementia and retains very little speech or understanding of the speech of others.

#### I  What challenges do you face in terms of communicating with your loved one?

Pre-training, Mark answered question 1 as follows:

> Lucy can't communicate *verbally* effectively, she finds it very difficult to understand anything *verbally*. Occasionally she can say the odd word too sometimes. Partial sentences come out occasionally but mostly it's nonsensical.

As such, Mark and Lucy can no longer include verbal communication as a key element of their interactions. On discussing the personal impact of the loss of verbal interaction within the relationship, Mark adds:

> As carers will know, it becomes quite a lonely life. You miss a lot of the little things, little conversations, it doesn't have to be an intellectual con- versation, it's just the little things like "what should we have for tea?" or "it's it great we could get three for the price of two" and things like that. You lose all that completely, so it's a big chunk of you missing from your life not being able to communicate verbally.

Clearly, Mark feels the loss of verbal communication deeply and misses the "little things" that are communicated between couples during their daily lives. The training focuses on changing perspectives about what communication is, i.e. to focus on connection over content. Trainees are informed that when speech is gone, the person living with dementia will use the fundamentals of communication to interact. For example, rubbing, tapping, signature sounds, eye contact, etc. The trainees' focus then becomes centred on the basic communication skills that are retained rather than the use and comprehension of speech which is severely impaired.

Post-training, Mark discusses how his approach to, and opinion of communication has changed because of the course:

> Before I used to say that the challenge I face is Lucy can't communicate. But of course, she can communicate. It's just you can't communicate verbally, so you just change your way of communicating really. So, what you do has taught me to communicate in different ways and you don't give up at all. Try everything you need to.

The previous quote illustrates that Mark is now focused on the non-verbal elements of his interactions with Lucy and how he can utilise those to connect with her.

### 2 How do you deal with these challenges?

Pre-training, Mark answered question two as follows:

> Various ways, you have to be sometimes repetitive, use simple language, Lucy will understand not always immediately, but most of the time. I still chat all the time and still talk as though she can talk. You use different actions, facial expressions, use objects – like sometimes if she might have a drink, I might pretend to have a drink though the straw and sometimes that might make her have a drink.

The previous quote illustrates how Mark has already made attempts to communicate with Lucy using the fundamentals, e.g., facial expressions, eye contact and modelling actions. However, he continued to talk to Lucy "as though she can talk", suggesting his attachment to speech as a form of connection and interaction. At this point, Mark was arguably unaware of the importance of non-verbal interactions on a conscious level. However, even pre-training, interacting with Lucy using the fundamentals of communication appeared to be a natural fit for him. Mark goes on to describe how the couple communicate non-verbally via affection:

> Our hugs are a great one. Being more affectionate and giving her (Lucy) hugs is wonderful, I give her a hug every time she gets up because she can't stand herself, and she loves that – she loves hugs. I say, "did you like that?" and she says "yes", which is one of the few times she talks or anything and its things like that.

Once more, the previous quote illustrates Mark's willingness to explore different methods of interacting with Lucy, finding that affection is particularly effective.

Mark's response to question two, post-training, suggests that he now views communication as something more than speech. Rather, he regards meaningful interaction to be grounded in shared experiences, observations and emotions.

> You adapt. You are using verbal communication, but you don't necessarily expect responses. So, you learned all the ways to communicate, but it doesn't stop you having conversation or talking, or, or anything like that. You just adapt. We started going out on trips again, a walk around ruined Abbey, and we have a picnic. You communicate with actions as well, don't you? We've started to go for little walks when we get back around the estate here. If she can physically, it just makes a nice walk, and you just observe. It's an excuse for you to have a nose at all the houses as well you see (laughs). Do things together, but it's just different, that's all.

The previous quote suggests that Mark now realises that Lucy is more aware/responsive than he thought previously and as such sees renewed value in going on trips, walking, observing, picnics and generally doing things together. Interestingly, Mark states that he still talks to Lucy but now does not expect or need a response. Instead, he relies on shared actions and non-verbal communication skills to connect with Lucy.

### 3 What would you like to be able to improve in terms of communicating with your loved one?

Pre-training, Mark provided the following response to question three:

> The one thing I'd love to be able to change but I don't think we can, is using Facetime and WhatsApp; Lucy being able to recognise someone on the phone because that's gone now. So, when her daughter rings, she can't really interact with the phone at all, which is a shame really. Her son tries to speak to her, but that's gone. I guess that's something we won't be able to improve but that would be ideal.

Mark's answer illustrates the recognition that there are aspects of Lucy's understanding and communication style that will not resurface. His response indicates an admission of this loss whilst also insinuating a desire for it to return.

This point is echoed in Mark's response to question three after training:

> Ah, I actually think that's one is the hardest of all of the questions, because in a way it goes without saying that you'd love to improve (verbal) communication, but your dreams will never be fulfilled for the way that Lucy is never going to have a conversation with me again.

Again, Mark acknowledges that conversation will not return yet expresses a desire for that not to be the case. Whilst Mark is undoubtedly hopeful that he can maintain a relationship with Lucy via nonverbal communication and is grateful for gaining this new perspective, he clearly continues to mourn the loss of verbal interaction.

### 4 What are your hopes and expectations for the training?

Pre-training, Mark answered question four as follows:

> I think I'd like it to be a two-way street. I like to try and give something based on my experience. I don't know if anyone ever finds it useful, but I like to try and help with these things and equally, I do enjoy learning and finding different ways of dealing with a loved one with dementia, and especially with communication because at the end of the day that's probably the most important thing. I can't claim to be an expert. So, I'd very much like to give and take back from it and hope that will be the case.

Here, Mark expresses the wish to both learn and educate during the course. He wishes to engage honestly with others and to share experiences with them. Mark demonstrates here that he is keen to engage with the learning process and is also happy to help and educate others on the course where possible. This quote also suggests that Mark recognises that changes in communication present a major challenge to all caregivers and that he hopes to find both camaraderie and educational value via taking part in the training.

### 4.1 How has the training met or failed your expectations?

Post-training, Mark provided the following response to question 4.1:

> I think this course has been inspirational because it opens a door for you that you didn't realise was there. So that sums up everything more, most importantly, what these things do, it helps you maintain your relationship with someone, which you struggle with otherwise. I'd have never understood some of the things that I've learned not least the rubbing being Lucy's way of saying that "I'm still here. I'm alive." I would never have had a clue with that and nor would most people so, and that's just one example. And I go on about that one because to me, it's so important, because she does it all the time, you know, I've heard other people say about tapping and everything and that's their way of communicating. So that's the thing is it gives you a new lease of life in your relationship, I think simply. Not only does it inspire you to believe that you can still communicate with people who lost their verbal skills, also it means so much more to all those whose loved ones are in homes or go to day centres

or just courses or anything like that, they're in the hands of people, who know how to communicate with on so many different levels. So, in an ideal world, it would be mandatory for all workers I would say. It's that important.

Mark's response here sums up participants' feelings about the course across the board. He recognised Lucy's leg rubbing actions to be communicative in nature which is something he was not aware of previously. He indicated that his relationship with Lucy was renewed, and he felt inspired by the realisation that it was still possible to communicate with her, albeit in a way that was relatively new to him. As such, Mark came to a realisation that AI provides PwAD and caregivers with a previously unrecognised method of connection albeit one that those with a diagnosis are already engaging in. As such, Mark became aware of the significance of non-verbal communication and that by *not* attempting to engage with our loved ones in this way we are preventing the continuation of a meaningful relationship. Mark also recognised that the use of AI may mean "so much more" to family members who visit their loved ones in care facilities. This quote echoes the research of Duggleby et al. (2013) who found that although family members feel ill-equipped to engage with their loved ones in care, they felt a sense of hope when a connection was made possible. Mark suggests there that AI could provide a way for relatives and PwAD to connect during visits. In addition to the significance of AI to family members, Mark also discussed the possible benefits of staff using the approach in care facilities. Of particular interest was his suggestion that AI training should be mandatory for professional caregivers who are employed in dementia care homes.

### Kate and Bella

Bella lives in a local nursing home and her daughter Kate visits her as often as she can. Bella retains some speech, but it is very difficult to understand and makes little sense to Kate. The situation is frustrating for both as they each try to be understood by the other.
Pre-training:

*I What challenges do you face in terms of communicating with your loved one?*

Pre-training, Kate answered question one as follows:

> You can tell by when they bring her through to the room where we've got to visit her now, what sort of visit it's going to be. Sometimes she can be a bit hysterical. Sometimes she can be crying. Sometimes she's coming through willingly and it is sometimes dependent on which carer is fetching her through. So, I really try and sort of like, "Oh come and have a sit-down mum, these chairs are really comfy. Come and tell me all about your week, and so we eventually get sat down and but in terms of a conversation, that doesn't really happen.

Kate indicates here that she can tell what sort of frame of mind her mum will be in the moment she sees her, perhaps suggesting that she is already using Bella's non-verbal communication to gauge how her mum is feeling. Naturally, her interpretation of her mum's mood impacts how Kate approaches her. Interestingly, although Kate demonstrates an awareness that her mum will not be able to hold a conversation with her, she suggests to Bella that she "tell her about her week". This prompt suggests both Kate's reliance on verbal interaction as an indication of connection and her lack of awareness of alternative avenues of communication that are open to her and Bella.

During the post-training interview, Kate's response to question one takes a very different turn. She states:

> Now, I think things seem a little bit easier and I don't know whether that's just getting a really good understanding of advanced dementia, all the different things, like everyone said. I've perhaps not noticed it or homed in on it before so that maybe what has been causing some of the challenges.

Post-training, Kate no longer discusses the challenges that she and her mum face in terms of communication. Rather, she is now focused on the solution, i.e. taking time, being patient and remaining open to how her mum is communicating at any given time. Kate also mentions the impact that gaining a thorough understanding of what happens to communication in advanced dementia has had on her approach to her mum. She states that this previous lack of knowledge may have served as a barrier to her communicating with her mum in a meaningful way.

## 2 How do you deal with these challenges?

Prior to the training programme, Kate answered question two as follows:

> I think I just try to reassure mum, because you can see she's getting frustrated and sometimes even though you can't really understand the words she's trying to say, I don't know whether she thinks they're coming out, right. And sometimes she'll go like this (looking frustrated), and I'll say, *"mum, I'm not going anywhere doesn't matter, just slow it down."* Just have think about it. You can tell sometimes she's running at a million miles an hour and she's trying to get all these words out. I will give her a hug. It's just reassurance and just trying to make her feel the best that she can, really *for me.*

Kate demonstrates her attempts to understand Bella's speech by asking her to slow down and to think about what she's trying to say. Understandably, this fails to help the situation as Bella may not understand either what Kate is saying or what she herself is trying to say. However, it is encouraging to hear that Kate is making valiant attempts to help Bella to interact, to minimise her frustration and to comfort her. Interestingly, Kate mentions that her attempts to make Bella feel the best she can is also an attempt to make Kate herself feel better. At first glance, this quote might come across as a little selfish on Kate's part but taken in context it is perfectly understandable that Kate would want to feel as though she had achieved something in helping Bella to be calm.

After training, Kate's response to question two was as follows:

> I think I need to be *realistic* and understand that a conversation might never come back. For me I think we always like to make people feel happy you know, because we care for them, and we love *them*. I think it's a case of I don't want her to struggle with anything or struggle with at least (sic) as possible. And it's, you know, while she's here, I just want her to get the best out of it. Nobody wants to be put through it (dementia), do we, but it's just trying to get the best that I can if there is just one little nugget that I can pick up that makes things better for her, then you know. That's, that's me.

Kate demonstrates here that AI training has encouraged her to be a little more realistic in terms of Bella's communication skills and to allow things to just "be" as they are. Kate talks of a desire to make Bella happy and to prevent her from struggling with communication as much as possible. Her overarching wish is for her to be able to make the best of it for Bella. As such, Kate is now more open to accepting the situation that she is presented with and rather than trying to change it, it happy to go with it to see where it takes her and Bella. The mention of "trying to get the best that I can" suggests that Kate now realises that communication her and Bella will not be as it once was but that attempting to interact with her via AI is still worth the effort to prevent her from struggling and to make her happy.

### 3 What would you like to be able to improve in terms of communicating with your loved one?

Pre-training, Kate's answer to question three illustrated her desire to remain pragmatic in her approach to communication. She stated:

> I think I need to be *realistic* and understand that a conversation might never come back. I think it's a case of I don't want her to struggle with anything or struggle as little as possible. Nobody wants to be put through it (dementia), do we, but it's just trying to get the best that I can and that's why I went on this course to see if there is just one little nugget that I can pick up that makes things better for her.

Here, Kate recognises the difficulties endured by those living with dementia and their families but that she wishes to minimise these as much as possible for

Bella. Her hope to pick up even one "tip" from the course speaks to her willingness to learn and engage with a new (to her) approach to interacting.

Post-training, Kate is far more focused not on improving communication between her and Bella but on making the most of the resources they already have. Kate states:

> Not to improve but I just want to make every interaction the best that it can be really, for her. Just being really aware if she sat on a chair and she's trying to reach for something that she's wanting something. Whereas I didn't really know what she was doing before and just understanding that she's looking for a need to be met and being aware of that.

Whilst Kate recognises that some of Bella's actions may be in response to an unmet physical need, she also demonstrates a recognition that those needs may be for communication itself. She states: "So, it's just putting everything into place, to communicate the best that I can." Here Kate is alluding to close observation of Bella's actions and to regarding them as having communicative purpose.

### 4 What are your hopes and expectations for the training?

Prior to training, Kate's response to question four was as follows:

> I just hope that I can pick something up to help so I don't feel, like sometimes she refuses to see me so I might not see her for three weeks. I've got an hour to try and have the best time. So, my hopes are just to see if I can pick something else up to put in the toolbox.

This quote demonstrates Kate's desire for her visits to Bella to go as well as they possibly can. Kate is aware that Bella's mood and therefore her readiness to communicate can fluctuate. As such, she is eager to make the most of the time they have together and is hopeful that training in AI will provide her with useful additional skills that will increase the chances of a successful interaction. Kate's comment stating that she only has an hour to "try and have the best time" suggests that she feels under pressure to "achieve" some sort of success when she visits Bella. Arguably, this additional time constraint can only add to the stress that both she and Bella feel when they attempt to communicate.

Kate answered question 4.1 post-training as follows:

> I think breaking it down really makes you home in just being more aware of it: that this is really important. And seeing a reaction when you put it into place, I know it's been a good one (laughs). But just being open to try things as well. I'll always have it in mind because all of these things might not happen in *every* interaction. They might not be happening now, but they might be happening a bit further down the line. I've so enjoyed doing

the training and it and it just I think a lot of the things we're, aware of but we just do automatically, it's not until somebody actually points it out that you think, "*okay*".

Here Kate affirms the significance of paying close attention to small details in Bella's communicative actions. She recognises that every interaction is likely to be different and that she does not expect them to be uniform. Kate mentions that the training has affirmed for her that some of the methods of interaction she had already been trying with Bella, quite naturally, are "*okay*".

## Conclusion

The participants in this study both recognise that communication with their loved one will never be as it once was. They allude to the challenges their loved ones face in terms of losing their ability to use and understand speech (see Azuma and Bayles, 1997; Hier et al., 1985; Ramanathan, 1997; Bayles, 1982). However, they both express a real difficulty in accepting this and Mark in particular notes a desire for the previous communication style to return (see Sanders and Swails, 2009; Foley et al., 2019; Duffy, 1999). This is perhaps the biggest difference between individuals with advanced dementia and those who are born with communication limiting conditions. Although unsurprising, this desire for things to return to how they were was present in all interviews to varying degrees. Increased knowledge of what happens to communication in advanced dementia and the fundamentals of communication impacted positively on participants in terms of their approach to their loved ones (see Kitwood, 1997; Perrin, 2001; Nind, 1996). Carers became more patient and curious about their loved ones' communicative repertoire, recognising things that they did not see previously.

The findings suggest that AI training impacts the family caregivers' experience of communicating with their loved ones. The training allowed participants to rekindle their relationship with their relative and see potential in their relative's communication. These new attitudes toward their loved one's communication abilities allowed them to find meaning in their communication again and hope for the future. Therefore, AI training could enable family caregivers to remain connected to their loved one, despite verbal-communication impairments, by teaching them to recognise and use non-verbal communication skills.

## References

Alzheimer's Association. (2019). 2019 Alzheimer's disease facts and figures. *Alzheimer's & Dementia*, 15(3), 321–387. doi:10.1016/j.jalz.2019.01.010

Astell, A. J., Shoaran, S. & Ellis, M. P. (2022). Using adaptive interaction to simplify caregiver's communication with people with dementia who cannot speak. *Frontiers in Communication*, 6. doi:10.3389/fcomm.2021.689439

Azuma, T., & Bayles, K. A. (1997). Memory impairments underlying language difficulties in dementia. *Topics in Language Disorders*, 18(1), 58–71.

Bayles, K. A. (1982). Language function in senile dementia. *Brain and Language*, 16(2), 265–280. doi:10.1016/0093-934X(82)90086-4

Bowie, P. & Mountain, G. (1993). Using direct observation to record the behaviour of long stay patients with dementia. *International Journal of Geriatric Psychiatry*, 8, 857–864.

Day, K. (1997). The validation therapy approach to the management of dementia. *Asian Journal of Occupational Therapy*, 1(1), 22–25.

Duffy, M. (1999). Reaching the person behind the dementia: Treating comorbid affective disorders through subvocal and nonverbal strategies. In M. Duffy (ed.), *Handbook of counseling and psychotherapy with older adults* (pp. 577–589). Wiley.

Duggleby, W., Schroeder, D. & Nekolaichuk, C. (2013). Hope and connection: the experience of family caregivers of persons with dementia living in a long-term care facility. *BMC Geriatr*, 13, 112. doi:10.1186/1471-2318-13-112

Ellis, M. P. & Astell, A. J. (2004). The urge to communicate in severe dementia. *Brain and Language*, 91(1), 51–52. doi:10.1016/J.BANDL.2004.06.028

Ellis, M. & Astell, A. J. (2008). A new approach to communicating with people with advanced dementia: a case study of adaptive interaction. In S. Zeedyk (ed.) *Techniques for Promoting Social Interaction for Individuals with Communication Impairments*. London: Jessica Kingsley.

Ellis, M. P. & Astell, A. J. (2011). Adaptive Interaction: a new approach to communicating with people with advanced dementia. *Journal of Dementia Care*, 19(3), 24–26.

Ellis, M. & Astell, A. (2017). Communicating with people living with dementia who are nonverbal: the creation of Adaptive Interaction. *PLoS one*, 12(8), e0180395. doi:10.1371/journal.pone.0196489

Feil, N. (1993). *The validation breakthrough: Simple techniques for communicating with people with "Alzheimer's-type dementia"*. Health Professions Press.

Firth, G. (2012). Background to Intensive Interaction. In D. Hewett, G. Firth, M. Barber & T. Harrison (eds) *The Intensive Interaction Handbook* (pp. 9–20). London: Sage.

Foley, S., McCarthy, J. & Pantidi, N. (2019). The struggle for recognition in advanced dementia: implications for experience-centered design. *ACM Transactions on Computer-Human Interaction (TOCHI)*, 26(6), 1–29. doi:10.1145/3359594

Hier, D. B., Hagenlocker, K. & Shindler, A. G. (1985). Language disintegration in dementia: effects of etiology and severity. *Brain and Language*, 25(1), 117–133. doi:10.1016/0093-934X(85)90124-5

Kitwood, T. (1990). The dialectics of dementia: With particular reference to Alzheimer's disease. *Ageing and Society*, 10(2), 177–196.

Kitwood, T. (1997). *Dementia Reconsidered: The person comes first*. Buckingham: Open University Press.

Klimova, B. & Kuca, K. (2016). Speech and language impairments in dementia. *Journal of Applied Biomedicine*, 14(2), April 30, 97–103.

Morris, J. C. (1993). The Clinical Dementia Rating (CDR): Current version and scoring rules. *Neurology*, 43(11), 2412–2414. *(Note: Manning & Ducharme may have used this version in their work.)*

Neal, M., & Briggs, M. (2003). Validation therapy for dementia. *Cochrane Database of Systematic Reviews*, (4), CD001394. doi:10.1002/14651858.CD001394.

Nind, M. (1996). Efficacy of Intensive Interaction: developing sociability and communication in people with severe and complex learning difficulties using an approach
based on caregiver–infant interaction. *European Journal of Special Educational Needs*,
11(1), 48–66.

Nind, M. & Hewett, D. (2012). *Access to Communication: Developing the basics of
communication with people with severe learning difficulties through intensive interaction.* London: David Fulton.

O'Connor, M. L., & McFadden, S. H. (2010). Development and psychometric validation
of the Dementia Attitudes Scale. *International Journal of Alzheimer's Disease*, Article
454218.

Perrin, T. (2001). Activity, occupation and stimulation: A care planning approach. In T.
Kitwood & S. Benson (eds), *The new culture of dementia care* (pp. 117–136). Hawker
Publications.

Ramanathan, V. (1995). Narrative well-formedness in Alzheimer discourse: an interactional examination across settings. *Journal of Pragmatics*, 23, 395–419.

Sanders, S., & Swails, P. (2009). A quest for meaning: Hospice social workers and
patients with end-stage dementia. *Health & Social Work*, 34(4), 275–283. (https://
www.jstor.org/stable/23719366)

Zarit, S. H., Reever, K. E., & Bach-Peterson, J. (1980). Relatives of the impaired elderly:
correlates of feelings of burden. *The Gerontologist*, 20(6), 649–655.

Chapter 7

# A parental and family view on using Intensive Interaction

*Graham Firth*

## Introduction

Better understanding the parental or family perspective on Intensive Interaction (Nind & Hewett, 1994) should allow for greater insight into the particular issues and challenges facing parental and/or family practitioners of the approach. Also, any such improved insight could provide parent and family practitioners with greater confidence in identifying and subsequently realising the potential communicative and emotional outcomes to be gained from using the approach within their own family setting.

Any such improved understanding of the parental or family perspective may also provide professionals, including those who advocate for, support and/or train parents in their use of Intensive Interaction, with greater insights into the specific challenges that parents and family practitioners are likely to encounter, perhaps particularly in the early stages of approach adoption. Providing more insightful and focused support should enable the use of Intensive Interaction to be more successfully adopted and better sustained by parents and family carers, making the potential emotional and developmental outcomes more likely to be realised.

This chapter therefore sets out to articulate the parental and/or family perspective on the use of Intensive Interaction; more specifically to identify the outcomes perceived from their use of the approach, both for their family member and for themselves as parental or family practitioners. The chapter includes the results of an online survey on the parental or family use of Intensive Interaction conducted by the author.

## The current Intensive Interaction literature on the parental and/ or family use of Intensive Interaction

Research or reports on the parental or family use of Intensive Interaction are limited. The first appearance in the Intensive Interaction literature of a parental perspective was included in Interaction in Action: Reflections on the Use of Intensive Interaction (Hewett & Nind, 1998). In this book one chapter, 'Gary's Story: Parents Doing Intensive Interaction' describes Beth and Steve Taylor's

DOI: 10.4324/9781003597933-7

story of using Intensive Interaction with their son Gary, a 12-year-old boy with severe learning difficulties and autism. Beth, Gary's mum, reported that it was only on discovery of Intensive Interaction as an entire philosophy guiding a way of being with a person that she felt it was completely appropriate to engage with her son in this manner. She revelled in the fact that her son now engaged in smiling, laughter, physical touch and close eye contact with her and that these interactions deepened their bond as a family. Steve, Gary's dad, recalls how different Gary is now in comparison to his life before Intensive Interaction. Steve discusses how Gary will now run to meet him at the door when he returns home, demonstrating obvious excitement, joy and affection.

Mary Kellet's 2005 paper 'Catherine's Legacy: Social Communication Development For Individuals with Profound Learning Difficulties and Fragile Life Expectancies' illustrates how Catherine's quality of life was transformed by Intensive Interaction in her last few months of life. The author notes that in the latter part of her life Catherine's mother had begun to use Intensive Interaction with her at home. Catherine's mother spoke of gleaning a great deal of pleasure from these interactions that included bubble-blowing games and tutting. Catherine also clearly enjoyed these activities and regularly reacted to her mother with close eye contact and smiles. On Catherine's death, her mother wrote to the author to thank her for including her daughter in the study, highlighting the immeasurable joy they experienced in connecting in a meaningful way. This connection was only made more potent as Catherine died only weeks after first connecting with her family using Intensive Interaction.

In her chapter 'Doing Intensive Interaction at Home' (in Hewett et al., 2012) mum Tandy Harrison reports on her use of Intensive Interaction with her son, using the approach as a method of being with him in the home environment. Tandy reported that even in the initial stages of using the approach, allowing her son to lead the interaction felt right and brought them closer together. However, over time communicative progress was identified, with Tandy describing increases in her son's eye contact, smiling and laughter whilst they were playing together. These increases in communicative action also occurred when Tandy's son interacted with other adults using Intensive Interaction, leading to him develop a range of relationships that were different in terms of their contents and tone.

Two parental respondents reported their experiences in the Firth et al. (2021) paper 'A Qualitative Study of the Practice-Related Decision-Making of Intensive Interaction Practitioners'. Both mothers noted that the parental relationship provided certain advantages in that they were able to identify any 'problems' that may not be related to communication difficulties. For example, both respondents felt that they were well placed to identify any physical issue or pain in their loved one owing to this close relationship. However, being a parent practitioner was also identified as carrying with it more complex and wide-ranging worries about the future life chances for their own child. For example, both mothers felt that they found it more difficult to use Intensive Interaction with their own children than with others owing to the worries they may harbour about the future of their own child.

Finally, Berridge & Hutchinson (2021) focused on 'Mothers' Experience of Intensive Interaction'. The researchers interviewed six mothers who used Intensive Interaction with their children with intellectual disabilities and/or autism. From the findings of this study, Intensive Interaction was seen by some mothers as giving them a way of connecting with their child through '*developing reciprocity*', indicating that using Intensive Interaction was beneficial in both relational and emotional terms for themselves and for their children. The findings also indicated a view that the benefits of using Intensive Interaction would be maximised if they, i.e. mothers, were given early opportunities to learn about and apply the approach.

## An online survey into the parental and/or family use of Intensive Interaction

The purpose in carrying out this qualitative survey was to gain a more detailed understanding of parental or family use of Intensive Interaction within their particular family settings. From this survey it was hoped that parents or family carers would articulate what they perceived to be the particular challenges and potential positive outcomes to be gained from its use.

The participants in this study identified themselves as: 11 mothers, one dad, one granny, one grandad and one aunty. These respondents all identified themselves as Intensive Interaction practitioners at some level i.e. having at times engaged with their son(s), daughter, grandchild or nephew using Intensive Interaction.

## Method

A 'parental and/or family use of Intensive Interaction questionnaire' was distributed via social media (via the 'Intensive Interaction Users' Facebook group on 23.11.22) or via email (using distribution lists historically developed by the author). Fourteen respondents returned a questionnaire (one being from a combined 'mum and dad') or answered the survey questions online via Survey Monkey (https://www.surveymonkey.co.uk).

The survey asked questions about their use of Intensive Interaction (frequency, context, form, etc.), how they came across the approach, why they use it, whether they had received any support in using it, the impacts they perceived from its use with their identified person (son, daughter, grandchild or nephew) and any perceived personal outcomes.

The returns were thematically analysed and coded using a Template Analysis methodology (King, 1998) thus producing a 'rich description' of the familial process and associated emotional and/or psychological outcomes. Template analysis is a qualitative method that involves developing a coding 'template' based on key 'a priori' conceptual issues pre-identified as likely to arise in the data, which in this case were defined as: 'communication and communication development', 'making and maintaining a connection', 'outcomes for identified child*', and 'outcomes for the parental/family practitioner'.

During the subsequent line-by-line transcript analysis, specific subordinate themes were added to provide further detail. The subordinate themes related to significant or common descriptors, issues or behaviours, emotional issues, etc. The survey responses were finally re-analysed with reference to the finalised thematic template (see Table 7.1).

[*In the findings section below, as in one 'a priori' theme, the recipient of Intensive Interaction is described as a 'child', this term being used to identify the person's familial relationship without any regard to their chronological age].

## Results

### Theme 1: Communication and communication development

#### Identifying fundamental communication as important

The parent or family carer's introduction to Intensive Interaction was varied and included coming across the approach via engagement with speech and language therapists, teachers, an 'LA support worker', 'a psychology assistant', 'through a

Table 7.1 Summary of developed analytic themes

| A priori theme 1 Communication and communication development | A priori theme 2 Making and maintaining a connection | A priori theme 3 Outcomes identified for the child* | A priori theme 4 Outcomes for parental/family member practitioner |
|---|---|---|---|
| Subordinate themes<br>• Identifying fundamental communication as important<br>• Communication development (including being better understood)<br>• Other Communication outcomes (including functional communication and/or language use) | Subordinate themes<br>• Relationship development, bonding and attachment<br>• The generalisation of sociability<br>• Being with the child in child-centred and non-demanding ways | Subordinate themes<br>• Showing or feeling positive emotions<br>• Dealing with negative emotions or behaviours<br>• Emotional Development - building agency and self-esteem | Subordinate themes<br>• Perceived positive emotional outcomes<br>• Experiences of feeling other emotions<br>• Dealing with the child's negative emotional states with Intensive Interaction<br>• Learning about themselves, their child and about the nature of communication |

*friend who also has a child with learning difficulties', 'through hearing it mentioned at work' and even 'at my son's drumming session several years ago'.*

This first exposure to the approach was often followed up by some more research, e.g. via the internet (YouTube and Facebook). Some respondents went further and read some Intensive Interaction journal articles or books or watched a relevant online video. Also, some respondents went on to attend some form of Intensive Interaction training course. In terms of further developing both their competence and confidence as Intensive Interaction practitioners, the respondents mentioned certain issues that they found difficult:

- *'It's a very isolated place to do Intensive Interaction [at home]. It's unclear how/ when parents should take a break. There is no-one there to help/watch/ comment but above all, there is no-one to give you a pat on the back'.*

These difficulties appeared to be more significant early in their adoption of the approach:

- *'In the beginning, I think like many that start Intensive Interaction, I kept wondering "what's next?"'*

The frequency of Intensive Interaction use within the family setting varied from *'daily'* to *'all the time'*. For one respondent frequency was identified as *'most days when I visit her ... at her residential placement'*. Some respondents didn't identify a specific frequency, instead stating that the approach just *'becomes part of daily life'*, being available during other daily activities, e.g. *'including when getting dressed'*. However, the frequency and form of Intensive Interaction engagements was indicated to potentially change over time:

- *'When they were babies, I used it every day, multiple times a day. Now they are older and able to express themselves through verbal speech, I use it less often, though still take elements of it'.*

The form these Intensive Interaction engagements took were various and included descriptions of *'tuning in'* and *'to and fro'* exchanges based on aspects of the person's current behaviour or activity, e.g. *'A back and forth of sounds, words, gestures and body language'*.

Some descriptions were more detailed, and evidenced variations in the tempo and form of the interactions, both within and across engagements over time:

- *'At home, I generally sit and join him in whatever activity he's engaged in. I spend some time observing first before trying to subtly join in with what he's doing. Our sessions can be very quiet and gentle, or they can be more energetic and fun (particularly when we're on the trampoline for instance!)'.*

- *'When they were babies, they would by lying down or sitting up and I would lean in, give open body language and eye contact, smile, mimic facial expressions and sounds, provide pauses and so on. This developed into showing interest in the toys and objects they showed interest in and exploring these with them and taking turns with them. Now they are older we tend to do things like sing songs together, dance, play games or role play'.*

Some respondents did not identify a sessional form of Intensive Interaction but saw it more as a basic communicative or social way of being with each other: *'Not sessions as such – just a basic part of our communication with each other'.*

### Communication development (including being better understood)

Generally, however, Intensive Interaction was seen as supporting positive communications exchanges between the parent or family member and the recipient child. A focus on the use and further development of the 'Fundamentals of Communication' (as identified by approach originators Nind & Hewett (1998)) within Intensive Interaction engagements was seen as important for some respondents:

- *'Understanding the importance of fundamental communication skills has really helped us all to understand that just because he doesn't speak, [that] doesn't mean he doesn't communicate'.*

For a significant number of respondents, Intensive Interaction was seen to support the continued or further development of the children's social and communication understandings and use:

- *'He is more vocal and has happy intonation in his voice'.*
- *'Increased smiles and eye contact which helps facilitate choices'.*

A whole family embracing the use of Intensive Interaction was seen as making such communication development possible: *'this approach has been adopted by the whole family and by those who know my youngster, and this had made the progress possible'.* This perceived communicative development was also indicated as being irrespective of age or apparent cognitive ability:

- *'She does new communications even now (she's 22)'.*

### Other communication outcomes (including functional communication and/or language use)

The use of Intensive Interaction was seen by some respondents as being incidentally supportive of other communication outcomes, with the strongest theme emerging being that of the parent or family member being better able to understand the child, and thus to respond appropriately:

- *'We often feel that our basic understanding of Intensive Interaction gives us the ability to understand W's "issues", to some degree, and to react accordingly'.*

Also very usefully, a particular feature of the child being better understood (according to the parental or family viewpoint) was being able to understand some aspects of their child's communication or behaviour indicating when they want to stop the interaction:

- *'When he indicates the interaction is finished, he usually does so by sitting on my knee for a cuddle'.*

Finally, there were comments from two respondents which seem to indicate outcomes extrapolated quite extensively from the initial use of Intensive Interaction. These comments focused on perceived improvements in being able to communicatively share emotional states and experiences via language use:

- *'They communicate well and are able to talk about their feelings and experiences easily'.*

### Theme 2: Making and maintaining a connection

#### Relationship development, bonding and attachment

Some of the main themes emerging from the survey data (across all the respondents) were those of improved connection, relationship development and perceived attachment formation. This was often stated explicitly about themselves, sometimes about the child, and sometimes more generally. A range of descriptors were used to define this phenomenon, including: *'relationship'*, *'connected'*, *'bond'*, *'attachment'* and *'loved'*:

- *'It has been the only approach we've used which has had a lasting benefit to our son and to our relationship with him. It has made him more sociable, connected and communicative … It has given us a relationship'.*

This *'connecting'* process was clearly indicated as being unconditional in nature by one respondent:

- *'I feel like I am connecting with my child, listening to her, talking to her and loving her as she is'.*

Also, this process of relationship development and perceived attachment was seen as having concurrent mutuality, and thus being seen to go in both direction:

- 'He feels acknowledged ... and loved'.

### The generalisation of sociability

Some respondents indicated a generalisation to this process of increased sociability. Some of the children were described as 'establishing relationships with others far more easily' or 'beginning to connect with others'. This two-way relationship development is described in more detail by one respondent as starting with the parents but then subsequently becoming easier with other members of the family:

- 'He has built positive relationships with a wider range of adults in the family (and they with him). He initiates interactions with his parents and is starting to be confident enough to do so with other family members'.

Going further still in evidencing such a generalisation of the social skills development attributed to Intensive Interaction, one respondent reported that this enabled their (adult) child to successfully interact and develop relationships with a range of other people outside of the immediate family:

- 'They are now able to use the skills they have learnt to interact with peers, tutors and employers and have a long-term relationship with another autistic person which gives them huge safety, security and love'.

However, this process was not seen to be necessarily quick or easy:

- '... I would add though that this requires someone to become very familiar with N, she also takes a few months to accept new people into her circle'.

### Being with the child in person-centred and non-demanding ways

Some of the respondents described their Intensive Interaction engagements with the children in ways that indicated a non-demanding and/or child or person-centred way, i.e. by creating sociability around the current actions or behaviours of the child and, as one respondent put it, 'to enter into his world'.

- 'I would join my nephew in whatever he is doing, mirroring his play and actions. After some time he will begin to repeat actions and look for me to mirror them. He often changes his actions and does different things to see if I will mirror him'.

- *'She's not stressed and under no pressure, and there's no demand on her ... it's really nice to see'.*

The descriptors used included terminology that indicated the development of a mutually equitable social state of *'being together'*:

- *'I still try to set aside a time, particularly after a busy school day, so that we can just be together using Intensive Interaction techniques'.*

### Theme 3: The outcomes of Intensive Interaction use for the child

As well as learning to understand and apply the fundamentals of communication in increasingly generalised social situations, other emotional or psychological outcomes were evidenced across the respondents' testimony.

#### Showing or feeling positive emotions

Despite one respondent indicating that *'with emotions it's hard to answer'*, generally across all the respondents there were consistent reports of positive emotional outcomes, both in the short term, and more cumulatively across the longer-term. A majority of respondents indicated that the recipient child was *'happy'* or *'happier'* during or after Intensive Interaction engagements, with this emotional state being recognised in *'increased smiles and eye contact'* or when they would *'laugh and smile'*.

- *'She's always pretty happy when the session has finished ... its because of the intense nature of the session, not because it's over'.*

For one respondent, this signalling of positive affect was even more pronounced:

- *'The joy on his face and in his body is overwhelming. He hugs and kisses and jumps'.*

This increase in positive affect was also at times combined with other positive emotional state outcomes, e.g. the child being seen to be *'calmer'*, *'more confident'* and *'less frustrated'*.

#### Dealing with negative emotions or behaviours

Not all the respondents only mentioned perceived changes in positive affect. Some reports indicated that the use of Intensive Interaction enable the recipient child to deal more successfully with negative emotional states. For one respondent this was attributed to an increased ability to express emotional difficulties in ways that could be understood, rather than masking or internalising them:

- *'He is happy to express joy and sadness and frustration more. I think he masked and internalised before'.*

Another respondent used Intensive Interaction quite deliberately to help relax the recipient child at or in the lead-up to emotionally challenging situations:

- *'I try to use it daily but need to use it when my son is stressed or anxious or ... before introducing something new. It relaxes him and I think helps him feel safe and connected'.*

A quite radical change (a decrease) in the presentation of certain challenging behaviours associated with negative emotional states was indicated by one respondent:

- *'My son used to lash out, pull my hair and scratch me for what I thought was no apparent reason. Not often but at times. Intensive Interaction technique alongside others which complement Intensive Interaction had made a huge difference to my son and my family. He is gentle, he seeks me out, he allows me to help him so much more with problem solving activities such as jigsaws and dressing, teeth brushing and combing hair'.*

One respondent saw the development of their social skills and the subsequent building of their self-esteem (through Intensive Interaction) as also helping repair previous psychological damage done earlier in life:

- *'They still misread situations and people and find it incredibly tiring. But the skills they have learnt have enabled them to study at a high level, impacting positively on their self-esteem and repairing damage done earlier in their school career when they were made to feel "stupid" (their word)'.*

### Emotional development – building agency and self-esteem

The previously mentioned development of the Intensive Interaction recipient's self-esteem was almost universally reported by the respondents. The terms used, in addition to 'self-esteem' included the development of, or perceived improvements in, 'confidence' and 'self-determination'.

- *'I feel my daughter in particular, having been a lockdown baby who barely saw anyone for first couple of years of her life, has proven to be more confident than her brother. I like to think all the intensive 1 to 1 work with her has paid off'.*

There were also reported improvements in emotional regulation and understanding:

- '... *more confidence, better emotional self-regulation, better emotional understanding*'.

This development of '*a sense of self*' and '*self-confidence*' was seen by one respondent as potentially a starting point of a process of much more involved emotional awareness and well-being:

- '*My youngster has developed a sense of self, self-confidence, is able to understand and explore ... many different emotions and has learned to integrate these into holistic awareness (rather than cognitive labelling) [of] different emotions ... they have a greater sense of well-being and are more resilient*'.

### Theme 4: Outcomes for parental/family member practitioner(s)

Interestingly, the respondents in this survey produced more comments on their own perceived outcomes from the use of Intensive Interaction than they provided about the outcomes for the children. Some of these identified outcomes were short-term, being realised during the '*very rewarding*' engagement with their children using Intensive Interaction, with some more longer-term changes identified relating to certain emotional states.

#### Perceived positive emotional outcomes

The in-the-moment positive outcomes of Intensive Interaction for the parental or family member are variously described as being '*fun*', being '*happy*', and also experiencing '*joy*'. These positive emotional states are indicated as being mutually and concurrently enjoyed by both parties:

- '*She's happy in the sessions and that makes me happy*'.

Indeed, as described by one respondent, these positive emotional outcomes are seen as being optimal from their parental perspective:

- '*Joy and love. What more could a mother want*'.

This '*positive*' feelings developed by the parents/family members was also indicated as providing an intrinsic motivation to want to do more, or at least try even harder to gain more from the interactions:

- '*When I have engaged in Intensive Interaction, and it has been successful, it makes me feel good and encourages me to try harder*'.

The cumulative, longer-term positive emotional outcomes of using Intensive Interaction within a family context are described by one respondent as increasing their own general psychological *'well-being'*.

- *'It has enabled me to build a strong loving relationship with my autistic youngster which has increased my sense of joy and well-being'.*

However, some short-term positivity experienced during Intensive Interaction engagements can lead to some more complex emotional outcomes, as candidly related in some detail by one parent:

- *'I do enjoy it but this is a complex question for me because (a) I enjoy it more, the more effort I put in and I frequently find myself doing it half-heartedly (I'm with him all day every day) which is less enjoyable for both of us, and (b) at the beginning when he was less able I found it very painful to do Intensive interaction because it stripped away some protective levels of denial I'd had regarding his abilities'.*

However, some of the other longer-term outcomes attributed to the use of Intensive Interaction included increased empathy, a reduction in parental stress and some improved *'emotional awareness'*:

- *'I feel I'm more empathic, generally happier and less stressed when faced with our daily challenges'.*
- *'The whole family has benefitted from Intensive Interaction entering into our daily life; it's created better emotional awareness for all of us'.*

### Experiences of feeling other emotions

As well as experiencing short-term feelings of *'joy'*, being *'connected'* and *'love'* (and being *'loved'*, and even for one respondent, being *'deeply loved'*) during or at the end of Intensive Interaction engagements, other positive feelings or emotional outcomes were indicated. These other feelings or emotional outcomes were variously listed as including being *'relaxed'*, and also of feeling *'purposeful'*, *'inspired'*, and even *'proud'*.

- *'I am less self-critical. I am no longer overwhelmed and instead feel empowered and relaxed and enjoy time with my son'.*

This increase in a relaxed state was attributed by one respondent to being so fully focused on the Intensive Interaction engagement that other thoughts were thus excluded when *'being with'* their daughter:

- '[I] feel grounded and calm, as the Intensive Interaction time doesn't allow you to think about anything else other than being with N'.

However, not all the emotional outcomes of using Intensive Interaction necessarily felt as positive. Strong negative feelings of *'frustration'* or self-criticism (and even being overcome by *'guilt'* for one respondent) can at times be the result of engagements that didn't go as well as wished:

- 'On a negative point when I get it "wrong" and we experience communication breakdown ... I am relentlessly hard on myself as I know I should know better. Being overcome by this guilt doesn't help in the moment when I am trying to manage/help and support someone in a state of [being] overwhelm[ed]!'.

For another respondent such feelings of *'guilt'* or *'negativity'* were identified as being particularly difficult at the start of the process, feeling that even though Intensive Interaction was generally seen (and felt) to be helpful in sociably or emotionally connecting with her son, this somehow exposed a previous personal weakness or failure in this area:

- 'I found it very hard at first ... even when I enjoy moments with my child there is an intense feeling of guilt/negativity that I need an intervention in order to interact with or enjoy my own child. Over the years Intensive Interaction has shown me that I need to take more care of myself in order to truly help my son'.

However, for another respondent, using the Intensive Interaction approach actually confirmed that they, as a mother in this case, had previously been *'getting it right in many ways'*, thus validating their previous parental style despite feelings of failure. Nonetheless, by focussing in more on specific areas of engagement practice, e.g. *'being playful'*, the adoption of Intensive Interaction was seen as being hugely significant for the entire family:

- 'Until I started Intensive Interaction, I really felt I'd failed as a mother, that I was incapable of helping him to develop. Intensive Interaction showed by that, in fact, I was already getting it right in many ways and that I just needed to concentrate more on those things that I was doing right (being playful with him, allowing him to take the lead ...) and that that was the best way I could help him. I truly believe that Intensive Interaction has saved both of us and the rest of our family'.

### Dealing with the child's negative emotional states with Intensive Interaction

Interestingly, some testimony about the use of Intensive Interaction during times of heightened or negative emotional states (for the recipient children) also emerged from the data. This seemingly deliberate use of Intensive Interaction techniques at such times (e.g. when *'angry or upset'*) was thought to enable better communication with, and emotional self-regulation by the child:

- *'I feel far more confident to face any challenging behaviour that might arise as I know that Intensive Interaction techniques will help him self-regulate better and help me to know how best to support him in those moments too'.*

### Learning about themselves, their child and about the nature of communication

The use of Intensive Interaction, or more precisely a more fully informed understanding of the practices and principles of Intensive Interaction, seemed to provide a range of learning opportunities and outcomes for the parental/family practitioners. Such learning outcomes were claimed to include being better able to understand their child, and thus how best to support them:

- *'It's created … a better understanding of how best to support and advocate for our son'.*

Coming to better understand of what could, or ideally should constitute communication for and with their children was also seen to develop with the adoption of Intensive Interaction:

- *'Understanding the importance of fundamental communication skills has really helped us all to understand that just because he doesn't speak, doesn't mean he doesn't communicate'.*

Learning about Intensive Interaction gave one respondent (a grandfather) some clearer perspective on their family's levels of preparedness for caring for a child with autism:

- *'I think it's made my daughter and I realise how inadequately prepared we were, and still are, to support W both now and particularly in the future'.* However, for some respondents, coming to know that Intensive Interaction techniques complemented, or even re-affirmed parental styles of care and engagement was also seen as a useful learning outcome. Such learning helped some parental practitioners feel more confident and capable in their overall parenting:
- *'When I learned about Intensive Interaction it gave me the research and science behind what I was doing naturally. Learning what is happening during these natural interactions made me feel more confident about what I was doing and secure in the approach we had adopted. So, yes, I feel it gave me confidence and reassurance in my parenting'.*

Respondents were also given the chance in the survey to provide 'any other comments' to take account of any views they wanted to express that sat outside the more specific survey questions. Below are a selected number of 'other comments' that the respondents gave about the Intensive Interaction approach:

- *'It's absolutely life-changing. I just feel sad that there are so many families out there who've not even heard of it yet'.*
- *'My son plays through Intensive Interaction: the only time he does'.*
- *'I know my child would be totally isolated without such an approach being used'.*

## Discussion

The findings of this study appear to be closely aligned with many of the existing (albeit limited) findings about parental or family use of Intensive Interaction. The similarities seem most obvious in terms of the perceived improvement in the quantity and quality of social communication and subsequently improved familial relationship development. The outcomes of the survey conducted for this chapter also appear to further indicate perceived improvements in emotional or psychological well-being for both the child recipient and the parental/family practitioners of Intensive Interaction.

Therefore, it would seem reasonable to propose that the findings of the included survey, and the previous relevant literature, should give parents and family members greater insight into the particular issues and challenges likely to affect them as parental/family practitioners. Also, they should perhaps take greater confidence in realising the mainly positive communicative and emotional outcomes indicated by using the approach; for both their children and themselves. Such improved insight should also be useful to other as yet non-Intensive Interaction practising parents/family members who might be new to the approach.

The findings set out in this chapter should also provide other practitioners and professionals, including those who support and/or train parents in their use of Intensive Interaction, greater insights into the specific issues and challenges facing parental/family practitioners, perhaps particularly in the early stages of approach adoption. The findings also should point towards implications for perinatal services, so that difficulties in attachment formation can be identified and responded to at the earliest opportunity, specifically when an infant has a diagnosis of learning disability and/or autism. However, it should also be noted that this survey had a number of limitations in terms of its scope and data generation. Its small sample size limits the generalisability of its findings, despite them correlating well with the previous literature and research data. Also, the respondents to the survey were already known users and advocates of the Intensive Interaction approach, and so no counter-positions questioning its efficacy or utility emerged. A future exploration of potential parental or family resistance to the use of Intensive Interaction would undoubtably be useful in terms of understanding or even countering negative views of the approach.

Finally, there is clear scope for further future research into this vitally important area of Intensive Interaction use. Insufficient research has so far been focused on this familial context of Intensive Interaction practice – much more research is required to more fully understand, and thus help support parents in their potential use of Intensive Interaction.

## References

Berridge, S. & Hutchinson, N. (2021) Mothers' experience of Intensive Interaction. *Journal of Intellectual Disabilities*, 26 (2), 391–406.

Firth, G., Glyde, M. & Denby, G. (2021) The decision-making processes of Intensive Interaction practitioners. *British Journal of Learning Disabilities*, 49 (2), 117–128.

Harrison, T. (2012) Doing Intensive Interaction at home. In Hewett, D., Firth, G., Barber, M. & Harrison, T. (eds) *The Intensive Interaction Handbook*. Sage: London.

Hewett, D. & Nind, M. (eds) (1998) *Interaction in Action: Reflections on the use of Intensive Interaction*. David Fulton: London.

Hewett, D., Firth, G., Barber, M. & Harrison, T. (2012). *The intensive interaction handbook*. UK: Sage.

Kellet, M. (2005) Catherine's legacy: social communication development for individuals with profound learning difficulties and fragile life expectancies. *British Journal of Special Education*, 32 (3), 116–121.

King, N. (1998) Template analysis. In G. Symon & C. Cassell (eds) *Qualitative Methods and Analysis in Organizational Research*. Sage: London.

Nind, M. & Hewett, D. (1994) *Access to Communication: Developing basic communication with people who have severe learning difficulties*. David Fulton: London.

Nind, M. & Hewett, D. (1998) Interaction as curriculum. *British Journal of Special Education*, 15 (2), 55–57.

Taylor, Beth & Taylor, S. (1998) Gary's story: Parents doing Intensive Interaction. In Hewett, D. & Nind, M. (eds) *Interaction in Action: Reflections on the use of intensive interaction*. David Fulton: London.

Chapter 8

# Exploring the barriers to implementing Intensive and Adaptive Interaction in practice

*Maggie Ellis and Arlene Astell*

This chapter examines the barriers preventing the effective implementation of Intensive Interaction (II) and Adaptive Interaction (AI) in practice, particularly within institutional, personal, and societal contexts. While research highlights the transformative potential of II and AI in fostering communication for individuals with profound and multiple learning disabilities (PMLD) and advanced dementia, significant obstacles hinder widespread adoption.

Institutional barriers include inadequate funding, rigid policies, and insufficient professional training. Personal barriers stem from resistance to change, lack of awareness, and caregiver apprehension. Societal misconceptions, stigma, and policy gaps further impede integration. Psychologists, in particular, face challenges such as theoretical disparities, limited training, and time constraints that prevent them from fully embracing II and AI approaches.

The chapter also explores strategies for overcoming these challenges, including successful funding models, professional development initiatives, and public awareness campaigns. By highlighting case studies and best practices, it demonstrates how II and AI can be effectively integrated into caregiving and therapeutic settings. Ultimately, the chapter argues that addressing these barriers is crucial to ensuring that II and AI fulfil their potential to improve communication and social inclusion for individuals with complex communication needs.

Research and practice indicate that both Intensive Interaction and Adaptive Interaction can be life-changing (Nind, 1996; Astell, Shaoran & Ellis, 2022). As described in previous chapters, Intensive Interaction increases social actions in people with Profound and Multiple Learning Disabilities (PMLD) and/or autism as compared to control and baseline conditions (e.g. Hutchinson & Bodicoat, 2015). These social actions can involve increases in mutual eye gaze, smiling, touch, communicative sounds, and joint attention (Bundock & Hewitt, 2017). Other examples of the positive impact of Intensive Interaction include facilitating the development of communication skills and increases in initiating social interaction (Irvine, Firth & Berry, 2010). For caregivers and family members, Intensive Interaction enhances their knowledge of those they care for, to create meaningful interactions that lead to improved care and person-centred practice. Caregivers also report increased feelings of self-efficacy and job satisfaction after engaging in

DOI: 10.4324/9781003597933-8

Intensive Interaction as a result of the positive impact on those in their care and the development of their own skills (Rayner et al., 2016).

Adaptive Interaction (Ellis & Astell, 2008) is a variant of Intensive Interaction designed to create meaningful connection between individuals with advanced dementia, caregivers, and family members. Reflecting its Intensive Interaction heritage, Adaptive Interaction focuses on the nonverbal fundamentals of communication to make connections with people who are no longer reliant on speech. The small but growing evidence base of the benefits of Adaptive Interaction include increased communicative actions such as eye gaze, smiling, bodily contact, laughter, and initiation of interaction by individuals with advanced dementia when compared to control and baseline conditions (Ellis & Astell, 2017b). Adaptive Interaction affords individuals with advanced dementia entry to a social world from which they are excluded, in some cases for years. For family members, Adaptive Interaction allows a rekindling of a relationship, albeit demonstrated in a new, nonverbal way (Ellis, Connell-McGrath, & Astell, in press). Training in Adaptive Interaction allows professional caregivers to recognise communicative actions that they may have previously missed in people with advanced dementia who are no longer reliant on speech (Currie, 2018). Prior to training, these communicative bids may have been misinterpreted as meaningless and random 'symptoms' of dementia, which were ignored or even discouraged (Astell & Ellis, 2011).

The availability and rollout of both Intensive Interaction and Adaptive Interaction is influenced by barriers and facilitators at individual, organisational, and systemic levels. Obstacles and facilitators to implementing Intensive Interaction have been addressed at numerous points over the years (see Barber, M., 2008; Berridge & Hutchinson, 2021, 2022; Clegg, Black, Smith & Brumfitt, 2018; Firth, Elford, Leeming & Crabbe, 2008; Firth, Glyde & Denby, 2021; Johnson & Hastings, 2002; Kormelinck, Janus, Smalbrugge, Gerritsen & Zuidema, 2021; Sri-Amnuay, 2012). Similarly, Ellis & Astell (2019) discussed at length the barriers and facilitators to implementing Adaptive Interaction. The purpose of this chapter is to discuss three inter-related domains – evidence, system, and perception – which need to be addressed if the potential of both Intensive Interaction and Adaptive Interaction are to be realised.

## Evidence

Despite its almost 40-year history, a lack of large scale studies, including randomised controlled trials, and a reliance on case or small 'n' studies, is a long standing limitation in Intensive Interaction (see for example Firth, 2006; Sharma & Firth, 2012). In their 2023 systematic review of Intensive Interaction for children with autism spectrum disorder (ASD), Papadopoulos and colleagues (2023) identified only four articles meeting their inclusion criteria for quantitative studies, including a total of 28 children, aged from 4 to 14 years old. The authors concluded that "children with ASD had a positive outcome from their involvement in the Intensive Interaction approach." But they added that methodological and design limitations, plus small sample sizes "preclude forming any definitive conclusions about the impacts of Intensive Interaction." (Papadopoulos et al., 2023, p. 1). Given the challenges to conducting ethical and sound research with individuals with PMLD and/or autism, it is perhaps unsurprising that the evidence base is not as large as it might be (Hutchinson & Bodicoat, 2015). However, some of these limitations may be addressed by the INTERACT trial, an NIHR funded research programme which commenced in March 2023 and runs until June 2027. Led by Jill Bradshaw and colleagues at the University of Kent in the UK, INTERACT is examining the clinical and cost-effectiveness of Intensive Interaction through a multi-setting pragmatic, two-arm, cluster-randomised superiority trial of an 18-week Intensive Interaction programme compared with usual care (NIHR, 2025). This research program addresses some of the recommendations from Papadopoulos and colleagues (2023) for larger sample sizes and control groups, tighter methodology, and improved reporting to increase replicability which will ideally further advance the field and inspire more research as well as take-up.

Adaptive Interaction has an even smaller evidence base, in part due to its shorter history than Intensive Interaction. Almost all articles to date have been produced by the originators (and authors of this chapter), focusing on developing the approach (Ellis & Astell, 2008), replicating its feasibility (Ellis & Astell, 2017b) and implementing training with nurses in Canada (Astell et al., 2015) and care home staff in the UK (Astell, Shoaran, & Ellis, 2022). A further study with family caregivers is forthcoming (Ellis et al., 2019 in press), with a book (Ellis & Astell, 2017b), chapters (Astell & Ellis, 2012; Ellis & Astell, 2019a) and articles on implementation in professional and practice publications such as the *PSIGE Newsletter* (Astell & Ellis, 2011) and the *Australian Journal of Dementia Care* (Ellis & Astell, 2019b). Whilst we have seen a growing interest in Adaptive Interaction among services including NHS and long-term care providers, and organisations including Alzheimer's Society, Alzheimer Scotland, and Social Care Institute for Excellence (SCIE), the lack of interest within the wider dementia research community is a concern. This may reflect a lack of research interest in the needs of people living with advanced dementia or lack of awareness of the potential of Adaptive Interaction to benefit this population. Research is also limited by lack of research funding, small participant numbers, and lack of buy-in to the research process in care facilities (Ellis & Astell, 2017a).

The challenges of implementing non-pharmacological approaches in dementia care is not confined to Adaptive Interaction. Whilst psychosocial approaches are recommended by the National Institute for Health and Care Excellence as a first line approach for people living with dementia, particularly for those experiencing distress, the evidence on their implementation is limited (Thompson, Hsu, Odell-Miller, Underwood & Wolverson, 2024). As with Intensive Interaction, this recent review identified a lack of good quality evidence including small sample size and single site studies, as limiting factors in the adoption of non-pharmacological approaches (Thompson et al., 2024). The authors also identified lack of staff time and training, plus high staff turnover (Thompson et al., 2024) as further limiting factors. Addressing these systemic issues is as crucial to increasing implementation and adoption of Adaptive Interaction and Intensive Interaction, and must be done alongside increasing the evidence base.

## System

Systemic barriers to the implementation of Intensive and Adaptive Interaction may be some of the most difficult to overcome. Among the barriers to sustained use of Intensive Interaction are staffing, management, and organisational structures, and ensuring that care staff have the necessary resources and support to implement these practices consistently (Nagra et al., 2017). Time constraints are a common and long standing barrier in both PMLD and dementia care. Staff in these settings are frequently dealing with heavy workloads, inadequate staffing levels, and numerous duties which limit the time available to engage in Intensive or Adaptive Interaction. Addressing the issue of time in terms of Intensive Interaction, Firth et al. (2008, p. 65) found that staff felt overwhelmed by their responsibilities, one of whom stated, "I've got quite a heavy workload anyway ... and [it's] getting bigger ... so sometimes you just think 'no, no I can't do anymore'". This situation is repeated in dementia care settings where staff have high workloads plus high staff turnover (Thompson et al., 2024).

Lack of training opportunities for staff to learn how to implement interaction-based techniques effectively, plus lack of awareness, have also been identified as significant barriers to effective engagement with Intensive Interaction (Clegg et al., 2018). In their 2010 report of "what works" in communication for PLMD, Goldbart and Caton commented on the need to not only provide skills and knowledge training for care staff, but also to explore their attitudes towards communication and interaction with the people they care for. Ongoing support and training are also essential for care staff to effectively maintain their use of Intensive Interaction when working with adults with PMLD.

Leadership and management play a significant role in prioritising relational care by allocating time for meaningful engagement rather than focusing solely on task-based activities. The importance of a team-based model with adequate support has been demonstrated (Barber, 2008; Kellett, 2003; Samuel et al., 2008) alongside supervision for caregivers as they developed and applied their newly acquired communication skills (Hutchinson & Bodicoat, 2015). Structured supervision provides staff with a secure environment to reflect on their experiences, refine their techniques, and receive constructive feedback. This process not only enhanced their confidence in using Intensive Interaction but also fostered consistency in practice, ensuring that interactions were delivered in a person-centred and effective manner (Hutchinson & Bodicoat, 2015). By addressing common challenges such as uncertainty, self-consciousness, and lack of institutional support supervision helped caregivers to overcome known barriers to implementing Intensive Interaction (Leaning & Watson, 2006; Firth et al., 2008).

A lack of awareness is also a problem facing Adaptive Interaction, which is not yet widely well-known or used in dementia care, owing in part to competing organisational culture and priorities. This is reflective of the lack of implementation in the whole field of non-pharmacological interventions in dementia care, not just Adaptive Interaction (Kupeli et al. 2018). In their investigation with health care professionals into the barriers to integrated care for people with advanced dementia, Kupeli et al. (2018) identified three main themes relating to the system, care home organization, and fragmented care. From this they developed a hierarchical model demonstrating "how societal attitudes and the governmental system can influence the organisation within care homes and a fragmented approach to care ... [which] interact, reducing the capacity of the care system to meet the end-of-life care needs of those with advanced dementia" (p. 167).

One way to address these challenges is to see what can be learnt from examples that have made their way into the care system. In their analysis of successful implementation of psychosocial interventions in residential dementia care, Boersma and colleagues (2015) concluded that multiple integration strategies are required, paying specific attention to maintenance post implementation, which can be particularly challenging for researchers. However, the most successful non-pharmacological intervention for dementia in the UK started out in research. Cognitive Stimulation Therapy (CST: Spector et al., 2003) was the first non-pharmacological intervention for dementia recommended by NICE in 2006.[1] Although originally developed in day centres and long-term care (Spector et al., 2001), CST has gone on to be a global intervention, primarily offered in the UK and other countries soon after diagnosis, rather than in the later stages. Targeting cognition as its primary outcome, Spector and colleagues conducted an intention to treat study, demonstrating that CST compared favourably with the existing anticholinesterase inhibitor treatments (Spector et al., 2003), followed by a cost effectiveness study demonstrating that CST may be more cost-effective than treatment as usual (Knapp et al.,, 2006). These studies undoubtedly contributed to the impact and widespread adoption of CST and could be seen as providing a model for evidencing psychosocial interventions for dementia. Whether this model could benefit Adaptive Interaction is discussed below, after considering a second example – Namaste Care (Simard & Volicer, 2010).

Namaste Care is more comparable with Adaptive Interaction as it is an approach intended for use with people living with advanced dementia (Simard & Volicer, 2010a). The aim of Namaste Care is to provide a "loving touch" approach to care, where care assistants carry out activities of daily living in a calm environment (Simard & Volicer, 2010b). The original Namaste Care research was delivered as an intervention with two-hour sessions twice daily, seven days a week, in a space set aside for this purpose with "lowered lighting, soft music playing, and the scent of lavender" (p. 46; Simard & Volicer, 2010b). Simard and Volicer (2010b) used Minimum Data Set indicators to identify impacts on clinical outcomes including distress, agitation, and delirium. In their recently published systematically constructed review Salvi and colleagues (2025) identified 25 articles reporting on Namaste Care from six countries, with the largest number (10) from the UK. The frequency and duration of Namaste Care sessions was identified as a significant barrier, alongside the need for a dedicated space, limited resources and staff engagement. The authors conclude with multiple recommendations including the need for standardised training programmes, greater involvement of family and volunteers, flexible scheduling and more research, including pragmatic trials reflecting the "real-world" of care homes.

Whilst not as successful as CST, Namaste Care has begun to gain traction in several countries, which provides an interesting point of comparison with Adaptive Interaction. One major difference is that while packaged as an approach to care, Namaste Care was designed and developed as an intervention. Rather than a training intended to be used in all care and interactions with people living with advanced dementia, Namaste Care is a separate intervention, delivered in a separate space requiring dedicated time and resources. Whilst these demands create barriers to the uptake of the approach (Salvi et al., 2025), it may be these very factors that make it of interest to care providers. Namely that it is an intervention that they can adopt to address priorities of concern to them, such as resident's distress, agitation, and delirium. Adaptive Interaction, on the other hand, is offered as a means of connecting and communicating with residents who are no longer reliant on speech. In this respect Adaptive Interaction is akin to using sign language or Makaton in all interactions as appropriate to the needs of the individual. Would testing and packaging Adaptive Interaction, and by extension Intensive Interaction, as a (time-limited?) therapy (such as CST) or intervention (such as Namaste Care) overcome the existing barriers to adoption?

## Perception

In addition to the need for a more robust evidence-base and changes within the care system to facilitate adoption of Intensive and Adaptive Interaction, additional barriers are rooted in social stigma or misconceptions surrounding the approaches. Unfamiliarity with Intensive and Adaptive Interaction among staff and families is common. While Goldbart and Caton found that Intensive Interaction was used by 85% of specialist practitioners they contacted for their evidence review, it was only reported by two parents. Lack of awareness or understanding of the benefits of the approaches may be compounded by fear or anxiety about adopting new methods (e.g. Nagra et al. 2017; Berridge & Hutchinson, 2021; Ellis & Astell, 2019). A qualitative study on practitioners' decision-making processes revealed that knowledge, personal confidence, and preconceived beliefs about Intensive Interaction influenced their willingness to implement it (Firth, Glyde & Denby, 2021). Conflict with previous ways of working (Leaning, 2006) plus low expectations about the abilities of certain individuals, can also discourage practitioners from attempting Intensive Inter-action (Sri-Amnuay, 2012).

Similar barriers occur in relation to Adaptive Interaction in dementia care. A desire to distance themselves from learning disabilities is common in older people's services. Additionally, the connection to infants via the nonverbal fundamentals of communication, have led to questions about the appropriate-ness of Adaptive Interaction for individuals living with advanced dementia. Of the 17 personal detractors defined by Kitwood (1997) *infantilisation* and *stig-matisation* are arguably most repeated by staff who have received training in person-centred care. Whilst the extent to which these and the other 15 personal detractors are actually understood and tackled within dementia care is a debate for another place, they are frequently brought up in discussions about Adaptive Interaction. To address this we bring up the connection between Adaptive Interaction and developmental psychology head on in our training at www.astellis.co.uk. Infant communication is introduced very early in the course, well before any mention of Intensive or Adaptive Interaction. This allows them to gain a sense of comfort and ease around seeing all human communication as being rooted in the building blocks of developmental psychology. As with Intensive Interaction, there is a shift during and after training, as trainees (both care staff and family) start to connect with and see the impact of Adaptive Interaction on the individuals with advanced dementia (Astell & Ellis, 2011).

However, an ongoing challenge faced by both approaches is the need for caregivers and other staff to 'employ themselves' as part of the approach. In the foreword to this volume, Dave Hewitt articulates the problem thus: "it could be a challenge to help them (services) become relaxed, less driven in interventions and happily employ themselves, face, voice, body language as the crucial learning facility". This may be why Intensive Interaction and Adaptive Interaction have received greater resistance than approaches such as Cognitive Stimulation Therapy (Spector et al., 2003) and Namaste Care (Simard & Volicer, 2010a) which are packaged as interventions that can be delivered or "done" to people living with dementia. In other words, is it easier for caregivers and staff to adopt something that is external to them, rather than having to change themselves?

How then do we overcome such a barrier in the real world? For this to happen, one might argue that we (advantaged communicators) must recognise and own responsibility for including disadvantaged communicators in the social world. However, such an attitude requires us to view ourselves as part of the problem, which of course we are. This viewpoint is unpopular for obvious reasons and as such requires a switch from "being part of the problem" to "being part of the solution".

Also helpful is normalising Intensive and Adaptive Interaction within every-day activities, such as meal times, personal care, and leisure activities, which helps integrate these practices seamlessly into caregiving routines. Avoiding the perception that such interactions require extra time or effort is key to ensuring their sustainability. A practitioner's account of the Intensive Interaction journey illustrated that embedding these approaches into daily routines reduces perceived workload and facilitates consistent implementation (Hutchinson & Bodicoat, 2015). In terms of Adaptive Interaction, Ellis and Astell (2019) discovered that presenting the approach as an integral part of interacting with individuals with advanced dementia, rather than as an optional or supplementary tool, significantly helps to overcome this barrier. In essence, trainees are encouraged to incorporate Adaptive Interaction naturally into all exchanges, including functional tasks (Astell et al., 2022).

## Conclusion

In conclusion, while Intensive and Adaptive Interaction demonstrate clear benefits for individuals with PMLD, autism, and advanced dementia, their widespread implementation continues to be hindered by a range of barriers. These obstacles include limitations in research, institutional resistance, personal and societal misperceptions, and competing organisational priorities. However, by embedding Intensive and Adaptive Interaction into routine care, fostering a supportive organisational culture, and providing practical training with opportunities for reflection, the adoption of these interaction-based methods can be significantly enhanced.

Finally, the simplicity and human-centred nature of Intensive and Adaptive Interaction should not be seen as weaknesses but rather as strengths, making meaningful engagement accessible to all. Ultimately, the challenge lies not in the simplicity of the approaches but in the willingness of services and individuals to embrace their role in nurturing inclusive communication. Overcoming these barriers requires a shift in perspective – from viewing communication as an intervention to recognising it as a fundamental human right, ensuring that individuals with limited verbal communication are not excluded from meaningful social interactions. By taking ownership of this responsibility, we can move beyond scepticism and hesitation, toward a future where Intensive and Adaptive Interaction are integral to person-centred care.

## Note

1  NICE recommendations 1.6.1.1 People with mild-to-moderate dementia of all types should be given the opportunity to participate in a structured group cognitive stimulation programme (2006).

## References

Astell, A. J., Amirkhanian, N., Hernandez, A. M., Nagulendran, S., Ruess, D. & Ellis, M. (2015) The psychological impact of Adaptive Interaction training on nursing staff in advanced dementia care. *Canadian Geriatrics Journal*, 18(4), 287–288, doi:10.5770/cgj.18.218

Astell, A. J. & Ellis, M. P. (2011) The challenges of equipping care home staff with psychosocial skills: reflections from developing a novel approach to communication. *PSIGE Newsletter*, 117, 26–32.

Astell, A. J. & Ellis, M. P. (2012) Communicating beyond speech. In *A Good Senior Life with Dual Sensory Loss* (pp. 24–31). Nordic Centre for Welfare and Social Issues.

Astell, A. J., Shoaran, S. & Ellis, M. P. (2022) Using adaptive interaction to simplify caregiver's communication with people with dementia who cannot speak. *Frontiers in Communication*, 6. doi:10.3389/fcomm.2021.689439

Barber, M. (2008) Using intensive interaction to add to the palette of interactive possibilities in teacher–pupil communication. *European Journal of Special Needs Education*, 23(4), 393–402.

Berridge, S. & Hutchinson, N. (2021) Staff experience of the implementation of Intensive Interaction within their places of work with people with learning disabilities and/or autism. *Journal of Applied Research in Intellectual Disabilities*, 34(1), 1–15.

Berridge, S. & Hutchinson, N. (2022) Mothers' experience of Intensive Interaction. *Journal of Intellectual Disabilities*, 26(2), 391–406.

Boersma, P., van Weert, J. C., Lakerveld, J. & Dröes, R. M. (2015) The art of successful implementation of psychosocial interventions in residential dementia care: a systematic review of the literature based on the RE-AIM framework. *Int Psychogeriatr.*, 27(1), 19–35. doi:10.1017/S1041610214001409

Bundock, K. E. & Hewitt, O. (2017) A review of social skills interventions for adults with autism and intellectual disability. *Tizard Learning Disability Review*, 22(3), 148–158. doi:10.1108/TLDR-05-2016-0015.

Clegg, J., Black, R., Smith, A. & Brumfitt, S. (2018) Examining the impact of a city-wide intensive interaction staff training program for adults with profound and multiple learning disability: a mixed methods evaluation. *Disability and Rehabilitation*, 42(2), 201–210. doi:10.1080/09638288.2018.1495769

Currie, L. (2018) Adaptive interaction as a method of non-verbal communication in individuals with dementia. *Practice Nursing*, 29(4), 176–180.

Ellis, M. P. & Astell, A. J. (2008) A case study of Adaptive Interaction: a new approach to communication with people with advanced dementia. In S. Zeedyk (ed.) *Techniques for Promoting Social Engagement in Individuals with Communicative Impairments*. London: Jessica Kingsley.

Ellis, M. & Astell, A. (2017a) Communicating with people living with dementia who are nonverbal: the creation of Adaptive Interaction. *PLoS ONE*, 12(8), e0180395. doi:10.1371/journal.pone.0180395

Ellis, M. P. & Astell, A. J. (2017b) *Adaptive Interaction for Dementia: How to communicate without speech*. London: Jessica Kingsley.

Ellis, M. P. & Astell, A. J. (2019a) Adaptive Interaction: facilitating connection in advanced dementia. In I. James & L. Gibbons (eds) *Communication Skills for Effective Dementia Care*. London: Jessica Kingsley.

Ellis, M. P. & Astell, A. J. (2019b) Implementing Adaptive Interaction in everyday care. *Australian Journal of Dementia Care*, 8(4), 26–28.

Ellis, M. P., Connell McGrath, C. & Astell, A. J. (in press) Connection at the end of life: what is possible? In C. Johnson & S. Pasupuleti (eds) *Dementia Revisited*. Oxford University Press.

Firth, G. (2006) Intensive Interaction: a research review. *Mental Health and Learning Disabilities Research and Practice*, 3(1), 53–62.

Firth, G., Elford, H., Leeming, C. & Crabbe, M. (2008) Intensive interaction as a novel approach in social care: care staff's views on the practice change process. *Journal of Applied Research in Intellectual Disabilities*, 21(1), 58–69.

Firth, G., Glyde, M. & Denby, G. (2021) A qualitative study of the practice-related decision-making of Intensive Interaction practitioners. *British Journal of Learning Disabilities*, 49(2), 117–128.

Goldbart, J. & Caton, S. (2010) Communication and people with the most complex needs: What works and why this is essential. Mencap. https://www.mencap.org.uk/sites/default/files/2017-05/Mencap%20Comms_guide_dec_10.pdf

Hewett, D. (2025) Foreword. In Doswell, S. & Ellis, M. (eds) *Intensive Interaction as Psychologically Informed Practice* (pp. xi–xiii). Routledge.

Hutchinson, N. & Bodicoat, A. (2015) The effectiveness of intensive interaction: a systematic literature review. *Journal of Applied Research in Intellectual Disabilities*, 28(6), 437–454.

Irvine, C., Firth, G. & Berry, R. (2010) *Understanding Intensive Interaction: Context and concepts for professionals and families.* Jessica Kingsley.

Johnson, E., & Hastings, R. P. (2002) Facilitating factors and barriers to the implementation of intensive home-based behavioural intervention for young children with autism. *Child Care, Health and Development*, 28(2), 123–129.

Kellett, M. (2003) Sam's story: evaluating Intensive Interaction in terms of its effect on the social and communicative ability of a young child with severe learning difficulties. *Support for Learning*, 15(4), 165–171.

Kitwood, T. (1997) *Dementia Reconsidered: The person comes first.* Buckingham: Open University Press.

Knapp M., Thorgrimsen, L., Patel, A., Spector, A., Hallam, A., Woods, B. & Orrell, M. (2006) Cognitive stimulation therapy for people with dementia: cost-effectiveness analysis. *Br J Psychiatry*, 188, 574–580. doi:10.1192/bjp.bp.105.010561

Kormelinck, C. M. G., Janus, S. I., Smalbrugge, M., Gerritsen, D. L. & Zuidema, S. U. (2021) Systematic review on barriers and facilitators of complex interventions for residents with dementia in long-term care. *International psychogeriatrics*, 33(9), 873–889.

Kupeli, N., Leavey, G., Harrington., J, Lord, K., King, M., Nazareth, I., Moore, K., Sampson, E. L. & Jones, L. (2018) What are the barriers to care integration for those at the advanced stages of dementia living in care homes in the UK? Health care professional perspective. *Dementia*, 17(2), 164–179. doi:10.1177/1471301216636302

Leaning, B. (2006) Using intensive interaction to work with people with profound and multiple learning disabilities: care staff perceptions. Doctoral thesis, University College London.

Leaning, B. & Watson, T. (2006) From the inside looking out – an Intensive Interaction group for people with profound and multiple learning disabilities. *British Journal of Learning Disabilities*, 34, 103–109.

Nagra, M. K., White, R., Appiah, A. & Rayner, K. (2017) Intensive interaction training for paid caregivers: 'Looking, looking and find out when they want to relate to you'. *Journal of Applied Research in Intellectual Disabilities*, 30(4), 648–660.

NIHR (2025) Intensive Interaction for children and young people with profound and multiple learning disabilities: INTERACT trial. https://fundingawards.nihr.ac.uk/award/NIHR151428

Nind, M. (1996) Efficacy of Intensive Interaction: developing sociability and communication in people with severe and complex learning difficulties using an approach based on caregiver-infant interaction. *European Journal of Special Educational Needs*, 11(1), 48–66.

Papadopoulos, A., Vogindroukas, I., Tsapara, A., Voniati, L., Tafiadis, D. & Plotas, P. (2023) Intensive interaction as an intervention approach in children with autism spectrum disorder: a systematic review. *Neuroscience Research Notes*, 6(4), 276.1–276.9.

Rayner, K., Bradley, S., Johnson, G., Mrozik, J. H., Appiah, A. & Nagra, M. K. (2016) Teaching intensive interaction to paid caregivers: using the 'communities of practice' model to inform training. *British Journal of Learning Disabilities*, 44(1), 63–70.

Salvi, S., Preston, N., Cornally, N., Walshe, C, and on behalf of the In-Touch Consortium. (2025) Implementing Namaste Care in nursing care homes for people with advanced dementia: a systematically constructed review with framework synthesis. *BMC Geriatrics*, 25(17), 1–24.

Samuel, J., Nind, M., Volans, A. & Scriven, I. (2008) An evaluation of Intensive Interaction in community living settings for adults with profound intellectual disabilities. *J Intellect Disabil.*, 12(2), 111–126. doi:10.1177/1744629508090983

Sharma, V. & Firth, G. (2012) Effective engagement through intensive interaction. *Learning Disability Practice*, 15, 20–23.

Simard, J. & Volicer, L. (2010a) *Namaste Care and Dying in Institutional Settings: Supportive care for the person with dementia*. Oxford: Oxford University Press.

Simard, J. & Volicer, L. (2010b) Effects of Namaste Care on residents who do not benefit from usual activities. *Am J Alzheimer's Disease Other Dementias*, 25(1), 46–50. doi:10.1177/1533317509333258

Spector, A., Orrell, M., Davies, S.*et al.* (2001) Can reality orientation be rehabilitated? Development and piloting of an evidence-based programme of cognition-based therapies for people with dementia. *Neuropsychological Rehabilitation*, 11, 377–397.

Spector, A., Thorgrimsen, L., Woods, B.*et al.* (2003) Efficacy of an evidence-based cognitive stimulation therapy programme for people with dementia: randomised controlled trial. *British Journal of Psychiatry*, 183(3), 248–254. doi:10.1192/bjp.183.3.248

Sri-Amnuay, R. (2012) Perceptions of teaching pre-verbal pupils with autism and severe learning difficulties: factors influencing the application of intensive interaction in the Thai culture. Doctoral dissertation, Northumbria University.

Thompson, N., Hsu, M. H., Odell-Miller, H., Underwood, B. R. & Wolverson, E. (2024) Characteristics, outcomes, facilitators and barriers for psychosocial interventions on inpatient mental health dementia wards: a systematic review. *BMC Geriatr.*, 23–24(1), 364. doi:10.1186/s12877-024-04965-8

# Training in Intensive Interaction and Adaptive Interaction for trainee and qualified psychological practitioners

*Sarah Dunstan, Alison Spencer, Judith Samuel and Maggie Ellis*

## Introduction

In this chapter, the current situation regarding training of psychologists in Intensive Interaction and Adaptive Interaction in the UK is described, and a research project exploring the place of Intensive Interaction and Adaptive Interaction teaching on Doctorate in Clinical Psychology Programmes is presented.

Opportunities for learning about Intensive Interaction and Adaptive Interaction include self-study via reading books or watching free online videos, or attendance at face-to-face or online training sessions. The content of such training has evolved over time with developments in the evidence base and any inclusion of the approaches in UK healthcare or education guidance, however there is no current agreement regarding content of training or length of time allocated. For example, in their review of Intensive Interaction, Hutchinson and Bodicoat (2015) found significant variation in training time offered, from less than a day's training to up to ten sessions of training, with follow-up support. There is currently no external accreditation of Intensive Interaction or Adaptive Interaction training. The different types of training currently available are described below.

### Intensive Interaction: general training

Introductory level training may be delivered by a more experienced in-house practitioner or bought in from an external provider. Such training may be in person or online and range in duration from an hour or more to a day. Attendance at peer support groups where case material is discussed might constitute introductory training experience too. Where there is an employed Intensive Interaction specialist (see Chapter 10), bespoke training often occurs as part of the offer to a referred person's network of support. Alternatively, a certain "dose" of training may be given to practitioners as part of a research study

DOI: 10.4324/9781003597933-9

(e.g. Samuel et al. [2008] for residential social care staff, or the Interact study www.interacttrial.com for staff of SEND units).

Follow-up training may include a session of a longer duration and/or some degree of supervised practice or peer group experience.

Advanced level training offered includes three modular online courses run by The Intensive Interaction Institute www.intensiveinteraction.com: Reflective Practitioner (3–6 months), Mentoring Practitioner (6–8 months) and In-service Trainer (6–8 months).

### Adaptive Interaction: general training

Training in Adaptive Interaction is offered both online and in person at https://www.astellis.co.uk/. Professor Arlene Astell and Dr Maggie Ellis developed the approach, which is based on Intensive Interaction with an emphasis on the possible goals and outcomes specific to people with advanced dementia, their families and professional caregivers. The certification programme covers everything from basic knowledge of the approach to becoming an Adaptive Interaction Trainer. The three-day programme provides deep insight into the Adaptive Interaction approach to communicating with individuals with advanced dementia. Trainees are armed with the necessary foundations, skills and tools to interact with people with advanced dementia who may appear to be "unreachable". The programme has been undertaken by a wide range of professionals including caregivers, speech and language therapists and clinical psychologists. However, there is as yet no specific training available to trainee clinical psychologists.

### Training for trainee clinical psychologists

Doctorate in Clinical Psychology training programmes in the UK determine their curriculum using the "*Standards for the accreditation of doctoral programmes in clinical psychology*" (BPS, 2019) and the "*Standards of proficiency for practitioner psychologists*" (Health & Care Professions Council [HCPC], 2023). The British Psychological Society [BPS] (2019) accreditation criteria emphasise the importance of meeting core competencies, including communication. This involves delivering teaching and training on adapting communication to meet the needs of service users with varying cognitive abilities. Moreover, the Health & Care Professions Council (2023) standards assert that practitioner psychologists should "use effective and appropriate verbal and non-verbal skills to communicate with service users … and others … [and] understand the characteristics and consequences of verbal and non-verbal communication" (p. 11).

On behalf of BPS Division of Clinical Psychology (DCP) Faculty for people with intellectual disabilities (FPID), a list of competencies to support courses to equip trainee clinical psychologists in addressing the needs of people with intellectual disabilities was developed (The British Psychological Society, 2021). A key competency noted is the "ability to communicate …including [with] individuals who are nonverbal, together with an awareness of communication uses and mediums to facilitate accessible communication" (p. 8). Similarly, the DCP Psychologists Special Interest Group in the Elderly (PSIGE) Training Subgroup (2006), specified the "[ability] to effectively communicate … [and] overcome cognitive and sensory impairments" (p. 4) as a competency required for working with older people. Yet, neither guidance specifically references any approach to address these competencies for people with severe and profound intellectual disabilities or other atypical communicators such as those with autism and/or individuals with advanced dementia. As this book shows, Intensive Interaction and Adaptive Interaction are two related psychological approaches of relevance to these clinical populations.

To embed Intensive and Adaptive Interaction as approaches clinical psychologists use, we believe they should be consistently taught on training courses, as a means of meeting the psychological needs of "atypical communicators". Authors across this book do offer training onto doctorate courses, but this is varied with regard to time allocated. For example, Jules McKim provides face-to-face Intensive Interaction teaching on three Clinical Psychology training programmes; for two, three and a half, and six hours in duration.

### Training for qualified psychologists: Intensive Interaction and Adaptive Interaction

If Intensive and Adaptive Interaction were not taught during clinical training, Practitioner Psychologists have typically learned about this approach through attending more general training described above. Although this will provide an introduction to the background, theory and practice of Intensive and Adaptive Interaction, attending more general training does not support psychologists to think together about how Intensive Interaction can be utilised as a psychological intervention, as suggested in earlier chapters as a therapeutic session or alongside another approach such as PBS.

Authors of this book have begun to offer Intensive Interaction training to psychologists, for example at the FPID Annual Conference. Feedback from these sessions indicated there is a long way to go before Intensive Interaction is considered as a psychological intervention. This recognition led to this book being proposed as a way of supporting psychological practitioners to embrace Intensive and Adaptive Interaction, but also led to research being undertaken to understand more about the current training offered on clinical psychology courses, and what potential barriers to this being offered might be.

### Initial scoping exercise into availability of training

In 2021, the FPID approached 27 UK Doctorate in Clinical Psychology Training Programmes to ask if they provided training in Intensive Interaction and if so, how it was positioned. Four courses responded that they provided such training. None responded that they did not. The limited response rate was disappointing, nonetheless the qualitative comments provided useful information (Spencer, 2021):

- Intensive Interaction is included in teaching on working with people with severe and profound Intellectual Disability.

  (mentioned by all four)

- It is also included within teaching on Positive Behaviour Support as a way of improving communication promoting positive engagement and building relationships.

  (mentioned twice)

- It is positioned as an intervention and covered in detail – delivered by a clinical psychologist.

  (mentioned once)

- Phoebe Caldwell videos are used.

  (mentioned once)

- It is positioned as a way of supporting communication development and is delivered by a speech and language therapist

  (mentioned once).

- It has been difficult to find someone to provide the teaching.

  (mentioned once)

The findings from the pilot study were shared with the authors of this book. In response, a brief description of Intensive Interaction and Adaptive Interaction was shared with the Doctorate in Clinical Psychology courses (Samuel & Ellis, 2022) [Appendix 1] in October 2022, January 2023 and October 2023. This document included key references and hyperlinks to free online resources.

## Further research

Following the pilot study, a small-scale research project was proposed, supported by both FPID and the DCP Faculty of the Psychology of Older People (FPOP). Sarah Dunstan undertook this project, following obtaining University Ethics Committee approval.

The research question was "What information can Doctorate in Clinical Psychology courses in the UK provide about their Intensive Interaction and Adaptive Interaction teaching?"

## Method

An online survey was undertaken, followed by semi-structured interviews. Initial questions in the survey were closed, providing quantitative information about whether and how Intensive Interaction and Adaptive Interaction was taught, whilst later questions focused on eliciting qualitative information on the usefulness of Intensive Interaction and Adaptive Interaction as an approach, barriers to teaching these approaches and suggestions for future guidance.

All 32 courses in the UK were sent the survey. Module leads for intellectual disabilities and older adults on each course were expected to complete the relevant survey. At the end of the survey, participants were asked if they would be happy to engage in a follow-up interview. One Adaptive Interaction and four Intensive Interaction participants engaged in online interviews.

## Results

Of the 32 universities contacted, 21 (65.6%) responded to the Intensive Interaction survey and nine (28.1%) to the Adaptive Interaction survey. One programme submitted two responses about Intensive Interaction so these were amalgamated. The data in Table 9.1 indicate that just over half the respondents were teaching Intensive Interaction, whereas Adaptive Interaction teaching was much less likely.

Table 9.1 Frequency of respondent universities providing Intensive Interaction (II) or Adaptive Interaction (AI) teaching

| Survey type | Yes (N) | No (N) | Do not know (N) | Total (N) |
|---|---|---|---|---|
| AI | 1 | 5 | 3 | 9 |
| II | 12 | 9 | 0 | 21 |

Eleven (92%) universities taught Intensive Interaction during lectures, six (50%) used videos to support teaching and four (33%) incorporated teaching into supervised practice. Some courses also used experiential exercises or delivered it within Positive Behavioural Support teaching. For Intensive Interaction, nine (75%) courses employed external teachers. Of these six (50%) employed Clinical Psychologists whilst five (42%) used others, i.e. Intensive Interaction specialists or Speech and Language Therapists (indicating some co-teaching). The one course teaching Adaptive Interaction reported that lectures were given by external professionals and incorporated in supervised practice.

With regard to the resource document described above, only 14/21 (Intensive Interaction) and 1/9 (Adaptive Interaction) respondents stated that they recalled receiving this. Fewer admitted to having read all of it (seven Intensive Interaction and no Adaptive Interaction respondents) or some of it (five Intensive Interaction and one Adaptive Interaction respondent). The document was found to be "very useful" by one and "useful" by six Intensive Interaction respondents.

We asked how Intensive Interaction and Adaptive Interaction were positioned in teaching (respondents could give more than one answer), and responses were as follows:

- Intensive Interaction: psychological intervention (8/12), communication technique (10/12), wellbeing activity (6/12), other (2/12) (within PBS teaching).
- Adaptive Interaction: psychological intervention (1/1) and communication technique (1/1).

### Thematic analysis

Braun and Clarke's (2019) reflexive thematic analysis generated six themes and four sub-themes, The themes are presented below with supporting quotes from survey and interview data. Participant identifying numbers or pseudonyms are used.

### 1 Value of Intensive Interaction and Adaptive Interaction

A repeating narrative was the value of teaching Intensive Interaction and Adaptive Interaction.

> Intensive Interaction feels like a very important and valuable tool.
>
> (ii26)

> A very valuable technique for all psychologists to be aware of to use with people with communication difficulties.
>
> (ii39)

Two sub-themes emerged: *Supporting awareness of unmet needs* and *Addressing unmet needs*.

Participants explained that Intensive Interaction and Adaptive Interaction teaching raised awareness of groups with additional communication needs and helped trainees to understand how to address these needs in clinical work.

> Opportunities to ... help people ... think about how ... they support somebody with dementia
>
> (April)

> A framework within which the needs of people with profound learning disabilities can be understood
>
> (ii09)

## 2 Role in supporting communication

The importance of teaching Intensive Interaction and Adaptive Interaction to support communication was evident.

> Part of a broader conversation about communicating effectively with people with learning disabilities
>
> (Julie)

> Clinical psychologists must be able to adapt communication to make what we offer accessible.
>
> (ai88)

Intensive Interaction and Adaptive Interaction were viewed as person-centred approaches, holding a unique value that met the service user at their level of communication. Moreover, some trainees had successfully used the approaches in practice.

> An important approach for ... connecting with them in ways that work for them
>
> (ii22)

> Trainees have used it in client work and as a way of building rapport and establishing communication.
>
> (ii13)

## 3 Practicalities of delivering Intensive Interaction and Adaptive Interaction teaching

Barriers to delivery were described. These included practical difficulties such as limited time to teach a large amount of content, inadequate space for face-to-face teaching, lack of teaching staff and a long-standing curriculum.

> There is extremely limited time in the curriculum so we have needed to prioritise.
>
> (ai13)

> So much to cover across so many client groups that it is difficult to find sufficient time.
>
> (ii26)

> We've got lots of topics to cover and are trying to balance the needs of the different ... topics.
>
> (Douglas)

I asked around the local services and our special interest group ... and nobody came forward to do it.

(Julie)

The topics have long been decided.

(April)

## 4 Transferability to real world settings

The approaches' limited use in clinical settings, reducing practice opportunities for trainees.

Adaptive interaction isn't commonly being talked about and used within older people's services.

(ai12)

Lack of local clinicians trained in this

(ii10)

I am struggling to find clinicians who ... have this work as part of their role

(ii55)

This perceived lack of real-world applicability became a factor in why Intensive and Adaptive Interaction teaching was not being delivered. This was supported by survey data which indicated that teaching which was not practical and transferable was unlikely to be continued.

It wasn't being directly relevant to the work [trainees] were then doing out on placement.

(Julie)

Trainees are often wanting teaching that's aligned with ... what they get to use on placement.

(Douglas)

## 5 Guidance

Participants reflected on helpful guidance for the future. Three sub-themes emerged: content, format and expected standards and guidelines.

*Content:* Participants described the type of guidance they would like to receive, for example, resources, standard teaching packs and case examples to support theory practice links.

Links to good quality resources, video lectures etc.

(ai13a)

Case studies written by psychologists who have used the approach

(ii21)

Examples of how it maybe has successfully been used with clients

(Natalie)

It'd be really useful to get some teaching materials.

(Julie)

*Format:* It was suggested that any guidance should be brief and embedded within existing standards for Doctorate in Clinical Psychology courses.

I think something very brief

(ai13a)

The best guidance is always brief

(Douglas)

Less on very specific topics and more ... embedded within how should we be teaching learning disabilities

(Douglas)

Some participants suggested that training, workshops or e-learning could be a helpful way of delivering this guidance.

Perhaps a training event

(ii03)

Probably a workshop

(ii17)

One interviewee suggested a similar format to "Let's Talk Sessions" which are already run by FPOP and would provide an opportunity for courses to talk about the teaching.

A let's talk session ... connecting people to bring it

(April)

### 6  Expected standards and guidelines

Interviewees described how teaching was shaped by BPS and DCP guidelines. Thus these needed to include the importance of teaching and practising Intensive Interaction and Adaptive Interaction.

It would be helpful for the BPS to maybe say ... Intensive Interaction ... needs to be part of your curriculum.

(Natalie)

Participants also expressed that they needed access to a good evidence base for teaching and using Intensive Interaction and Adaptive Interaction in practice.

You have to really have a really strong reason and evidence base to fight to carve out bits of curriculum time.

(Julie)

An intervention and approach that has like a good ... evidence base

(April)

Programmes asserted that it was important to know what teaching was expected by Doctorate in Clinical Psychology courses.

Indication of minimum content – knowledge and skills development – that programmes should aim to include in the curriculum

(ii33)

## Discussion

This exploratory study indicated that Intensive Interaction is being taught in at least a third of Doctorate in Clinical Psychology courses, with Adaptive Interaction being rarely taught. It is unknown if there was a response bias, in that module leads where Intensive Interaction is taught were more likely to respond. However, it is also known to the authors of this chapter that one university who did not respond has teaching in Intensive Interaction, so the response rate may have been impacted by other factors such as not having identified curriculum leads and lack of time to respond when courses are so busy. Additionally, it would seem from the interview data that in one university at least, Intensive Interaction was "talked about" (Julie) in sessions on communication and about autism but was not considered to be taught. Data about Adaptive Interaction is much more limited.

Survey respondents consider Intensive Interaction and Adaptive Interaction as psychological interventions, communication techniques and for Intensive Interaction at least, wellbeing activities. It is helpful that courses are considering Intensive and Adaptive Interaction as not only as a communication intervention but recognising that there are wide psychological benefits to these approaches. The survey did not ask specifically about their use for distress or trauma to be processed. Nor did it differentiate between wellbeing for both participants (i.e. the atypical and typical communicator) (see Chapter 11) and these could be areas for development in future teaching sessions.

As alternatives to teaching about Intensive Interaction and Adaptive Interaction, programmes fedback that they were using models, such as cognitive or behavioural, to support trainees in meeting the core competency of communication. Positive Behaviour Support was viewed as helping trainees consider the needs of people with severe and profound Intellectual Disability whilst teaching approaches for people with advanced dementia included Communication and Interaction Training (CAIT; James & Gibbons, 2019) and guidance from a dementia care specialist called Teepa Snow (Positive Approach to Care, 2023). As demonstrated in Chapter 5, it may be helpful for courses to consider Intensive and Adaptive Interaction as interventions that can augment approaches such as PBS.

A number of factors were identified as determining curricula, including accreditation standards from the British Psychological Society (BPS) and Division of Clinical Psychology (DCP), feedback from trainees, and approaches known to be used within local services. The survey responses indicated that Adaptive Interaction was less well-known than Intensive Interaction, possibly because it is a newer approach with a smaller evidence base, the first case study being conducted in 2006 (Ellis & Astell, 2011). Despite the value placed on Intensive Interaction and Adaptive Interaction by many participants, others said they were lacking in awareness of the approaches, or confidence in teaching them.

The survey did not ask if any course teachers were also practitioners. Teaching tended to be delivered by external practitioners, usually specialists within the field of Intensive Interaction or Adaptive Interaction. Participants inferred that increasing knowledge and ability to teach about Intensive Interaction and Adaptive Interaction would be needed. Respondents said they required practical guidance such as a teaching pack including resources, case examples and contributions from experts by experience. Participants also indicated that training events, workshops or CPD sessions for teaching staff provided by FPID and FPOP would be helpful to increase knowledge and confidence about the approaches. Participants highlighted that guidance should be brief, with a clear evidence base supported by standards expected by the BPS and DCP on the teaching of core competencies.

## Conclusion and recommendations

There is a lack of agreement about the content and timings of Intensive and Adaptive Interaction training across the UK, leading to significant variety in training offers. This recent survey has highlighted that this variation is echoed across training for trainee Clinical Psychologists.

Challenges in offering Intensive and Adaptive Interaction training include a lack of expertise within course staff and local clinical supervisors, pressures on time allocated for training and these approaches not being specifically named in training guidance. Feedback from courses, reflections from authors across this book and research (Hutchinson & Bodicoat, 2015) suggest that:

- The DCP training guidance should explicitly include Intensive Interaction and Adaptive Interaction as approaches that may be helpful for individuals including those with severe and profound intellectual disability and dementia.
- Courses should be supported to offer Intensive Interaction and Adaptive Interaction teaching, through guidance regarding what should be taught and a teaching pack including examples and the approaches being used.
- Qualified psychologists should be offered training on Intensive and Adaptive Interaction so they can not only support training courses but can also offer supervised practice to trainees on placement.
- Training should highlight not only the benefit to the "atypical communicator" but also to family members and support staff utilising these approaches.
- Training outcomes should be collected to develop the evidence base, including the length of training needed and which elements lead to the most successful implementation of the approaches.

## References

Adu, P. [drphilipadu]. (2023, April 21). *NVivo for Beginners: How to categorize codes to develop themes* [Video]. YouTube. https://www.youtube.com/watch?v=mrioduYXWE4

Bhattacherjee, A. (2012). *Social science research: Principles, methods, and practices* (2nd edn). Creative Commons Attribution.

Braun, V. & Clarke, V. (2019). Reflecting on reflexive thematic analysis. *Qualitative Research in Sport, Exercise and Health*, 11(4), 589–597. doi:10.1080/2159676X.2019.1628806.

British Psychological Society (2019) *Standards for the accreditation of Doctoral programmes in clinical psychology*. UK: BPS.

Byrne, D. (2022). A worked example of Braun and Clarke's approach to reflexive thematic analysis. *Quality & Quantity*, 56, 1391–1421. doi:10.1007/s11135-021-01182-y

Dunstan, S. (2024). *Intensive Interaction (II) and Adaptive Interaction (AI) teaching: What can Doctorate in Clinical Psychology (DClinPSy) courses in the United Kingdom (UK) tell us?* [Unpublished service related project]. University of Essex.

Edwards, K. (2024, March 22). What is a good response rate for a survey?SurveyLab. https://www.surveylab.com/blog/what-is-a-good-response-rate-for-a-survey/#:~:text= A%20good%20survey%20response%20rate%20often%20depends%20on,acceptable% 20response%20rate%20is%20between%2010%25%20and%2030%25

Ellis, M. P. & Astell, A. (2011). Adaptive interaction: a new approach to communication. ResearchGate. Retrieved 31 March, 2024, from https://www.researchgate.net/p ublication/292924818_Adaptive_interaction_A_new_approach_to_communication

Health & Care Professions Council. (2023). The standards of proficiency for practitioner psychologists. HCPC. https://www.hcpc-uk.org/standards/standards-of-proficiency/pra ctitioner-psychologists/

Hutchinson, N. & Bodicoat, A. (2015). The effectiveness of Intensive Interaction: a systematic literature review. *Journal of Applied Research in Intellectual Disabilities*, 28(6), 437–454.

James, I. A. & Gibbons, L. (2019). *Communication Skills for Effective Dementia Care: A practical guide to communication and interaction training (CAIT)*. Jessica Kingsley Publishers.

Jones, T. L., Baxter, M. A. & Khanduja, V. (2013). A quick guide to survey research. *Annals of The Royal College of Surgeons of England*, 95(1), 5–7. doi:10.1308/003588413X13511609956372

McCombes, S. (2019, May 8). What is a case study? Definition, examples & methods. Scribbr. https://www.scribbr.com/methodology/case-study/

Naeem, M., Ozuem, W., Howell, K. & Ranfagni, S. (2023). A step-by-step process of thematic analysis to develop a conceptual model in qualitative research. *International Journal of Qualitative Methods*, 22. doi:10.1177/16094069231205789

Office for Health Improvement and Disparities. (2020). Guidance: mixed methods study. https://www.gov.uk/guidance/mixed-methods-study#:~:text=combining%20quantitative%20and%20qualitative%20approaches,results%20than%20each%20individual%20method

Positive Approach to Care. (2023, November 14). *Radically transforming the experience of dementia*. Positive Approach to Care. https://teepasnow.com/.

PSIGE Training Subgroup. (2006). Good practice guidelines for UK clinical psychology training providers for the training and consolidation of clinical practice in relation to older people. The British Psychological Society. https://cms.bps.org.uk/sites/default/files/2022-05/PSIGE%20BPS%20Nov%202006%20Good%20Practice%20Guidelines%20Training%20Providers.pdf.

Ramshaw, A. (n.d.). The complete guide to acceptable survey response rates. GENROE. https://www.genroe.com/blog/acceptable-survey-response-rate-2/11504.

Regnault, A., Willgoss, T. & Barbic, S. (2018). Towards the use of mixed methods inquiry as best practice in health outcomes research. *Journal of Patient-Reported Outcomes*, 2(19), doi:10.1186/s41687-018-0043-8

Samuel, J., Nind, M., Volans, A. & Scriven, I. (2008) An evaluation of Intensive Interaction in community living settings for adults with profound intellectual disabilities. *The Journal of Intellectual Disabilities*, 12(2), 111–126. doi:10.1177/1744629508090983

Samuel, J. & Ellis, M. (2022). Intensive Interaction and Adaptive Interaction: Resources for UK clinical psychology doctoral training programmes September 2022. Unpublished document.

Spencer, A. (2021). Intensive Interaction and clinical psychology training programmes. Unpublished document.

Surveyplanet. (2022, November 23). Average survey response rate: what is a good survey response rate?Surveyplanet. https://blog.surveyplanet.com/average-survey-response-rate-what-is-a-good-survey-response-rate

The British Psychological Society. (2019). Standards for the accreditation of doctoral programmes in clinical psychology. BPS. https://cms.bps.org.uk/sites/default/files/2022-07/Clinical%20Accreditation%20Handbook%202019.pdf

The British Psychological Society. (2021). Training and consolidation of clinical practice in relation to adults with intellectual disabilities. BPS. https://www.bps.org.uk/guideline/training-consolidation-clinical-practice-adult-intellectual-disabilities

The British Psychological Society. (2024). Standards for the accreditation of doctoral programmes in clinical psychology (Draft). Retrieved 26 July from https://cms.bps.org.uk/sites/default/files/2024-03/Draft%20Accreditation%20Standards%20-%20Committee%20on%20Training%20in%20Clinical%20Psychology.pdf

# Chapter 10

# Intensive Interaction within psychological service structures

*Jules McKim, Judith Samuel and Julie Elsworth*

## Background

Intensive Interaction has been used within one NHS Trust[1], since 1996 (McKim, 2013; McKim & Samuel, 2019). In this chapter we offer suggestions about how Intensive Interaction can be established within a Psychological Service. These suggestions are based on nearly 30 years of experience and much reflection on what has worked well and what might be done better. We offer ideas about initial steps that could be taken to develop a similar service, as well as thoughts on sustainability.

In 1996, the Specialist Learning Disability NHS Trust provided multi-disciplinary clinical support across Oxfordshire. The Trust also employed over 300 domiciliary social care staff. This connection with and knowledge of people with intellectual disabilities and the staff who worked with them enabled a focus on person-centred support as well as developing an understanding of the challenges that the support of some individuals posed.

Conversations with staff around the concept of engagement and what 'good' interactions looked like were key. Intensive Interaction was identified by the Multiple Disability Resource Team (a specialist multi-disciplinary team for people with profound and multiple learning disabilities (Samuel & Pritchard, 2001)) as essential for those people with profound and multiple learning disabilities who the support staff found difficult to engage in any meaningful activity. An intervention called 'Individualised Sensory Environment' (Bunning, 1996) had been tried for a few individuals. In this, structured sensory stimulation increases the opportunity for purposeful interaction. However, people with profound and multiple learning disabilities were generally passive recipients of sensory input and any communication and interaction were perceived as limited by staff, even with continuous support (Samuel & Pritchard, 2001).

Initially, the use of Intensive Interaction was exploratory. Staff were encouraged to 'have a go'. A few staff said they had been using some of the principles, e.g. vocal mirroring, based mainly on intuition and the positive feedback gained when they tried. The training and support on Intensive Interaction gave them "permission to be playful" (Samuel & Maggs, 1998, p. 143). Addressing

DOI: 10.4324/9781003597933-10

outdated notions of chronological age-appropriateness (Nind & Hewett, 1996) and stressing the relevance of the model of early human development and its place in respectful person-centred support was key to encouraging focused, skilled use of the approach.

To ensure sustainability of Intensive Interaction it was soon identified that ring-fenced resources were required. In 2009, a business case was made by the Head Psychologist for a full-time coordinator role within the Psychology Department. The Oxford Health NHS Foundation Trust Intensive Interaction Service currently consists of the full-time Specialist Care Coordinator (minimum Agenda for Change band [AFC] 7); 0.1 whole time equivalent clinical psychologist (minimum AFC band 8a) with occasional support from assistant psychologists, honorary assistants in psychology (third year undergraduates on placement) and trainee clinical psychologists. Professional management is provided by the Psychological Service lead and the budget is held by the Community Learning Disability Team (CLDT) manager.

Over the years, Intensive Interaction has been introduced to all parts of what constituted the Trust at the time: social care (residential and day), inpatient and community services. The Intensive Interaction Service is now located within the two adult CLDTs serving the county and provides input to the Intensive Support Team (IST), a nursing-led multi-disciplinary team working with adults and children who present with behaviours of concern/challenging behaviour, hence reducing the likelihood of hospitalisation (Department of Health, 2018). Chapter 5 provides more information about the work of this team.

In this chapter, we outline the place of Intensive Interaction within the Trust's care pathways. We describe how to conduct assessment of need, detail our multi-disciplinary working and training practices, discuss ways we have worked to embed evidence-based practice, our approach to outcomes measurement, audit and review, and the sustainability of Intensive Interaction. We conclude with recommendations for practice and for further research.

## Development of care pathways

The Trust's Learning Disability Care Pathways are called Clinical Areas of Practice. Those where Intensive Interaction is included are *Behaviours of Concern, Complex or Physical Health, Dementia* and *Autism*. Intensive Interaction Service representation on working groups developing and reviewing these pathways has ensured that the approach is considered from the earliest stages of a referral. Joint working between psychologists, speech and language therapists and occupational therapists has been essential as areas of professional interest overlap.

Referrals to the Intensive Interaction Service are made from service managers, parents and care managers as well as internal referrals from other clinicians. Those referred include people with profound and multiple learning disabilities, severe intellectual disability and autism and people with intellectual disability and advanced dementia.

## Assessment of need

A prompt to consider the relevance of Intensive Interaction is included in both the CLDT and the IST initial assessment process. Questions include: *Who [does the client] have rapport with? Who gives [the client] a sense of safety and security?* (Skelly, 2017). We (McKim & Samuel, 2021) recommend the rapid increase of one-to-one time when safe and possible, and when the initial assessment suggests that the person's behaviours of concern partly function to meet their social needs (see Chapter 5 for more information about functions of behaviour).

The *Intensive Interaction Assessment of Need* designed by the Leeds Partnership NHS Trust (Firth, 2012) is used by clinicians as a way of screening potential referrals to the Intensive Interaction Service. This form can also be used to assess the need within a defined population, for example: a health, social care or educational establishment. We have updated this form for our use within Oxford Health NHS Foundation Trust and it is presented below in Table 10.1 (McKim, 2021).

*Table 10.1* Intensive Interaction Assessment of Need Form

| *Intensive Interaction Assessment of Need Form* | | | |
| --- | --- | --- | --- |
| Name of individual | | | |
| Address | | Date of assessment | |
| Staff involved in discussion | | | |
| Intensive Interaction is a communication and interaction approach that can help to develop a person's communication skills, can facilitate their social inclusion, can attend to their emotional well-being and be used to develop rapport with their staff and carers. It is part of the following CAPs: Autism, Challenging Behaviour (to form part of the person's PBS plan), Dementia and Physical Health. | | | |
| *Statement* | *Yes* | *No* | *Comments* |
| The person has a severe or profound learning disability (and/or severe autism) and mainly uses body language and/or limited vocalisations to communicate with those around them. | | | |
| The person has a diagnosis of dementia. | | | |
| The person is described as engaging in repetitive non-social routines (e.g. stereotypy or self-stimulatory behaviour) and/or seeking sensory activity/stimulation. | | | |
| The person's reasons for communicating are described as limited by staff/carers, i.e. their communication behaviour is reported as mainly functional. | | | |
| The person is described as being dependent on others to initiate social contact. | | | |

| Statement | Yes | No | Comments |
|---|---|---|---|
| The person is reported to be generally passive and unengaged. | | | |
| Inconsistent staff responses to the person are reported. | | | |
| Intensive Interaction is mentioned in any context as an activity that is or has been used with the person. | | | |
| The person has a Positive Behavioural Support plan and developing rapport with those around them has been identified as a proactive strategy to improve their life quality. | | | |

If any of these statements are answered with a "yes" Intensive Interaction will be a relevant approach for communicating with this person.

## Consent

For people who lack capacity to make decisions about their health care, assessment and intervention are considered using the Best Interests procedure (Mental Capacity Act, 2005). A key component of Intensive Interaction implementation is the identification of the physical and behavioural cues indicating the person's interest in the interaction. This is decided by discussions with care-givers who know the individual well and analysing video footage of interactions and could include such things as changes in vocal tone, breathing rate, position, eye contact and/or gestures. Recording and sharing these details, both in written guidelines and video examples where possible, enables staff to be more tuned in and only engage with the person when they are in agreement. This also underpins more general person-centred support.

## Multi-disciplinary work

### Initial contact and observation

Once a referral is received, visits are made to observe and get to know the individual, their family and their network of support: personal assistants and other social care staff, teachers and teaching assistants, healthcare workers, and the service(s) they attend. Where agreement to use video is obtained, observations and interactions are filmed (see Video use section below).

### Building a strong partnership

Supporting staff and carers to adjust their practice is complex. It is necessary to build rapport with the network of support to understand their priorities and concerns. Recognition, validation and building on the positive aspects of support is essential to influence changes in practice. This is as true for parents and family carers as it is for paid staff (Moroza-James, 2019). Presentation of even excellent new ideas as an external expert can be met with resistance. It is important to carefully and collaboratively formulate training and support strategies to influence change (Firth, 2019).

### Video use

Video footage of interactions, with appropriate consents in place, is a powerful training tool. The development of guidelines and video care plans can be used for future in-house induction. Social Learning Theory (Bandura, 1977) suggests learning from experienced peers through observation and modelling can be more effective than learning from an external 'expert.' In addition, the skills learned in this way, particularly with the use of video, will be person-centred.

### Training

Video-informed training is provided by the Intensive Interaction Service to the individual's network. Face-to-face training is the preferred option, though since the start of the Covid-19 pandemic, virtual sessions have occurred and have been appreciated. The insistence that managers attend training has been present from the beginning of the local development of Intensive Interaction (Nind & Hewett, 2001, p. 89; Samuel, 2009; Donnelly et al., 2015). Management support is crucial for sustainability, since managers are key partners in timetabling, mentoring and supervision of staff and in creating systems of monitoring and record-keeping. Family members are also invited to attend training events, with exclusive sessions arranged if preferred. In-house coaching is required for any staff who are unable to attend the training.

Where possible the team around an individual should be designed to meet their specific needs. In congregate care settings this is impossible. Such person-centred and values-based recruitment is more luxury than reality when recruitment is difficult and use of agency staff high.

### Guidelines

Both written and video guidelines are developed for each client. Draft guidelines are produced during the training and are reviewed and revised as staff use Intensive Interaction with the individual and discover what works best. Risk assessments are drawn up in collaboration with the network of staff and family. Discussions about the use of physical contact take place around every individual referred and person-specific touch guidance is developed.

Video guidelines are used to summarise both the general definition and background of Intensive Interaction, the aim(s) of its use with an individual, a summary of the technique, followed by edited examples of how to use it specifically with them. Video guidelines can be a stand-alone resource or uploaded onto relevant protected web pages as appropriate depending on the organisation supporting the person. Due to an initiative within a local further education college, online platforms for collaborative development of guidelines (Multi Me, 2020) are contributed to by the Intensive Interaction Service. When a client does not attend a care planning meeting about themselves (out of Best Interests considerations) such videos can be shown instead. This focuses the participants' attention on the individual and may positively influence decision making.

### Follow up support

The quality of Intensive Interaction improves with training and the self-reflection that is encouraged. However, training itself is insufficient. Follow up support is required to maintain motivation and fidelity, to trouble-shoot, to embed in daily practice, all of which guards against initiative decay (Firth et al., 2008).

Within the Positive Behavioural Support (PBS) framework (Gore et al., 2013) as used by the IST, a Periodic Service Review (PSR) (LaVigna et al., 1994) measures adherence to clinical recommendations and aims to ensure the ongoing use of the approach.

### Peer support

Peer support groups have been helpful in normalising Intensive Interaction and developing reflective practice. This type of group has been described as a community of practice (Wenger, 1998) and has long been used in Oxfordshire (Nind & Hewett, 2001, p. 50). Open access face-to-face meetings occur in a central accessible location with easy parking; however, reflecting changing working practices during the Covid pandemic, virtual sessions remain available.

### Wider support and influence

CLDT staff are encouraged to attend a one-day introductory course. It has long been proposed that this should become essential training, but despite our best intentions this is still not the case due to conflicting pressures on clinicians' time. The introductory course is considered essential for the IST. Building rapport with service users is relevant for all staff regardless of the reason for their involvement. Raising awareness amongst clinicians allows for informal monitoring where Intensive Interaction is already in place and consideration of referrals where it might be introduced. Joint working with the network of support aids the embedding of recommendations and ensures sustainability.

The service also promotes the use of Intensive Interaction across the wider Trust. The Introductory course has been attended principally by clinical psychologists and speech therapists working in older people's mental health wards. They have found the approach both of great interest and practical value when used with certain individuals. For example, a trainee clinical psychologist reported improved rapport between ward staff and a gentleman with Parkinson's and dementia when Intensive Interaction principles were used.

Teaching is delivered to some clinical psychology doctoral courses, and trainee clinical psychologists on placement have a range of clinical and research opportunities. Teaching is being provided to local undergraduate occupational therapy, physiotherapy and learning disability nursing students. Specialist experience is encouraged and both short and long placements taken up.

A summary of the key points about multidisciplinary working is given in the table below.

## Embedding evidence-based practice

Our vision is that all who could benefit from Intensive Interaction are able to receive it. In order to work towards this goal we have taken steps to promote the approach both locally and nationally. This has included the use, with appropriate permissions, of videos in meetings, training courses and on local intranet pages. These videos are powerful tools and have shown the relevance of Intensive Interaction for other client groups, e.g., older adults with advanced dementia (see Chapter 6).

To increase reach, open access training courses are advertised on the Trust intranet and via networking with other relevant bodies: the Care Home Best Practice group (a cross-county health and social care multi-disciplinary advisory group), the wider Trust psychology department, national and international Special Interest Groups (SIGs), e.g. Video Interaction Guidance SIG (Association for Video Interaction Guidance UK, 2022) and the Intensive Interaction Oxfordshire Regional Support Group.

Research and service development have been key in raising the profile of Intensive Interaction across the wider organisation and contributing to the evidence base. Publications have included case studies, case descriptions, an audit, commentaries and discussions of ethical issues, research and several book chapters. For example: Samuel and Maggs (1998), Elsworth (1999), Samuel and Pritchard (2001), Gray and Chasey (2005); Samuel et al. (2008), Samuel (2009), McKim (2013), Donnelly et al. (2015) and McKim and Samuel (2019 and 2021).

### Outcomes and output measurement

Capturing anecdotal and narrative feedback is a regular part of the service's process. However, the development of an informant-based outcome measurement tool is under way. This is based on the "Fundamentals of Communication" (Nind & Hewett, 2001, p. 7) and the *Mood, Interest and Pleasure Questionnaire* (Ross & Oliver, 2003). The aim is to pick up subtle communication changes (e.g. frequency of eye-contact) as well as perceived mood and well-being changes. Service outputs are easier to measure than individual outcomes. Service outputs include: completion of training; an identified champion; Intensive Interaction specified in care plans with person-centred guidelines; systems of record-keeping; etc.

People referred via the IST regularly have several clinicians involved, and, where possible, rapid changes to the person's support will be made: levels of

*Table 10.2* Multidisciplinary working: key points

| | |
|---|---|
| **Establishing Relationships**<br>Why: promoting changes in practice is complex, takes time and requires trust | *How:*<br>• Take time to get to know the client and their support network, including family<br>• Build rapport and emphasise partnership working |
| *Training*<br>*Why:* Ensure shared practice amongst all those who will interact with a person.<br>Ensure buy-in from managers who will influence on-the-ground implementation | *How:*<br>• Deliver training to support staff and family (either together or separately)<br>• Ensure managers, as key stakeholders, attend training<br>• Offer training in an accessible medium, face-to-face if possible, or virtually if required |
| *Use of Video*<br>*Why:* provides a useful medium for learning through modelling, allows transmission of skills, allows support to remain person-centred | *How:*<br>• Use video (with appropriate consents) during training and for care-planning to allow direct modelling of key Intensive Interaction skills |
| *Guidelines*<br>*Why:* ensure safety, maintain fidelity, build on experience | *How:*<br>• Develop initial (written and video) guidelines for II during staff training and amend these as experience using II with the person develops over time<br>• Conduct risk assessment involving family and support system<br>• Specify person-specific guidelines around physical touch |
| *Video-based Care plans*<br>*Why:* to provide a more accessible format to present guidelines | *How:*<br>• Use video within care plans to communicate the intentions of II and demonstrating/documenting its use with an individual client<br>• Consider safe storage of these within existing clinical guidelines |
| *Ongoing Training*<br>*Why:* to support implementation, to guard against initiative decay | *How:*<br>• Provide an opportunity for ongoing support to improve implementation, maintain fidelity over time and allow staff to deepen their practice and troubleshoot any difficulties that arise. |
| *Peer Support*<br>*Why:* continue to build skills, ensure fidelity of implementation over time | *How:*<br>• Develop a community of practice using reflective practice within peer supervision, either in person or virtually |
| *Wider Training*<br>*Why:* increase institutional awareness and buy-in, embed practices, allow more staff to be involved in monitoring fidelity of implementation | *How:*<br>• Offer training to CLDT staff<br>• Increase awareness of II to encourage referrals and/or re-referrals and enable staff to monitor fidelity<br>• Encourage broader reach to other clinical services (e.g., older adult services) |

| Teaching | How: |
|---|---|
| Why: Develop interest and skills to increase knowledge and build capacity supporting longer-term sustainability | • Offer training to clinical psychology doctoral trainees, occupational therapy, physiotherapy and learning disability nursing students<br>• Offer short and long placements for those interested in deepening their understanding of Intensive Interaction |

support, medication, training of staff and adjustment to the person's social and sensory environment. Given all these variables makes it problematic to identify what specifically influenced the outcomes.

## Audits

The first round of an audit was completed in 2011 (Donnelly et al., 2015). This is to be repeated shortly. Data collected includes training feedback and evidence of completion of all stages of the Standard Operating Procedure (outlined above in the ideal service proposal) for clients discharged.

Based on Hewett (2007)'s ideas about the importance of social touch, an audit of provider agency touch guidance has been conducted (Collett et al., 2023) and further cross-agency guideline development work is planned.

## Sustainability

### Sustaining provision of Intensive Interaction for an individual

Change within peoples' networks of support is inevitable: change of staff or of provider, age-related changes in the individual and their families. Whilst Intensive Interaction guidelines need regular reviews their use must be lifelong. However, written and video guidelines are not always transferred when changes of service provider occur. Digital versions, shared with families, provide a valuable back-up.

A General Data Protection Regulation (Data Protection Act, 2018)-compliant register of people with profound and multiple learning disabilities has been created to monitor the ongoing use of Intensive Interaction. At the point of discharge from the Intensive Interaction service, with permission, a person with profound and multiple learning disabilities is added to the register with the understanding that the service will get back in touch after two years. People with profound and multiple learning disabilities are under-referred to psychological support (Nadany & Hunter, 2010; Sheehy & Nind, 2005). It should not be assumed that this is because services are providing good quality Intensive Interaction. A simple questionnaire will ask if Intensive Interaction is still being used and if not, a re-referral is needed.

For referrals through the IST, the Periodic Service Review (PSR) (LaVigna et al., 1994) requires scrutiny of evidence of the use of Intensive Interaction and its outcomes. Initially this is led by the IST clinicians themselves to ensure general guidelines are being followed. Findings are used to inform the decision to discharge the client from the IST caseload and handover the monitoring responsibility to the lead provider.

### Service sustainability

Sustaining the service requires direct attention and a champion to provide leadership. Maintaining links with the wider Intensive Interaction community (e.g. The Intensive Interaction Institute (www.intensiveinteraction. org)) and the Facebook Intensive Interaction Users (2023) group has been important for sharing the latest research and ideas on best practice.

Presentations at conferences and publications contribute to the evidence base and promote the service's work both internally and externally, demonstrating its value and the rationale for continued funding.

The Health and Care Act 2022 has resulted in the development of an Integrated Care System (ICS) across NHS local authorities and community and voluntary provider organisations in three adjoining counties. We have recently proposed to extend the use of Intensive Interaction across this wider geography, offering the following skills and experience:

- A consultation model of support on how to set up an Intensive Interaction service through sharing skills, knowledge and experience, specifically:
- Experience of a well-established service model
- Formulation of clinical pathways
- Sharing online resources, our own resources (printed, videos, forms, links)
- Management supervision/remote support and guidance including support with video analysis
- An online steering group meeting regularly via Teams
- Access to Regional Support Group
- Training recommendations – external and possibly local

We spent time envisioning an "ideal Intensive Interaction service". We were ambitious with our proposal, which can be seen in Table 10.3. At the time of writing, we await feedback on our proposals from the ICS. Within our Trust there are plans for a part-time assistant post.

*Table 10.3* Service 'wish list'

*Context*

A full-time co-ordinator for adults with learning disability working across Oxfordshire

A full-time assistant for adult learning disability work – administration and video editing support

A full-time co-ordinator for other client groups across Oxfordshire

A full-time assistant for other client groups – administration

Additional resources to allow service development across three counties

Part time clinical and management supervision

Service based within and supervised by psychology, speech and language therapy or occupational therapy

Clinical input across all ages, other diagnostic categories as well as learning disability, e. g. autism, dementia

Service covering all settings – including Supported Living and in-patient

All associated clinicians are aware of the service, assessment of need criteria, national guidance on best practice and referral process

All clinicians have had basic one-day training

*Referral Standard Operating Procedure*

Referral begins with observations of the service user and existing interactions

Pre-intervention outcome measurements using local tools and specific Intensive Interaction tools

The wider circle of support (family, advocates, day services, etc.) are involved

Consent/agreement to use video is obtained with appropriate paperwork and assurances

Observation and interaction videos are obtained and stored following data protection guidance

One-day bespoke Intensive Interaction training is delivered to all staff/carers/family members as appropriate

A set of draft guidelines is produced

An action plan is developed

Service to commit to videoing and paper record keeping

A minimum of six follow-up/mentoring visits to the service/home (ideally)

Mentoring and feedback given to all staff

Guidelines updated

Video guidelines/care plan developed and shared

Outcomes are measured using tools developed along with narrative outcomes

Discharge letter sent to all, including GP, with future recommendations

*Teaching, Training and Mentoring*

Delivering training events across the organisation and externally as required with a suite of options; general open-access, bespoke person-specific, three-day good practice course

Monitoring and evaluating the training

Developing the training further in line with national developments and the evidence base

Running Regional Support Groups in Oxfordshire

Offering training placements across a range of disciplines

Teaching on Intensive Interaction Institute level courses to continue to develop the future of the approach

*Research, Service Development and Audit/Evaluation*

Maintaining a register of individuals with Profound and Multiple Learning Disabilities

Outcome tool development

Touch guidelines (development and research)

Research and audit

## Recommendations for practice

The following recommendations for practice are made:

- Ring-fenced time via a dedicated Intensive Interaction post (full or part time) within NHS Learning Disability clinical services (CLDTs and ISTs).
- Introductory training on Intensive Interaction is deemed essential for all clinicians and social care staff working with people with intellectual disabilities.
- Intensive Interaction is an essential component of support for people with profound and multiple learning disabilities and is expected as such by commissioners and inspectors.
- Intensive Interaction is made available to other potential beneficiaries: people with severe intellectual disabilities, autistic people with high support needs and those with advanced dementia (with or without intellectual disabilities).
- Guidelines are in both written and video format (with appropriate agreements in place).
- Links with local university courses, both undergraduate and postgraduate are made and maintained.

## Recommendations for further research

Within *Video Interaction Guidance* (Kennedy et al. 2011), video shared with the practitioner only includes segments where moments of attunement were achieved, even if only of a few seconds in duration. In our experience, showing unedited video enables a more rounded conversation, though it could in some cases increase resistance to change. Research exploring what develops and sustains practice and the effectiveness of different styles of coaching using video feedback would be useful.

How Intensive Interaction differs when someone has experienced trauma and PTSD would be usefully examined.

Biofeedback measures used during Intensive Interaction "sessions" might reveal a range of physiological changes associated with emotional states.

Kellett and Nind's (2003) framework of "emerging, established and advanced" Intensive Interaction practice in educational settings could be used to evaluate this in psychological services within health and social care.

In the *Raising Our Sights* report about provision for people with profound and multiple learning disabilities, Mansell (2010 p. 13) wrote:

> There is great potential here to provide a better quality of life for the person with profound intellectual and multiple disabilities, if staff are helped to build on the foundation of a good relationship with the person they support by using person-centred approaches, such as intensive interaction and person-centred active support. Intensive interaction is a method of developing reciprocal interaction. These approaches are not yet widely understood or implemented.

A re-examination of national progress for people with profound and multiple learning disabilities seems timely.

## Conclusions

Intensive Interaction is an essential component to improving the quality of life for people with profound and multiple learning disabilities. It can also be used with a wider group of beneficiaries: people with severe intellectual disabilities, autistic people with high support needs and people with advanced dementia.

A structure and a pathway are required of Psychological Services and associated provision to ensure the approach is sustained and its quality maintained. Resources must be allocated and ring-fenced; there needs to be a commitment to partnership working and management support and governance structures are required.

Intensive Interaction can, and should, be within the remit of clinical psychologists working with people with severe learning disabilities, autistic people with high support needs and those with advanced dementia. As a minimum, during doctoral training via teaching and supervised clinical practice, they should have an awareness of the approach and what it can achieve. Beyond this, service commitment to dedicated time and resources is required to secure the best outcomes for people for whom Intensive Interaction would be beneficial.

## Note

1 The local NHS services have been part of different Trusts over the years: Oxfordshire Learning Disability NHS Trust up to 2012; Southern Health NHS Foundation Trust from 2012 to 2017; Oxford Health NHS Foundation Trust from 2017 onward.

## References

Association for Video Interaction Guidance UK. (2022). Homepage. [online] Available at: https://www.videointeractionguidance.net [Accessed 25 Jan 2023].

Astell, A. & Ellis, M. (2017). *Adaptive Interaction and Dementia: How to communicate without speech.* Jessica Kingsley.

Bandura, A. (1977). *Social Learning Theory.* Englewood Cliffs, NJ: Prentice-Hall.

Bunning, K. (1996). The principles of an individualised sensory environment. *Royal College of Speech and Language Therapy Bulletin,* January, 9–10.

Collett, Z., Moll, D., Colston, A., McKim, J. & Elsworth, J. (2023). Expressive touch in health and social care: a review of touch guidance to explore the extent to which social and communication needs of adults with learning disabilities are considered. *British Journal of Learning Disabilities,* 1–10. doi:10.1111/bld.12523

Department of Health. (2018). *Transforming Care: A national response to Winterbourne View Hospital: Department of Health Review Final Report.* London: Department of Health.

Donnelly, C. M., Elsworth, J. & McKim, J. (2015). An Evaluation of an Intensive Interaction service. *Tizard Learning Disability Review,* 20 (3), 111–116.

Elsworth, J. (1999). A preliminary study exploring the use of Intensive Interaction with people with profound and multiple learning disabilities living in small group homes. Small scale research project, University of East London, Doctorate Course in Clinical Psychology.

Firth, G., Elford, H., Leeming, C. & Crabbe, M. (2008). Intensive Interaction as a novel approach in social care: care staffs' views on the practice change process. *Journal of Applied Research in Intellectual Disabilities,* 21, 58–65.

Firth, G. (2012). Intensive Interaction Assessment of Need Form. Leeds: LYPFT NHS.

Firth, G (2019). A view on organisational and institutional issues: the theory of change management. In Mark Barber & Graham Firth (eds) *Delivering Intensive Interaction across Settings: Practice, Community and leadership* (pp. 175–185). Melbourne: private publication.

Georgiades, N. J. & Phillimore, L. (1975). The myth of the hero-innovator and alternative strategies for organizational change. In C. Keirnan & F. P. Woodford (eds) *Behaviour Modification with the Severely Retarded* (pp. 313–319) Amsterdam: Elsevier.

Gore, N. J., McGill, P., Toogood, S., Allen, D.*et al.* (2013). Definition and scope for positive behavioural support. *International Journal of Positive Behavioural Support,* 3(2), 14–23.

Gray, G. & Chasey, C. (2005). SMILE: a new service development for people with profound and multiple learning disabilities. *Living Well,* 5 (4), 22–27.

Hewett, D. (2007). Do touch: physical contact and people who have severe, profound and multiple learning difficulties. *Support for Learning,* 22 (3), 116–123.

Hutchinson, N. & Bodicoat, A. (2015). The effectiveness of Intensive Interaction: a systematic literature review, *Journal of Applied Research in Intellectual Disabilities,* 28, 437–454.

Intensive Interaction Users (2023) Discussion [Facebook] 27 February. Available at: https://www.facebook.com/groups/13657123715?locale=en_GB (Accessed 28 February 2023).

Kellett, M. & Nind, M. (2003). *Implementing Intensive Interaction in Schools: Guidance for practitioners and coordinators*. London: Routledge.

Kennedy, H., Landor, M. & Todd, L. (2011). *Video Interaction Guidance: A relationship-based intervention to promote attunement, empathy and well-being*. London: Jessica Kingsley.

Kellett, M. & Nind, M. (2003). *Implementing Intensive Interaction in Schools. Guidance for practitioners, managers and coordinators*. London: David Fulton.

Kennedy, H., Landor, M. & Todd, L. (2011). Video Interaction Guidance: A relationship-based intervention to promote attunement, empathy and well-being. London: Jessica Kingsley.

LaVigna, G. W., Willis, T. J., Shaull, J. F., Abedi, M. & Sweitzer, M. (1994). *Periodic Service Review: A total quality assurance system for human services and education*. Baltimore MD: Paul Brookes Publishing.

Mansell, J. (2010). *Raising Our Sights: Services for adults with profound intellectual and multiple disabilities*. London: Department of Health.

McKim, J. (2013). Developing the use of Intensive Interaction in the Oxfordshire Learning Disability NHS Trust (Ridgeway Partnership). *Clinical Psychology and People with Learning Disabilities*, 1–2, April, 12–19.

McKim, J. (2021). *Intensive Interaction Assessment of Need Form*. Oxford: OHFT. Based on: Firth, G. (2012). *Intensive Interaction Assessment of Need Form*. Leeds: LYPFT NHS.

McKim, J. & Samuel, J. (2019). Twenty years of developing Intensive Interaction in a National Health Service setting. In Mark Barber & Graham Firth (eds) *Delivering Intensive Interaction Across Settings: Practice, community and leadership* (pp. 44–59). Melbourne: private publication.

McKim, J. & Samuel, J. (2021). The use of Intensive Interaction within a Positive Behavioural Support framework. *British Journal of Learning Disability*, 49(2), 129–137. doi:10.1111/bld.12367

Moroza-James, S. (2019). At home with Tom: maximising my son's potential with Intensive Interaction. In Mark Barber & Graham Firth (eds) *Delivering Intensive Interaction across Settings: Practice, community and leadership*. (pp 129–139). Melbourne: private publication.

Multi me. (2020). My Wiki and multi me [online]. Available at: https://www.multime.com/programs [Accessed 25 Jan 2023].

Nadany, S. & Hunter, C. (2010). Are we meeting the emotional and mental health needs of adults with profound and multiple learning disabilities? *Clinical Psychology and People with Learning Disabilities*, 8 (1 and 2), 21–25.

Nind, M. & Hewett, D. (1996). When age-appropriateness isn't appropriate. In J. Coupe O'Kane & J. Goldbart (eds) *Whose Choice? Contentious issues for those working with people with learning difficulties* (pp. 48–57.) London: David Fulton.

Nind, M. & Hewett, D. (2001). *A Practical Guide to Intensive Interaction*. Kidderminster: British Institute of Learning Disability.

Ross, E. & Oliver, C. (2003). Preliminary analysis of the psychometric properties of the Mood, Interest & Pleasure Questionnaire (MIPQ) for adults with severe and profound learning disabilities. *British Journal of Clinical Psychology*, 42, 81–93.

Samuel, J. (2009). Intensive Interaction for people with profound and complex learning disabilities. In Helen Beinart, Paul Kennedy & Sue Llewelyn (eds) *Clinical Psychology in Practice* (pp. 175–185). Oxford: Blackwell.

Samuel, J. & Maggs, J. (1998). Introducing Intensive Interaction for people with profound learning disabilities living in small staffed houses in the community. In D. Hewett & M. Nind (eds) *Interaction in Action: Reflections on the use of Intensive Interaction* (pp. 119–148). London: David Fulton.

Samuel, J., Nind, M. E., Volans, A. & Scriven, I. (2008). An evaluation of Intensive Interaction in community living settings for adults with profound intellectual disabilities. *The Journal of Intellectual Disabilities*, 12 (2), 111–126.

Samuel, J. & Pritchard, M. (2001). The ignored minority: meeting the needs of people with profound learning disability. *Tizard Learning Disability Review*, 6 (2), 34–44.

Sheehy, K. & Nind, M. (2005) Emotional well-being for all: mental health and people with profound and multiple learning disabilities. *British Journal of Learning Disabilities*, 33, 34–38.

Skelly, A. (2017). Maintaining bonds: positive behaviour support and attachment theory. *Clinical Psychology Forum*, 290, 36–41.

Wenger, E. (1998). *Communities of Practice: Learning, meaning, and identity*. Cambridge: Cambridge University Press.

# Chapter 11

# Development of a psychological model and recommendations for measuring Intensive/Adaptive Interaction when used as a psychological intervention

*Sophie Doswell and Maggie Ellis*

## Introduction

The authors of this book believe that Intensive and Adaptive Interaction can improve psychological wellbeing, and have demonstrated across our chapters that these approaches can be considered and applied from a wide range of psychological perspectives. In Chapter 2, Sophie Doswell highlighted that one of the barriers to approaches being accepted as psychological interventions appears to be the lack of a coherent model, alongside other barriers highlighted in Chapter 8. We have therefore come together as a group of psychological practitioners to develop a model describing the psychological processes that we believe occur when Intensive and Adaptive Interaction are used. This chapter highlights how this model came to be, linking elements from the previous chapters, and also how this model can help us to consider the psychological outcomes that we can measure, to strengthen the research body to support the use of Intensive and Adaptive Interaction as psychological interventions.

## Introducing the new model

Graham Firth's 'Dual Aspect Process Model' (Firth, 2009) recognises that Intensive Interaction practitioners appear to use the approach in two ways; one, with the primary aim of responding to the communication of a person with 'atypical' communication (for example a person with intellectual disability, dementia or autism) and the second identifying educational or developmental goals. The model we have developed builds on this, and suggests Intensive and Adaptive Interaction can serve four different functions relevant to the promotion of psychological wellbeing.

### Intensive and Adaptive Interaction as interventions for developing and maintaining positive attachments

In Chapter 1, Graham Firth describes Intensive Interaction as providing 'positive and developmentally useful experiences of being socially included and

DOI: 10.4324/9781003597933-11

emotionally connected, where previously such experiences had been absent'. For psychologists, there is a particular focus on the importance of this 'emotional connection' and in this new model, while communication is recognised as the essential process through which connection is made, the difference for the psychological practitioner is that this 'emotional connection' is explicitly noted to be supporting the development of positive attachments, which are vital for psychological wellbeing. As described in Chapter 2, Bowlby's attachment theory (1969) is considered a key theory by a number of psychologists using Intensive Interaction.

Jules McKim and Judith Samuel confirm, in Chapter 5, the importance of these underpinning attachment experiences when supporting individuals with behaviours of concern, highlighting Skelly's work (2017) on 'Conditions for Security', which include emotional availability, predictability and warmth. This chapter demonstrates the need for connection in the description of a staff member recognising that, following the introduction of Intensive Interaction for an individual with behaviours of concern, there was a move from the previous task-orientated care to emotionally connected care.

Graham Firth also identifies this 'emotional connection' as being something that family members recognise as being a key element of their experience undertaking Intensive Interaction, and this was noted as one of four themes described in Chapter 7.

### Intensive Interaction and Adaptive Interaction as interventions for promoting positive emotions

In Chapter 4, Rachel Ann Jones highlights the role of Intensive Interaction in providing experiences that lead to positive emotions. Examples from Positive Psychology literature that reference positive subjective experiences and shared mutual pleasure are described. In our model, the importance of these positive emotions is highlighted.

Across chapters, the ability of Intensive and Adaptive Interaction to promote positive emotions has been highlighted, for example 'Ellen' in Chapter 3 and 'Gary' in Chapter 7. 'Showing or feeling positive emotions' was also identified as a key outcome of Intensive Interaction by family members (Chapter 7).

### Intensive Interaction and Adaptive Interaction as tools for managing individual distress

In Chapter 2, Sophie Doswell identifies a further role for Intensive Interaction, also identified in the model, which is the ability to enable an individual to express and process their distress. This is described as being more akin to 'therapy', where sessions are offered on a more regular basis and where there is a conscious effort on the part of the psychological practitioner to provide a safe space for distress to be expressed and held.

Ruth Berry and Ditte Rose Anderson, in Chapter 3, highlight the adversity, pain and suffering experienced by many children and adults with disability and note that attempts to 'manage' these difficulties can actually make things worse. The authors suggest that a detached stance by the 'typical' communicator results in lack of connection with the 'atypical' communicator, leading to distress not being recognised or responded to helpfully. They argue that Intensive Interaction enables compassionate, immediate responses to suffering and that this has great therapeutic potential.

This ability of Intensive Interaction to create a space for processing distress is also noted in Chapter 7, with parents describing the ability to deal with negative emotions or behaviours as an outcome of Intensive Interaction. The capacity of Intensive and Adaptive Interaction to provide a restorative function, following the expression and processing of negative emotion, is a key element of this new model and is of particular relevance for psychological practitioners.

### Intensive Interaction and Adaptive Interaction as approaches to improve the psychological wellbeing of supporters

A clear theme across the chapters is the positive impact of Intensive and Adaptive Interaction on the family member, staff member or psychological practitioner.

Maggie Ellis and Arlene Astell describe, in Chapter 6, how training in Adaptive Interaction enabled family carers to rekindle their relationship with their relative and see potential in their relative's communication. The importance of this connection being powerful for 'typical' communicators has been highlighted in the model.

In Chapter 7, parents mention a range of benefits from the use of Intensive Interaction including positive emotional outcomes, dealing with their child's negative emotional states and learning about themselves, their child and about the nature of communication.

## The model – Intensive Interaction and Adaptive Interaction as psychological interventions

In the model, we have highlighted four core functions of Intensive and Adaptive Interaction: developing attachment, promoting positive emotions, holding distress and improving the psychological wellbeing of supporters. The model describes how, prior to Intensive or Adaptive Interaction, attempts at communication and connection by the 'atypical' communicator are missed, leading to a negative feedback loop of attachment difficulties, a lack of engagement and social exclusion for the 'atypical' communicator and detachment and disconnection for the 'typical' communicator. However, with Intensive or Adaptive Interaction, we see a positive feedback loop, where attempts to communicate and connect are responded to, leading to improved psychological wellbeing for both the 'atypical' and 'typical' communicators.

**Proposed Model**

**Pre-Intensive/Adaptive Interaction**

| Atypical communicator | Lack of connection | Typical communicator |
|---|---|---|

| Atypical communicative expression of emotions/desires/distress | | Lack of recognition of communication style of the atypical communicator (either over- or under-estimation of recipient's communication skills); communication bids unanswered |
|---|---|---|

-ve  Feed back

| Attachment difficulties; lack of engagement; exclusion from the social world; human right to communication denied; social withdrawal | Loop | Individual seen in terms of 'deficits'; disregarded as a social agent; leads to detachment and disconnect; 'doing for' and 'doing to' the recipient |
|---|---|---|

**Intensive/Adaptive Interaction**

| Atypical communicator | | Typical communicator |
|---|---|---|

| Communicative bids are recognised and responded to; awareness of status as active participant in the social world; development of rapport/relationships/positive attachment and a place for distress to be shared and processed/restorative function | +ve  Feed back  Loop | Recognition and use of communication repertoire of the atypical communicator; individuals' communicative bids seen in terms of skill set; accepted as social agent; 'doing with' and 'being with' the recipient |
|---|---|---|

| Human right to meaningful communication fulfilled; improved quality of life; improved emotional wellbeing/positive emotion | Mutually meaningful relationship | Connection made possible; increased self-efficacy; improved quality of life/job satisfaction |
|---|---|---|

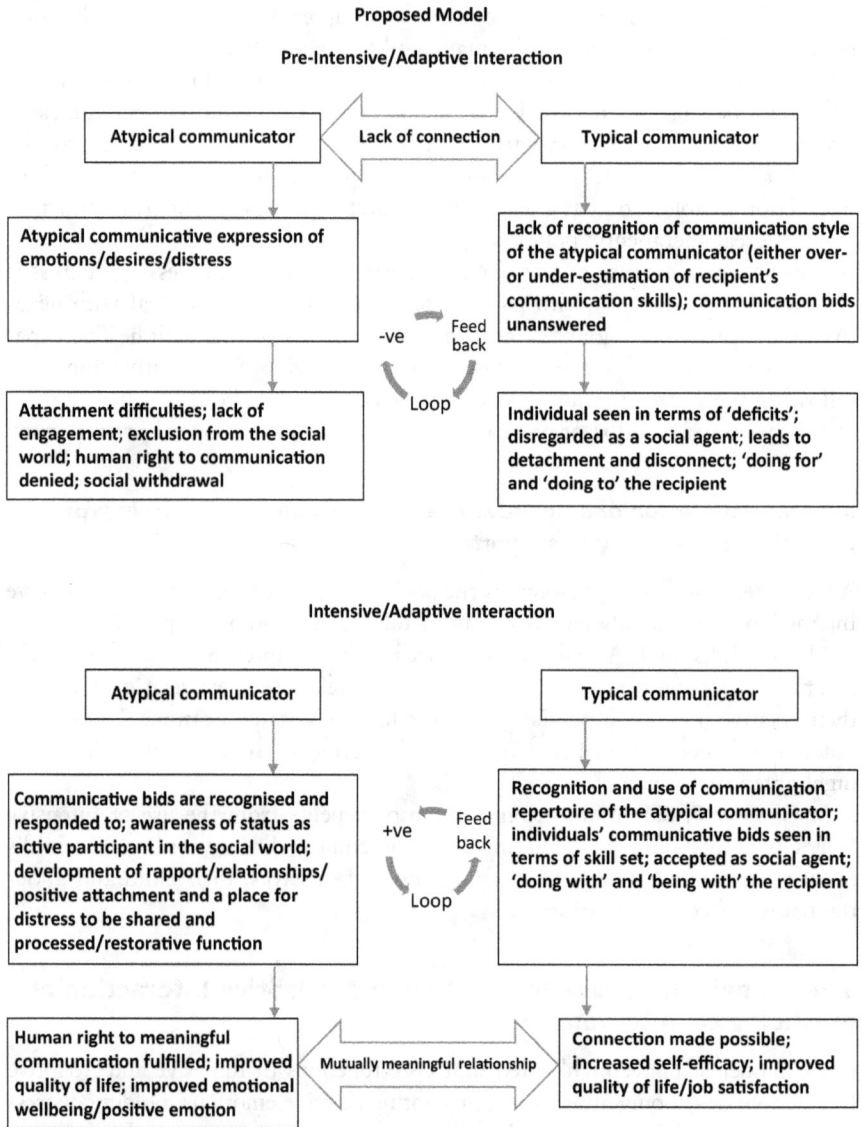

*Figure 11.1* A model describing psychological processes influenced by Intensive Interaction and Adaptive Interaction

## Outcomes

Sophie Doswell argues in Chapter 2 that even when psychological practitioners have engaged in Intensive Interaction, outcomes reported have typically remained focused on social and communication benefits, rather than measuring psychological domains. Of course, when supporting individuals with 'atypical' communication, gaining access to their internal psychological processes can be challenging. However, we believe that the new model provides a framework for developing psychologically focused outcome measures.

### Measuring positive attachment

Attachment has traditionally been measured through two processes: through the use of the formal Adult Attachment Interview (George et al., 1985) and also through self-report scales such as the Experiences in Close Relationships Scale (Fraley et al., 2006). Due to the cognitive and communication requirements of these approaches, neither are likely to be useful for many of the individuals who benefit from Intensive and Adaptive Interaction.

However, psychological practitioners interested in understanding the attachment experiences of individuals with learning disability, who cannot necessarily tell us about their attachment experiences, have developed an observational measure of attachment, called the Manchester Attachment Scale – Third Party Observational Measure (MAST) (Penketh et al., 2014). The MAST requires an informant to rate observable attachment behaviours and make inferences about the needs and feelings of individuals with a learning disability. This therefore may be a useful tool when considering the current attachment behaviours of an individual with learning disability, and charting any development of attachment behaviours over time, following the introduction of Intensive Interaction.

For autistic individuals, measurement of attachment is acknowledged as being a potential challenge as there can be overlaps in how autistic individuals present and the behaviour of individuals with attachment difficulties. This potential overlap led to the development of the Coventry Grid (Moran, 2010) an observational tool designed to be completed by professionals. It has also been developed into an interview schedule (Flackhill et al., 2017).

Within dementia services, similar observational tools to assess attachment have been utilised, such as the Ward Attachment Observation Questionnaire (Miesen, 1990).

### Capturing positive emotions

A second area of measurement indicated by the model is the display of positive emotions, an aspect that is likely to be easier to measure, as informants can highlight observable aspects such as smiling and laughing. This is an area that Intensive Interaction clinicians are already considering, as noted in Chapter 10 (Webster & McKim, 2022), with the Mood, Interest and Pleasure Questionnaire (MIPQ) (Ross & Oliver, 2003) being considered as a helpful tool for measuring psychological well-being (Flynn et al., 2017). The MIPQ is an informant-based questionnaire specifically designed to measure affect in people with severe and profound learning disabilities.

Other tools, for example the PERMA Profiler (Butler & Kern, 2016) may be useful in capturing wellbeing, and has been successfully utilised with autistic individuals who are able to self-report (Grosvenor et al., 2023).

A number of instruments that may be useful for measuring positive emotions and expressions in individuals with dementia have been developed; however, it is recognised that different tools may be needed, depending on the stage of dementia (Madsø et al., 2021). An example is the Observed Emotions Rating Scale (OERS) (Lawton et al., 1996) which is an observational tool considered to have good content validity and psychometric properties and is recommended by Madsø et al. for measuring positive emotions in individuals with dementia.

### Monitoring levels of distress

Oliver et al. (2022) recognise the importance of measuring psychological distress in individuals with profound or severe learning disabilities. They highlight different measurement tools available, including observational schedules and informant questionnaires, including the MIPQ.

Mazefsky et al. (2018) developed the Emotion Dysregulation Inventory which is a caregiver-report measure developed to assess the severity of autistic children's struggles with negative mood and reactivity.

Similar tools have been developed for individuals with dementia, recognising the need to measure negative elements alongside positive emotions. For example, Casey et al. (2014) developed the Behaviour, Engagement and Affect Measure (BEAM) which captures, from observers, a number of areas which are of interest in considering the psychological impact of Adaptive Interaction, including agitation, affect and contentment, as well as level of interaction with others.

### Assessing supporter wellbeing and experiences

Within the model, we note the benefits of Intensive and Adaptive Interaction, not just for individuals with 'atypical' communication but also for those using Intensive or Adaptive Interaction with them. We believe this is an area which also warrants robust measurement to demonstrate the wider psychological benefits of this approach.

Attachment is a two-way process (Rees, 2007) thus it makes sense that we should understand the attachment experiences of Intensive and Adaptive Interaction practitioners, including family members. A potential tool is the 'Experiences in Close Relationships – Relationship Structures Questionnaire' (Fraley et al., 2011) which is a self-report measure focusing on attachment behaviours and attitudes within the particular relationship with the 'atypical' communicator rather than attachment representations more generally.

Staff and parent enjoyment has also been highlighted as a direct impact of Intensive Interaction and Adaptive Interaction and could be measured, for example, by a self-report measure such as the Discrete Emotions Questionnaire (Harmon-Jones et al., 2016).

As described in several chapters, Intensive and Adaptive Interaction can provide a change in attitude and knowledge, for example seeing potential in the communication of individuals with dementia and greater ability to deal with the negative states of children with learning disability and/or autism. Questionnaires such as the Approaches to Dementia Questionnaire (Lintern, 2001) or the Parental Stress Scale (Berry & Jones, 1995) may provide helpful information regarding caregiver changes over time in these areas.

### Qualitative measurement

The model we have posited describes four functions of Intensive and Adaptive Interaction that can be formally measured to highlight the psychological benefits of these approaches. However, a consistent finding in the literature is that there is a difference between quantitative outcomes and qualitative feedback, with qualitative responses being more positive than quantitative measures demonstrate (e.g. Webster & McKim, 2022; Hutchinson & Bodicoat, 2015).

We therefore recommend that, alongside any quantitative measurement, Intensive and Adaptive Interaction practitioners collect qualitative data.

## Training

In Chapters 2 and 9, there is reference to a survey of clinical psychology training courses (Dunstan, 2024), which highlights that fewer than half the training courses contacted offer teaching on Intensive Interaction (12 of 32), and hardly any offer Adaptive Interaction teaching (one of 32). Prior to this survey being undertaken, courses were twice provided with a summary of Intensive and Adaptive Interaction, along with a useful reference and resources list (Samuel & Ellis, 2022). This can be found in Appendix 1.

Feedback from the courses indicate that only eight courses describe teaching Intensive Interaction as psychological intervention, with ten considering it a communication technique, six a wellbeing activity and two linking it with Positive Behaviour Support teaching. Adaptive Interaction was positioned by the one course teaching it as both a psychological intervention and communication technique.

Dunstan (2024) noted barriers exist to teaching, including access to experienced practitioner/teachers (either within the course team or in external local services) and suitable teaching materials that make theory–practice links clear. Curriculum time pressures were also cited. Programmes have to meet standards of accreditation (BPS, 2019) and proficiency (Health & Care Professions Council, 2023). With regard to teaching on learning disability, Barter et al.'s 2019 guidance is used to decide priorities to meet expected standards, and Intensive Interaction is not referenced in this document.

## Conclusions and next steps

We hope that if you are new to Intensive and/or Adaptive Interaction, we have inspired you to learn more about the approaches and to apply these to your work with individuals who could be described as 'atypical' communicators. For all readers, we hope we have convinced you that Intensive and Adaptive Interaction can improve psychological wellbeing for 'atypical' communicators through supporting positive attachments, producing positive emotions and managing individual distress. We hope we have also persuaded you that Intensive and Adaptive Interaction can improve the wellbeing of supporters. Finally, we hope that we have empowered you to overcome barriers that can exist to the utilisation of Intensive and Adaptive Interaction within psychological services.

The publication of this book is the next step in promoting these approaches within the psychological practitioner community. We are keen that there are opportunities to learn more through training from psychological practitioners already using Intensive and Adaptive Interaction. This training needs to be accessed across the professional lifespan; from trainee psychologists and therapists to qualified staff.

To embed Intensive and Adaptive Interaction into everyday psychological practice, ongoing support is needed, via supervision and consultation.

An important focus is the building of the evidence base. We are keen that our new model, with its four functions, is analysed and developed through further research.

The use of Intensive and Adaptive Interaction as psychological interventions will be strengthened by their inclusion in professional guidance, including training requirements and professional practice standards.

The international Intensive and Adaptive Interaction practitioner community is small but passionate and growing. We encourage anyone interested to get in touch with any of the authors via our dedicated email address iiaipsych@gmail.com

## References

Barter, B., Phillips, M., Spencer, A., Steel, J. & Theodore, K. (2019). *Training and consolidation of clinical practice in relation to adults with intellectual disabilities*. The British Psychological Society.

Berry, J. O. & Jones, W. H. (1995). The parental stress scale: Initial psychometric evidence. *Journal of social and personal relationships*, 12(3), 463–472.

Bowlby, J. (1969). *Attachment. Attachment and loss: Vol. 1. Loss*. New York: Basic Books.

The British Psychological Society. (2019). *Standards for the Accreditation of Doctoral Programmes in Clinical Psychology*. BPS.

Butler, J. & Kern, M. L. (2016). The PERMA-Profiler: a brief multidimensional measure of flourishing. *International Journal of Wellbeing*, 6(3), 1–48.

Casey, A. N., Low, L. F., Goodenough, B., Fletcher, J. & Brodaty, H. (2014). Computer-assisted direct observation of behavioral agitation, engagement, and affect in long-term care residents. *Journal of the American Medical Directors Association*, 15(7), 514–520.

Dunstan, S. (2024). *Intensive Interaction and Adaptive Interaction teaching: What can Doctorate in Clinical Psychology courses in the United Kingdom tell us?* Unpublished service related research report. Colchester: University of Essex.

Firth, G. (2009). A dual aspect process model of intensive interaction. *British Journal of Learning Disabilities*, 37(1), 43–49.

Flackhill, Charlotte & James, Sarah & Milton, Karen & Soppitt, Richard. (2017). The Coventry Grid Interview (CGI): exploring autism & attachment difficulties. *Good Autism Practice*, 18(1) 62–80.

Flynn, S., Vereenooghe, L., Hastings, R. P., Adams, D., Cooper, S. A., Gore, N.*et al.* (2017). Measurement tools for mental health problems and mental well- being in people with severe or profound intellectual disabilities: a systematic review. *Clinical Psychology Review*, 57, 32–44.

Fraley, R. C., Niedenthal, P. M., Marks, M. J., Brumbaugh, C. C. & Vicary, A. (2006). Adult attachment and the perception of emotional expressions: probing the hyperactivating strategies underlying anxious attachment. *Journal of Personality*, 74, 1163–1190.

Fraley, R. C., Heffernan, M. E., Vicary, A. M. & Brumbaugh, C. C. (2011). The experiences in close relationships – Relationship Structures Questionnaire: a method for assessing attachment orientations across relationships. *Psychological Assessment*, 23(3), 615–625.

George, C., Main, M. & Kaplan, N. (1985). *Adult Attachment Interview (AAI)* [Database record]. APA PsycTests.

Grosvenor, L. P., Errichetti, C. L., Holingue, C., Beasley, J. B. & Kalb, L. G. (2023). Self-report measurement of well-being in autistic adults: psychometric properties of the PERMA Profiler. *Autism in Adulthood: Challenges and Management*, 5(4), 401–410.

Harmon-Jones, C., Bastian, B. & Harmon-Jones, E. (2016). The discrete emotions questionnaire: a new tool for measuring state self-reported emotions. *PloS one*, 11(8), e0159915.

Health & Care Professions Council. (2023). *The Standards of Proficiency for Practitioner Psychologists*. HCPC.

Hutchinson, N. & Bodicoat, A. (2015). The effectiveness of intensive interaction: a systematic literature review. *Journal of Applied Research in Intellectual Disabilities*, 28(6), 437–454.

Lawton, M. P., Van Haitsma, K. & Klapper, J. (1996). Observed affect in nursing home residents with Alzheimer's disease. *The Journals of Gerontology Series B: Psychological Sciences and Social Sciences*, 51(1), P3–P14.

Lintern, T. (2001). Quality in dementia care: evaluating staff attitudes and behaviour. Thesis submitted for the degree of Ph.D. University of Wales–Bangor.

Madsø, K. G., Flo-Groeneboom, E., Pachana, N. A. & Nordhus, I. H. (2021). Assessing momentary well-being in people living with dementia: a systematic review of observational instruments. *Frontiers in Psychology*, 12, 742510.

Mazefsky, C. A., Yu, L., White, S. W., Siegel, M. & Pilkonis, P. A. (2018). The emotion dysregulation inventory: psychometric properties and item response theory calibration in an autism spectrum disorder sample. *Autism Research*, 11(6), 928–941.

Miesen, B. (1990). *Gehechtheid en Dementie* [Attachment and dementia]. Almere: Versluys.

Moran H. (2010). Clinical observations of the differences between children on the autism spectrum and those with attachment problems: the Coventry Grid. *Good Autism Practice (GAP)*, 11, 46–59.

Oliver, C., Ellis, K., Agar, G., Bissell, S., Chung, J. C. Y., Crawford, H., ... & Woodcock, K. (2022). Distress and challenging behavior in people with profound or severe intellectual disability and complex needs: assessment of causes and evaluation of intervention outcomes. *International Review of Research in Developmental Disabilities*, 62, 109–189. Academic Press.

Penketh, V., Hare, D. J., Flood, A. & Walker, S. (2014). Attachment in adults with intellectual disabilities: preliminary investigation of the psychometric properties of the manchester attachment scale-third party observational measure. *Journal of Applied Research in Intellectual Disabilities (JARID)*, 27(5), 458–470.

Rees C. (2007). Childhood attachment. *The British Journal of General Practice: The Journal of the Royal College of General Practitioners*, 57(544), 920–922.

Ross. E. & Oliver. C. (2003). Preliminary analysis of the psychometric properties of the mood, interest and pleasure questionnaire (MIPQ) for adults with severe and profound learning disabilities. *British Journal of Clinical Psychology*, 42, 81–93.

Samuel, J. & Ellis, M. (2022). *Intensive Interaction and Adaptive Interaction: Resources for UK clinical psychology doctoral training programmes*. Unpublished document.

Skelly, A. (2017). Maintaining bonds: positive behaviour support and attachment theory. *Clinical Psychology Forum*, 290, 36–41.

Webster, S. & McKim, J. (2022). Reflections on developing an outcome measurement tool for use with people with profound and multiple learning disabilities within an Intensive Interaction service. *PMLD Link*, 34(3) 32–34.

# Appendix

# Intensive Interaction and Adaptive Interaction: resources for UK Clinical Psychology Doctoral Training Programmes

UK Clinical Psychology Doctoral Training Programmes enable trainees to work with people with a wide range of levels of cognitive ability (British Psychological Society, 2006, 2019, 2021). The general standards for accreditation of doctoral programmes in clinical psychology (BPS, 2019) as part of the nine core competencies (Section 2.1.3) expects trainees to be "*adapting style of communication to people with a wide range of levels of cognitive ability, sensory acuity and modes of communication*" (p. 20).

For people with intellectual disabilities, the BPS, Division of Clinical Psychology FPID guidance for doctoral programmes (BPS, 2021) specifies the need for trainees to have the "*ability to communicate ... including [with] individuals who are non-verbal*" (page 7). In the section on Academic Teaching the guidance specifies "*working with people across the spectrum of intellectual disabilities, including people with severe and profound intellectual disabilities*" (p. 12). Other populations who may have social communication differences or difficulties include those with severe autism and/or individuals with advanced dementia.

Intensive Interaction (Nind & Hewett, 2005, https://www.intensiveinteraction.org) and Adaptive Interaction (Ellis & Astell, 2017) are two related psychological approaches of relevance to these populations.

Intensive Interaction is a transactional approach which enhances the responsiveness of families, other carers and professionals in supporting people with severe or profound intellectual disability and/or severe autism to develop the fundamentals of human interaction: how to use social communication and how to enjoy being with others. It was developed in the 1980s by Dave Hewett and Melanie Nind, who were teachers in a UK long-stay institutional setting. It was informed by "augmented mothering", the work of the clinical psychologist Geraint Ephraim (cited by Berry et al., 2013) who drew on the theory that early human learning occurs within a dynamic social context in which both infant and caregiver initiate interaction and mirror each other with mutual enjoyment. Through this process the infant develops a sense of self and of agency and attachment grows. Firth (2008) describes Intensive Interaction in terms of its dual aspect: the process of enhancing social inclusion through responsiveness to an individual's communicative initiations however expressed, and the process of facilitating the development of interactional skill through education and/or therapy.

Intensive Interaction is now used internationally in a variety of educational, health and social care settings (Barber & Firth, 2019) and has been recommended by UK Government policy (e.g. Department of Health, 2009). It is described as an intervention within a Positive Behavioural Support framework (McKim & Samuel, 2021) and as a therapeutic response within trauma informed care (Samuel & Doswell, 2021).

Adaptive Interaction is an approach to facilitating meaningful communication between individuals living with advanced dementia and their communication partners. Adaptive Interaction is closely based on Intensive Interaction differing only in its range of basic aims (Ellis, 2022, personal communication).

Below are some key references and videos about Intensive Interaction and Adaptive Interaction. Thanks to Jules McKim (Specialist Intensive Interaction Practitioner) and Julie Elsworth (Principal Clinical Psychologist) both with Oxford Health NHS Foundation Trust and who teach on the Oxford Clinical Psychology Doctoral Training Programme, for contributions to this list.

Dr Judith Samuel (retired Head of an NHS Psychological Service for people with Learning Disabilities and former Chair BPS DCP FPID, team member at the Intensive Interaction Institute). Judith.Samuel9@gmail.com tel.07879626587. and

Dr Maggie Ellis MBE (Senior Lecturer/Wellbeing Officer University of St Andrews). mpe2@st-andrews.ac.uk tel. 01334 462017.

*Maggie is currently co-editing with Dr Sophie Doswell (Chair of BPS DCP FPID), a book about Intensive Interaction and Adaptive Interaction as a psychological approach. Judith is a chapter author.*

September 2022

## References

Astell, A. J., Shoaran, S. & Ellis, M. (2022). Using Adaptive Interaction to simplify caregiver's communication with people with dementia who cannot speak. *Frontiers in Communication* 6, 689439.

Barber, M. & Firth, G. (eds) (2019) *Delivering Intensive Interaction across Settings: Practice community and leadership.* Melbourne: KDP. Also available as a Kindle or Amazon book).

Berridge, S. & Hutchinson, N. (2021). Staff experience of the implementation of Intensive Interaction within their place of work with people with learning disabilities and/or autism. *Journal of Applied Research in Intellectual Disabilities* 34, 1–15.

Berridge, S. & Hutchinson, N. (2022). Mothers' experience of Intensive Interaction. *Journal of Intellectual Disabilities* 26(2), 391–406.

Berry, R., Firth, G., Leeming, C. & Sharma, V. (2013). Clinical psychologists' views of Intensive Interaction as an intervention in learning disability services. *Clinical Psychology and Psychotherapy* 21, 403–410.

British Psychological Society (2006). *Good Practice Guidelines for UK Clinical Psychology Training Providers for the Training and Consolidation of Clinical Practice in Relation to Older People*. Leicester: BPS.

British Psychological Society (2019). *Standards for the Accreditation of Doctoral Programmes in Clinical Psychology*. Leicester: BPS.

British Psychological Society (2021). *Training and Consolidation of Clinical Practice in Relation to Adults with Intellectual Disabilities, for UK Clinical Psychology Training Providers*. Leicester: BPS.

Clegg, J., Black, R., Smith, A. & Brumfitt, S. (2020). Examining the impact of a city-wide Intensive Interaction staff training program for adults with profound and multiple learning disability: a mixed methods evaluation. *Disability and Rehabilitation* 42(2), 201–210.

Department of Health (2009). *Valuing People Now: A three year strategy for people with learning disabilities*. London: HMSO.

Ellis, M. & Astell, A. (2017). *Adaptive Interaction and Dementia: How to communicate without speech*. London: Jessica Kingsley.

Ellis, M. & Astell, A. (2019a). Implementing Adaptive Interaction in everyday care. *Australian Journal of Dementia Care* 8(4), 26–28.

Ellis, M. & Astell, A. (2019b). Communicating without speech. *Australian Journal of Dementia Care* 8, 30–34.

Ellis, M. (2022). Personal communication.

Firth, G. (2008). A dual aspect process model of Intensive Interaction. *British Journal of Learning Disabilities* 37, 43–49.

Firth, G., Glyde, M. & Denny, G. (2021). A qualitative study of the practice related decision making of Intensive Interaction practitioners. *British Journal of Learning Disabilities* 49(2), 117–128.

Hutchinson, N. & Bodicoat, A. (2015). The effectiveness of Intensive Interaction: a systematic literature review. *Journal of Applied Research in Intellectual Disabilities* 28, 437–454.

McKim, J. & Samuel, J. (2021). The use of Intensive Interaction within a Positive Behavioural Support framework. *British Journal of Learning Disabilities* 49(2), 1–9.

Nind, M. & Hewett, D. (2005). *Access to Communication: Developing the basics of communication in people with severe learning difficulties through Intensive Interaction* (2nd edition). London: David Fulton.

Samuel, J. & Doswell, S. (2021). The use of Intensive Interaction in trauma informed care for people with severe and profound intellectual disabilities. In Nigel Beail, Pat Frankish & Allan Skelly (eds) *Trauma and Intellectual Disability: Acknowledgement, identification & intervention*. Brighton: Pavilion.

## Further resources

*Adaptive Interaction* [video]. https://www.youtube.com/watch?v=L6JmzNEQZjk.

*Intensive Interaction* [video]. https://www.intensiveinteraction.org.

Rosie. *The Intensive Interaction handbook* [Video]. https://youtu.be/MH1z1qNQ5bg.

'*So… what is Intensive Interaction?*' [video] Interview with Dave Hewett. https://youtu.be/gJruQPRx3Jk.

# Index

For Product Safety Concerns and Information please contact our EU
representative GPSR@taylorandfrancis.com
Taylor & Francis Verlag GmbH, Kaufingerstraße 24, 80331 München, Germany

www.ingramcontent.com/pod-product-compliance
Lightning Source LLC
Chambersburg PA
CBHW050656280326
41932CB00015B/2927

9 781032 982892